Praise for *THE MIRACLE COLLECTORS*

"Miracles happen. But why, where, how, and to whom? That's a bit more mysterious. This lively, charming, and inviting new book clears up some of those mysteries by exploring the fascinating stories of miracles that happen in real life. Open this book and have your faith strengthened, challenged, and, most of all, deepened in the God who makes all things possible."

—James Martin, SJ, author of *Learning to Pray*
and *The Jesuit Guide to (Almost) Everything*

"The word 'miracle' might bring to mind an image of someone walking on water or jumping out of a wheelchair, but sometimes a miracle occurs when the phone rings at just the right time, or a certain car drives by just when your life depends on it. In my own life, I've come to define a miracle as a moment when God reveals his presence to me. It turns out I'm not alone. Joan Luise Hill and Katie Mahon—beneficiaries of miracles in their own lives—have done a fantastic job of compiling and sharing these beautiful testimonies that remind us not only how God's got our back, but he created us to have each other's backs.

"Today, when the world is reeling from the destructive forces of the global pandemic and unjust racial, social, and economic inequality, THE MIRACLE COLLECTORS could not have come at a better time. The recognition of miracles in our lives is a necessary remedy for the human family to begin rebuilding a culture that has sadly descended into 'us and them' tribalism and has closed ourselves off to the beauty of fraternal love. The hundreds of deeply personal testimonies of courage, faith, forgiveness, and hope in this book will help open your eyes to unlikely angels and miraculous events—ones that can't simply be chalked up to coincidence or luck. THE MIRACLE COLLECTORS will remind you how God is revealing himself all over the place through the gift of other people.

"By sharing the witness of others and waking us up to the beauty, love, and—yes—supernatural power of the God who unifies us all, this book challenges us to collect miracles in our own lives. THE MIRACLE COLLECTORS reminds us that we can be better than we are, and more connected with each other as brothers and sisters. Thank you, Joan and Katie, for this wonderful book that very well may be the miracle someone has been looking for."

—Jeannie Gaffigan, producer, writer, philanthropist, mother of five, and author of the *New York Times* bestseller *When Life Gives You Pears*

"There were so many stories and pages that reminded me of something about my life. I believe in miracles, but it's always wonderful to be reminded that we must keep our eyes and minds open to these beautiful blessings that are presented to us."

—Laura Schroff, author of the #1 *New York Times* bestseller *An Invisible Thread*

"The heartfelt stories in THE MIRACLE COLLECTORS take readers on a journey of the soul. Remarkable stories of coincidence, love, rescue, forgiveness, and peace reveal the wisdom and grace that are accessible to all and allow access to deeper connections with one another. THE MIRACLE COLLECTORS offers a refreshing and uplifting opportunity to rediscover your own dreams, change your aperture on the world, and possibly find the miracles in your life."

—Lee Woodruff, #1 *New York Times* bestselling author of *In an Instant: A Family's Journey of Love and Healing*

"The miracle chasers have paused in their quest to share some of the amazing treasure they have collected, and there are dazzling gems here! Tales of inexplicable healing; random acts of kindness; timely interventions by strangers who appear without summons and disappear, often without thanks, as if they were "earthly angels"; luminous moments of gratitude and forgiveness that transform lives; and acts of inspiring courage that will leave you agape with wonder and touched by joy. The authors tell these stories with respect, aware that they are gifts entrusted to their care, and set them within their own wise reflections on their meaning. Throughout, they challenge us to become a miracle for someone else, to practice a generosity of spirit that 'makes anything, perhaps it is everything, possible.' Perfect reading in a time of anxiety and isolation, when we need the bracing reminder that 'miracles abound' when hope overcomes fear and love holds us together in an embrace neither disease nor death can pry loose."

—David L. Weddle, professor emeritus of religion, Colorado College, and author of *Miracles: Wonder and Meaning in World Religions*

"Looking for miracles? This wondrous little collection is a rush of good feelings, showing us how to find, recognize, and ultimately *be* that miracle for another. In a weary world, THE MIRACLE COLLECTORS causes ripples of wonder to spread across a parched land.

"In THE MIRACLE COLLECTORS, the reader realizes that—aha, so even *I* have a miraculous life!

"A collection of stories pointing out what really fills our lives—daily miracles that spring everywhere, large and small. And this book is the lens to see them through."

—Mary Lea Carroll, author of *Saint Everywhere: Travels in Search of the Lady Saints* and the upcoming *Somehow Saints*

"THE MIRACLE COLLECTORS inspires us to see our heartbroken world in a new light, alive with beauty and possibility. In these pages, Joan and Katie rekindle our relationship with vulnerability, compassion, and awe. And in so doing, they call us to connect with ourselves and each other by sharing our stories and recognizing our unique gifts. This book and its authors are on a mission that our world needs right now. Read it and breathe again."

—Laura Munson, *New York Times*, *USA Today*, and international bestselling author of *This Is Not the Story You Think It Is*, and *Willa's Grove*, and founder of the acclaimed Haven Writing Programs

"Imagine a world imbued with more gratitude and love. This book reminds the reader that this is possible, no matter the external circumstances. Be open and present, embrace the uncertainty between life and death, and let your unique gifts shine a light within and around you. Every word and every action we take going forward has the power to change the world for the better. Be the miracle."

—Dr. Laura Ciel, MA, MBA, PsyD, CEO of NineQ LLC,
and former consultant to ICU, ER,
and palliative care teams and patients

Miracles Abound,
Joan Luise Hill

The Miracle Collectors

UNCOVERING STORIES OF WONDER, JOY, AND MYSTERY

JOAN LUISE HILL
AND KATIE MAHON

WORTHY®

New York • Nashville

Worthy
Hachette Book Group
1290 Avenue of the Americas, New York, NY 10104
worthypublishing.com
twitter.com/worthypub

First Edition: March 2021

Worthy is a division of Hachette Book Group, Inc. The Worthy name and logo are trademarks of Hachette Book Group, Inc.

The publisher is not responsible for websites (or their content) that are not owned by the publisher.

The Hachette Speakers Bureau provides a wide range of authors for speaking events. To find out more, go to www.hachettespeakersbureau.com or call (866) 376-6591.

Scriptures noted ESV are taken from The Holy Bible, English Standard Version, copyright © 2001 by Crossway Bibles, a division of Good News Publishers. Used by permission. All rights reserved.

Scriptures noted KJV are taken from the King James Version of the Bible.

Scriptures noted NASB are taken from the New American Standard Bible®, Copyright © 1960, 1962, 1963, 1968, 1972, 1975, 1977, 1995 by The Lockman Foundation. Used by permission.

Library of Congress Cataloging-in-Publication Data
Names: Mahon, Katie, author. | Hill, Joan Luise, author.
Title: The miracle collectors : uncovering stories of wonder, joy, and mystery / Katie Mahon and Joan Luise Hill.
Description: New York : Worthy, [2021] | Includes bibliographical references. | Summary: "Do you want to believe that miracles can happen? Perhaps you need something greater than yourself to hold you, safely guide your way through a desperate situation, and answer your fervent prayer. Have you wondered if something you experienced could be considered a miracle? Perhaps, at just the right time, you receive an encouraging text from a friend across the country. Or maybe it was much more dramatic. Something life-altering such as a split-second decision, an instinct, to slow your car just before the vehicle in front of you lost control. Regardless of its nature, once you have a miracle experience, big or small, you are never the same. You are changed by your miracle. By exploring their own experiences, searching out religious texts, and collecting stories shared by others, the authors have compiled what they believe is the truest meaning of miracles. The Miracle Collectors offer inspirational stories of miracles that ripple through time and space changing the lives of others. Readers will learn to recognize and celebrate miracles for the gift of grace that they are"—Provided by publisher.
Identifiers: LCCN 2020042923 | ISBN 9781546018025 (hardcover) | ISBN 9781546018001 (ebook)
Subjects: LCSH: Miracles.
Classification: LCC BT97.3 .M335 2021 | DDC 231.7/3—dc23
LC record available at https://lccn.loc.gov/2020042923

ISBNs: 978-1-5460-1802-5 (hardcover), 978-1-5460-1800-1 (ebook)

Printed in the United States of America

LSC-C

Printing 1, 2021

To all the soul sisters and miracle misters
who graced us with their stories.

To Shiloh, Ronán, Rory, and Finn:
May you never lose your sense of wonder,
or your ability to find joy in the moment.
As you grow in wisdom and grace, may you always
find the miracles that life holds.

—Katie Mahon

With thanks for the abundance of miracles in my life:
most especially my husband, Gene, our three children,
David, Alyssa, and Gregory, and their growing families,
all of whom bring wonder, joy, and mystery.

—Joan Luise Hill

Contents

Foreword

If you picked up this book, it is likely that you are someone who wants to believe that miracles can happen. You want to feel that when you are in the foxhole of life, something or someone greater than you will hold you, safely guide your way through a desperate situation, and answer your fervent, if silent, prayer.

Chances are you've entertained the possibility of divine intervention because of an experience: Perhaps, at just the right time, a song on the radio spoke to you with a message you knew was meant for you. You felt a sense that your deceased loved one had an arm around your shoulders, guiding your next step. Or maybe it was something much more dramatic. These are luminous moments when the known and rational world trembles at the edge of the divine world. At first you may label these moments as "unreal." You may mentally dismiss or ignore them, struggle to make sense of them, or wish you could return to the unknowing place of your former sense of reality. But you cannot: once you have a miracle experience, big or small, you are never the same. You are changed by your miracle.

Embracing your miracle story is not for the faint of heart, though it does have transformational power as the authors of this book and I came to understand. Two decades ago, Katie, Joan, and I, friends through our children, met one morning in a coffee shop in the small provincial town where we lived. Unexpectedly, we discovered over cups of coffee that we had each experienced a miracle, times when death had been diverted and tragedy had been overcome. As incredulous as this seems, we quickly learned once you enter the world of the miracle, once you acknowledge to yourself and others that you have experienced your miracle, your journey becomes deeply personal but not just for you alone. Others are changed by your miracle.

Miracles impact the world far beyond the scope of the receiver. In our case, when we acknowledged our individual miracles together, we were catapulted into an unknown world. This is how we became miracle seekers. By exploring our own stories, searching out religious texts, and collecting stories shared by the many people we encountered along the way, we tried to compile the truest meaning of miracles.

To help us understand how miracles work, we were insatiable in looking for answers to questions like, "Why me and not them?" "What if you prayed for one miracle and got another?" "Can a miracle be experienced even if it is not asked for?" Or, like Einstein asked, "Does God play dice?" We sought answers by reaching deep within religious history, which, no matter how wise the philosophers, scientists, and theologians seemed at the outset, never felt completely satisfying.

Engaging with the transformational potential of every miracle we "met" to the best of our individual abilities, we learned so much more than we anticipated. What we learned became much more meaningful when we worked and shared that knowledge collaboratively. For over ten years, we followed this path, which led us deeper toward miracles, life, friendship, and an increased understanding of how the Divine works within our lives. In 2010, through some sort of miracle of its own, our book, *The Miracle Chase*, was published. While Katie and Joan continued on the path of miracles conducting seminars and workshops across the country, God had a different plan for me.

The miracles in my life, including what I learned from writing *The Miracle Chase*, have taken me on a path I never planned for, nor expected. I write this foreword from my hotel balcony, looking toward Waikiki Beach and the beautiful Pacific Ocean. I am here to support the people of the state of Hawaii as they work to improve their childcare systems. Chasing miracles has led me here. It reminds me that miracles ripple through time and space like waves upon the shore, returning to the source to ripple time and time again.

My journey—the journey that began when a neighbor's nanny shook my six-month-old baby, leaving her with seemingly little hope for survival—has now taken me into the fields of childcare, child abuse prevention, and supporting families with children who have special needs. One of the most amazing synchronicities of my life is that the advocacy for legislation we did long ago has come full circle and now funds states and territories to improve the quality and accessibility of childcare for all families.

Creating meaning from our family's tragedy became my personal mission statement: to support others less fortunate, to understand the impact of trauma on families—the homeless, families who are very low income, families with children with special needs, and families experiencing violence or addiction—that they may find support through quality childcare and early education as well. I know that through divine grace my daughter, Liz, not only lived, but thrived. I will never say that what happened to her and to our family was good: we endured too much suffering for that. However, there were miracles to guide our way, helping us as we raised our voices to make sure what happened to Liz as a baby didn't happen to another family. While my miracle led me to this specific field of work, Katie and Joan have continued to carry the message of *The Miracle Chase* to countless groups across the country. The result of their efforts and ongoing journey is this book, *The Miracle Collectors: Uncovering Stories of Wonder, Joy, and Mystery.*

I believe that you picking up this book is no accident, that it is another wave of grace and it is part of the miracle journey the three of us started when we wrote *The Miracle Chase* together. Like Hawaii's waves that begin far beyond the horizon, there is an illusionary line I can see from my balcony where the infinite sky meets the blue, blue sea. To let a miracle guide you, to choose to make the most of any life experience, good or bad, is like focusing on the horizon and trusting that even if we cannot see them, waves of grace are surely forming and moving forward toward our shore.

My wish for you is that you find within these pages connection and camaraderie with others who have had a luminous experience and are trying to make sense of it. May you honor the miracle(s) in your life with courage, and follow the path you are given with hope, faith, and inspiration. And most importantly, I hope you share the miracle stories you uncover with others. We need to celebrate these gifts of grace with gratitude and open hearts. Welcome to the world of miracles!

Happy to have you on the journey.

—*Mary Beth (Meb) Phillips, Honolulu, Hawaii*

September 2019

The Miracle Collectors

Prologue

*When the question "What is a miracle?" is posed, people don't wait
to hear the answer before they want to hear or tell the stories.
It is stories that carry the power as they have for millennia.*
—*The Miracle Chase: Three Women, Three Miracles,
and a Ten Year Journey of Discovery and Friendship*

What if you had been given a miracle and didn't know it? Or, you knew
you had experienced one but never told anyone about it? There are plenty
of reasons to distance yourself from miracles. For some, miracles conjure
up ideas of magical thinking, falling outside the limits of what is possible.
Others are leery of miracles because they fear being ridiculed or thought to
be odd, too religious, or just plain crazy. And yet, 80 percent of Americans
say they believe in miracles, a statistic that has remained steady for decades.[1]

The question of what constitutes a miracle is one the two of us have
been contemplating for the better part of two decades, and the answer has
been a moving target. Is a miracle biblical in proportion, which arrives like
a crackling thunderbolt from the sky? Is it a personal sign that only you can
recognize, or a coincidence that changes your outlook or your life? Miracles
can be big and bold, immediately having consequences for the whole world,
or nuanced and personal, having consequences for one person at a time.

There are those who instantly recognize a divine hand at play wherever they look. "Hallelujah!" and "Amen!" We were not those people, at least not back then. That was twenty years ago, when an ordinary meeting among friends sparked a spiritual journey, one we wholeheartedly embarked on, but with no idea where it would lead.

The three of us (Katie, Meb, and Joan) were meeting at the local coffee shop, having made the morning drop-offs at school, eight children among us. Busy mothers, professional careers on hold, we had our hands in every volunteer pot you could imagine, from women's health to childcare advocacy, from classroom helping to fundraising for ballot measures supporting the local public schools. We were more "doings" than "beings," Catholics by varying degrees, and certainly with no time to become spiritual seekers.

Joan and Meb knew each other through their sons, Katie and Joan through their daughters. As the common denominator, Joan saw how much the three of us had in common: Jesuit universities, nonprofit passions for the underdog and underserved, and a burning desire to make the world a better place. Joan was determined to find a cause we could all embrace. A spiritual odyssey was not on the list of options she imagined. And yet, we each had our story.

Meb was well known in our small town just east of San Francisco. Her oldest child, Liz, six months old at the time, had been shaken so violently by a neighbor's nanny that one doctor said it was equivalent to being thrown out of a second-story window onto concrete. If she survived, she would likely be "a vegetable," he said. One night in the hospital, when Meb was at her lowest point and felt that Liz was losing her battle to survive, she was approached by a kind man in a white coat. He told Meb that though Liz suffered from shaken baby syndrome, she would be fine. Despite Meb's efforts to locate the man later, no one seemed to know who he was, and she was never able to find him. Liz became Meb's miracle. She not only survived but flourished, though the assault had caused retinal detachment in both eyes and Liz was irreversibly blinded. In spite of the severity of her injuries, Liz worked to regain her body function, learned braille, and with her PhD in hand, works to open the world to others with disabilities. When the nanny was given a slap on the wrist by the courts and a green light to be a nanny again, Meb sprang into action, fostering new legislation in California, creating the TrustLine Registry, so that what happened to her family would not happen to another. Meb was subsequently honored at the White House for changing the face of childcare in her own state and creating a blueprint for other states to follow.

Our meeting that morning was to get an update on the remarkable survival of Joan's eighth grade son, David.

We knew what had transpired over the past few months. Joan just happened to be at the middle school for a meeting at the exact time David was struck by crushing chest pain during his physical education class as he tried to break his own running record. Had Joan not been there, she would have chalked it up to too many push-ups at swim team practice the day before, as the on-call pediatrician she took him to had done. Instead, she was on high alert and scheduled a follow-up visit with his regular doctor, who insisted on a cardiac workup. The tests uncovered a lethal cardiac anomaly, usually discovered upon autopsy when someone drops dead, apparently, as David could have done that day.

David's right and left coronary arteries originated on the same side of his heart. That is a problem because his right coronary artery ran directly between his aorta and pulmonary artery. When they engorge with blood, as happens with exercise, the misplaced coronary artery is pinched closed, causing cardiac arrest. David was a walking, ticking time bomb. His diagnosis led to a terrible catch-22. Open-heart surgery could be performed to try and move the artery to its correct position on the other side of his heart, which no one with similar problems had ever survived. Or, bypass surgery could be performed in the hope that the bypass would work when needed. Unfortunately, it would need to be redone every ten to fifteen years, relegating this athletic, otherwise healthy child to the couch for the rest of his life. The week before surgery, Joan; her husband, Gene; and David had been told the optimal fix, moving the coronary artery, was not an option. There just was not enough room to maneuver between the two arteries, and the surgeon would have to do the less desirable bypass.

On the day of the surgery, David was sprinkled with water from Lourdes by his grandmother. Lourdes, France, represents a place of miracles and has been a shrine and pilgrimage site for Catholics for over a century. Bernadette Soubirous, a young girl the same age as David, had encountered the Blessed Mother there and had been directed to uncover a spring that had healing waters. Her story had captured Joan's heart as a child, and *The Song of Bernadette*, an Academy Award–winning movie from 1943, was her favorite.

In the agonizing hours in the waiting room, worrying about whether David would live or die, Joan and Gene made their way to a far corner, well away from the other parents who were crowded around the TV with its tales of the absurdity of life orchestrated by Jerry Springer. After several hours, Joan was called up to the nurses' station for an update. It was a call from the operating room to let them know David was on cardiac bypass, the most dangerous part of the surgery. As she put down the phone, someone called her maiden name, Luise. She searched for the source and noticed that the television, a moment ago as she walked to the phone tuned into inane talk show central, was now playing *The Song of Bernadette*. It turns out Bernadette's mother's name was Louise and someone in the movie had called to her, capturing Joan's attention.

But how had the channel changed? The other parents in the waiting room were confused because no one had touched the TV and they didn't understand what had happened. As Joan stared at the surreal scene on the television screen and explained the movie to the other parents, she was enveloped in a sense of peace and knew that everything was going to be all right. Just as the movie ended, the renowned surgeon they had tracked down to perform David's surgery came in with miraculous news. He had been able to do the optimal fix. The minimum space he needed to move the artery to its proper place, the width of no more than a nickel, had been there exactly! David could go on to live a normal and active life.

That morning in the coffee shop, Joan didn't seem to want to engage, at least not in the miraculous experience of what we knew had transpired; she was ready to sweep it under the carpet and move on. David was good—no point in dwelling on what might have been. Katie knew better. She could relate to Joan's reticence, but fearing Joan would dismiss something truly extraordinary, Katie finally decided to share her own miracle, an experience that had haunted her for her entire adult life. It was not a story she shared often or particularly willingly. This morning was different. That is the thing about miracles—they stop time, or maybe they open a space in time.

"I have a story," Katie began. Maybe it was the way she said it but the mood at the table shifted. Somehow, Joan and Meb understood this was not going to be any ordinary story.

"It was the summer after my freshman year in college. I worked until three every day near Union Square in San Francisco. I took the first ferry home to Tiburon, but it didn't leave until four, so I always had time to kill. As I window-shopped in front of I. Magnin, a man approached me. He was clean-cut, maybe thirty, a white-button-down-shirt-and-khaki-pants kind of guy. He said he was a stranger in town and that he'd had eye surgery; he needed to look up his best friend's parents in the phone book, and he couldn't do the close-up work, so could I please help him?

"My first reaction was to put to use what I'd learned in childhood—

'Don't take candy from a stranger'—and I said no I couldn't help him and moved to the crosswalk. He followed me and repeated his request. He was so persistent and finally he said, 'I'm staying up the street at the Hyatt. Won't you please help me out?' *Oh, the Hyatt,* I think to myself, *a place that will be crowded with people.* And I have the time and can put to use another mainstay of my childhood: 'Be a good Samaritan.'

"As you guys know, the Hyatt is built on a hill, and as I recall, we entered the building a floor below the lobby. Sure enough, there were plenty of people around. We got in the elevator, and when it stopped on the lobby level, everyone got out—except for the man. He had pressed the mezzanine button and I thought, *Okay, it will also have people milling about,* but when the doors opened on the mezzanine and we got out, it was deserted. At this point I began to feel uncomfortable and unsure of myself. I followed him down the hall and into a long conference room. In the back, against the wall, was a pay phone with a phone book resting on the metal shelf below it.

"He stood behind me as I began to look down the columns for a Brown family that lived on Marina Boulevard. Maybe a minute went by. Suddenly, I felt a wave of terror wash over me. It's not like I went down a checklist; it was an instantaneous understanding that none of this made sense: *He has no patch on his eye. Why doesn't he know the first name of his friend's parent? Why does he ask* me? I was in a deserted place with a stranger, just what I'd been taught my whole life not to do.

"I turned around to look at him. His face had completely changed; his eyes had darkened. He knew that I knew and that I was terrified. It was part of his sick game, as if he was waiting for me to figure out I was trapped.

"All of a sudden, there was movement at the door. A bellman walked in and said to me, 'Don't you think you should be going now?' I walked out with the bellman into a waiting elevator, the door already open. The man did not follow. We got off on the lobby level and it took me a few seconds to get my wits about me. I was completely shell-shocked. When I finally looked around to thank the bellman, he was nowhere in sight."

Meb and Joan looked pretty flabbergasted at this point; Katie felt spent, but there was more to the story.

"About fifteen years went by. I told very few people what had happened because I felt stupid and embarrassed, and I wasn't looking for, or wanting, a spiritual explanation for what had happened, even though my dear Irish Catholic mother did. 'The bellman was an angel,' she told me at the time. But I saw all that religious stuff as hocus-pocus. I was occasionally awakened in the middle of the night by a nightmare that included the man's face, my heart pounding. But, other than that, I was able to put it out of my mind.

"And then one evening, as Jim [Katie's husband] and I read the morning newspaper, toddlers tucked into bed, he handed me the front-page section and said, 'Oh my God, Katie, I think this is your guy.' There, on the front page, was a photograph of Ted Bundy. He'd been put to death in Florida the day before. The article went on to recount his victim profile: young women between the ages of nineteen and twenty-one, five foot six or five foot seven, thin, and with long blond or brown hair parted in the middle—just as I had looked back then. He lured many of his victims feigning injury and was a frequent visitor to San Francisco in the mid-1970s, when he was at the height of his murder spree. He was even a suspect in two murders in the Bay Area during that time. I felt it in the deepening pit forming in my stomach. Jim was right—this was my guy."

Meb and Joan had been speechless. If Katie had known it would be the last time in a long time for a moment of such blessed silence, maybe she would have savored it longer. Instead, after Katie shared her story, it was as if a collective light bulb went on in our respective brains. The three of us recognized our common cause: miracles. Defining, chasing, and researching them in religions, faith and wisdom traditions, and in history, philosophy, and science. All of a sudden, there were burning questions that needed answers. "Why me—why did I get a miracle and not someone else?" "How can we possibly believe in miracles when there is so much suffering in the world, and when so many don't seem to get one?"

The miracle chase was on. Like most journeys of the spirit, this one also included unexpected twists and turns—some were enlightening and full of wonder, while others were difficult and potentially tragic. Along the way, Joan was diagnosed with invasive breast cancer, Meb's marriage imploded, and Katie's husband survived the "widow maker," a nearly fully blocked main artery to the heart. No doubt, these experiences altered our initial thoughts on *The Miracle Chase*, because God and miracles look very different from the trenches. We discovered that miracles are chameleons and sometimes can be blessings in disguise.

Telling our stories beyond our own threesome took courage. After all, what would people think? Believing a miracle happened to you can be uncomfortable and messy; it may mean revisiting experiences of trauma, fear, and confusion that render you vulnerable. Miracles require a reordering of a seemingly ordered life. For Meb, this meant accepting the miracle she got and not the one she once prayed for. For Katie, it meant spiritual complacency was no longer an option. And Joan was forced to stop moving long enough to contemplate what had happened and the gift her family had been given.

In sharing our miracle stories, we navigated the waters of mystery and mishap together. Faith and friendship was a winning combination that we counted on again and again in order to survive. Before we knew what was happening, we became soul sisters—connecting on a more honest and deeper level—and it felt good. Which is not to say it was always easy.

Looking back, we could see that our miracle project was able to move forward because the three of us had to cultivate our best characteristics, without which we would have been doomed. We learned early on that our miracle chase was bigger than we were, and we had to check our egos at the door. We each had good ideas, but not surprisingly, some contradicted and clashed, so we had to develop the ability to listen without judgment or agenda. We were all pretty adept at giving help but discovered how hard, though necessary, it is to ask for help. We learned that it is okay to dream big and believe in yourself, and that cultivating a generosity of spirit pays untold dividends for your soul and your relationships. We remained curious, open to where the journey would take us.

In our first book, we share a definition of miracles that we developed through research and our own experience: "A miracle is a sign of divine intervention in the world that creates an unfolding and beneficial connection between God and humankind."[2] This notion that miracles *unfold* is unique; they burrow their way into your soul over time and ripple outward into perpetuity. Being open to the possibility of miracles is the first step. Soren Kierkegaard talked about miracles as manifestations of Divine incognito, understanding the concept that God works in anonymous and mysterious ways.

When *The Miracle Chase* was published and we traveled the country to promote it, a remarkable and unexpected consequence began to unfold. Sharing our own stories helped unearth more tales of miracles. Others were inspired to share stories they never had before, stories they didn't think mattered, stories they had forgotten. We had opened the door for them to tell the stories that in many cases represented defining moments in their lives, as our stories had been in ours. When we created an elixir of vulnerability and spiritual connection, others were willing to partake. Like treasures held close to the heart, we cherished each story we heard and we became aware of our own role in bringing these stories into the light of day. It was an unanticipated gift and it is where our miracle journey comes full circle and expands. As we continued in our quest, we became miracle collectors too. By sharing miracle stories, not only of our own, but now of others, we are connecting with each other through grace, acknowledging the presence of the Divine in each of our lives. The powerful and wondrous gift of grace encourages all of us to seek to experience the sense of hope and connection we have come to appreciate.

A spiritual path forward emerged in the insights we discovered along the way. First, to recognize a miracle you have to keep an open mind and become more aware of what is around you. This new level of awareness sometimes requires a change in perception or even a full-on paradigm shift. Second, sharing our stories deepens our connections with each other and sparks an understanding of how much we have in common. Finally, by opening ourselves up to a spiritual journey, we can find greater meaning and a sense of fulfillment and purpose in our lives.

Accordingly, this book is organized into three parts, each building upon the other. "Becoming Aware" focuses on how we need to notice and appreciate not only what we see in front of us, but what is beyond or behind what we see, in order to discover the miracles that surround us. While we are reminded of living in the moment and being present at every turn, this is far easier said than done. This section offers insights on how to foster a practice of increasing awareness of ourselves, those around us, and the places and things we encounter every day.

The second part of the book revolves around "Deepening Connection" with each other. It offers a road map for reengaging with one another in ways that peel back the protective layers we have put up over the years, unveiling our authentic selves. When we share our stories with each other, we discover we are far more interconnected with more in common than we could have imagined. By exercising a generosity of spirit, and offering one another a sense of forgiveness and understanding, we can reach a new level of trust, with deeper connection and faith in the human spirit as the result.

Once we become more aware and engage on a deeper level, our journey takes us to the third part of the book, "Finding Meaning." Discovering we are where we are meant to be and saying yes to the job we are meant to have take the courage to dream and to be grateful that we are the right person in the right place at the right time. It is empowering to contribute to the world in your own unique way and to perpetuate what we call the ripple effect of miracles.

Einstein once said, "There are only two ways to live your life. One is as though nothing is a miracle. The other is as though everything is a miracle." This notion of "everything" broadens our own definition. For in the center of the miracle debate is always the understanding that much of the time the inexplicable cure does not come, and tragedy and suffering continue to mar the near and far corners of our world. God does not use a magic wand to cure all evils, though we have all wished for that at one time or another. We have no answer to the unanswerable question, "Why?" But, as we came to learn on our own journey, if we can see miracles all around us, then we're all privy to divine gifts. Think of a sunset streaked with rays of pink and gold, of the collective goodness in a community that lifts lives up, of the unconditional love a parent has for her child. Think of stories of courage, forgiveness, gratitude, faith, hope, and love. If we learn to notice and appreciate the miracles that are available to each one of us, then none of us is left out of God's embrace.

In the pages that follow, you will find the stories that we have collected from many kind souls and generous spirits who shared them with us, and now with you. As you will see, miracle stories need no embellishment; the stories themselves are alive. These powerful tales illuminate the path before us. Join in as they guide us on our continuing miracle journey.

PART ONE

Becoming Aware

To look at everything always as though you were seeing it either for the first or last time: Thus is your time on earth filled with glory.
—Betty Smith, *A Tree Grows in Brooklyn*

CHAPTER ONE

Terminal Course

*All external expectations, all pride, all fear of embarrassment
or failure…fall away in the face of death, leaving only what is
truly important…there is no reason not to follow your heart.*
—Steve Jobs, Commencement Address, Stanford University

What if you found out you had a week to live? One week. Think about that
for a minute. Now, when you look at your calendar, your priorities change,
probably drastically. No need to keep that dentist appointment, or make
the board meeting, or even show up at work. It is time to call your mom or
your best friend, be home for after-school games and snacks, make amends.
Maybe it is time for a quick trip to paradise, wherever that may be for you,
and maybe you want to write down some words of love, encouragement,
and wisdom to leave behind for those you care about most. One thing is for
certain: with one week left on earth, it should be easy to separate the wheat
from the chaff. The clock is ticking.

What stays, what goes, and what gets added to the mix? For most of us,
when facing death, connecting with friends and family will be paramount.
The simple things in life that are taken for granted will gain new meaning:
the sound of the front door opening, the voice of someone you love, the
warmth of the sun on your face, the sound of the leaves rustling in the trees

or crunching beneath your feet, and the birds as they call. Regrets might surface: the dreams never realized, the changes never made, or the time wasted being unfulfilled, unhappy, or less than who you are meant to be.

If you have a week to live, time becomes a precious and scarce commodity. The seconds tick by in precise rhythm, becoming hours past until your seven days are up. You are handed the gift of roughly sixteen hours every morning. The question is, what would you do with it today if you only had a total of 112 hours left? If you are like Joan, you will sleep deprive yourself to the grave and stretch those sixteen-hour days into twenty; if you are like Katie, you will get the recommended daily allotment of sleep and hope one of the mornings you will wake up from the nightmare: reality meets denial.

Besides an acute awareness of diminishing time and the commensurate imperative to focus on the only things that really matter, some would also take a spiritual inventory. The big questions floating around for years would finally need answers. *Is there a God? Do we live on? Have we left the world a better place?* Others would cling to their great faith and certainty that they'll be with the Divine and in a better place.

There are some who identify with what John Lennon said: "I'm not afraid of death because I don't believe in it. It's just getting out of one car and into another."[1] From earth to heaven in one easy ride. Some have no faith at all and think there will be nothingness when the bell tolls at midnight on the seventh day. Although they say there are no atheists in foxholes, if you are dying in a week, you are in one. Will you hedge your bets and pray anyway?

The seventeenth-century mathematician Blaise Pascal had a famous wager about believing in God. "Let us weigh the gain and the loss in wagering that God is…if you gain, you gain all; if you lose, you lose nothing."[2] Well, perhaps you think you will look a fool, but you won't really care when you are dead. This reminds us of a woman we met who told us of an experience she had after being diagnosed with ovarian cancer. Feeling at her lowest point in a long, scary ordeal, she was lying in bed staring at the ceiling, when all of a sudden she saw the face of Christ in the contours of the chandelier. Later, the same image appeared in the grain of her oak closet door. Although she was not religious, she decided she should pray. Ultimately, she fully recovered and never encountered the strange images again. Though we don't know if she ever changed her mind about religion, she felt the encounter was important enough that years later she wanted to share the experience with us, as if for safekeeping.

A week might seem an eternity to live if you think you only have minutes. Take the gentleman who shared an elevator ride with Katie's daughter Laura the day after the Miracle on the Hudson, when on January 15, 2009, US Airways flight 1549 landed in the Hudson River. Offering a pleasantry, Laura asked, "How are you?" to which he declared, "I'm great! I was on that airplane yesterday and I am so thankful to be alive; my life will never be the same again!"

Not all of us are so instantaneously receptive to reaching the same conclusion. We miracle collectors belong to this group, and so we understand the reticence involved before admitting a miracle. At one book club meeting where Joan had Skyped in, a woman shared a story about a day many years ago as she sat in a London airport. Her flight was boarding but she had the urge to go peruse the nearby bookstore, grab some coffee, and take her time. She approached the desk and asked when the next flight to New York City would be. Informed it was in less than an hour and she could switch to that flight, she made the arrangements and was off to the bookstore. The flight she changed was Pan Am flight 103, the one that blew up over Lockerbie, Scotland. It had never occurred to her to see this event as deliverance until years later, when she was transformed by the response of her fellow book group members. Overwhelmed by her admission, her friends were shocked that they had never heard this story and immediately challenged her to consider that her life had been touched—saved, in fact— by the Divine. Unlike the wise gentleman who survived the US Airways flight, it takes some of us a while to join the ranks of the forever appreciative and to keep our eye on what is most important.

Katie received an email that had been circulated among her college classmates from their friend Martha who had just been diagnosed with an aggressive cancer. If you want to know what a death sentence feels like, Martha knows, and this is what she said:

> I was diagnosed last week with Stage IV pancreatic cancer that has spread to my liver. There it is…in black and white. The worst words you can hear when you are sitting across from the doctor in his office. Outside, the sun is still shining, the traffic is still moving, and inside that room your life has been turned upside down in a flash. You struggle to breathe and take it all in, but at the same moment wish you could pass out!
>
> You walk out of the door and start thinking about how you are going to live your life from that day forward. Everything has changed in an instant, and nothing seems to be the same…

Katie's college friend may have a better sense of the timing of her death, and this must be terrifying. However, we are all going to die—most of us just have the luxury to put it out of our minds from day to day. A Buddhist teacher, Sangye Khadro, suggested we "imagine being on a train, which is always traveling at a steady speed—it never slows down or stops, and there is no way that you can get off. This train is continuously bringing you closer and closer to its destination: the end of your life."[3] A customized one-way ticket, arrival date unknown.

The good news is it does not have to take a serial killer or a terrorist bombing or a terminal diagnosis or even a practice exercise to remind us of our eventual demise. Becoming more aware of every miracle moment you are alive is about bridging the gap between the death sentence you have been handed and the reprieve you are going to get at the end of the week when you realize it was all a mistake. Turns out you are not going to die in a week after all. Relief! Gratitude! And now, you have a changed outlook, kind of like Scrooge on Christmas morning. Katie can picture Martha, a mother of seven, doing a jig, a somersault—*anything*—if someone told her it was all a mistake.

What might it look like to feel like Scrooge did on Christmas morning, every morning? His profound appreciation when he realizes he hasn't missed Christmas; his enthusiasm as he imagines he could help Bob Cratchit and cure Tiny Tim; his exuberance as he delights in the faces of children whose very existence once annoyed him. Even the snow seems to sparkle. "Golden sunlight; Heavenly sky; sweet fresh air; merry bells. Oh, glorious. Glorious."[4] The Ghost of Christmas past showed him missed opportunities for a different life, the Ghost of Christmas present showed him the error of his ways, and the Ghost of Christmas Yet to Come—well, that is when he stared into his own grave and got religion. He sees the world anew through the eyes of one completely transformed.

If you are lucky, like the new and reformed Scrooge, maybe you know exactly what to do with the moments of your life that you have left. Or at least you know what not to do. No more detritus like so much tumbleweed allowed in your door, worry and uncertainty and time wasted on the things that do not matter. Regardless, we all have an opportunity to consider how to be more deliberate and happier, to find a way to see the world through fresh eyes.

Joan has never forgotten the invasive breast cancer diagnosis she received twenty years ago and the potential death sentence it was.

"Trust me, you don't have to remind me I could die tomorrow. The feeling has never left me. When I am overwhelmed by my responsibilities and commitments, I remember my cancer diagnosis acting as a free pass to rearrange my life. The busyness of my days should never mask the splendor in having them to live. It completely changed the way I think."

Mahatma Gandhi, among others, said, "Live as if you were to die tomorrow." Why? Because it keeps us focused on what is important and all that matters right now, this minute. Hansa Bergwall and Ian Thomas agree. They founded WeCroak, an app designed to notify you five times a day, "Don't forget, you're going to die." This is followed by a life-affirming, or death-affirming, quote, like "Your own positive future begins in this moment. All you have is right now" (Lao-tzu), or, "You could leave life right now. Let that determine what you do and say and think" (Marcus Aurelius). The app is based on the Bhutanese philosophy that to be a happy person, we must contemplate death five times a day. At recent count, nearly thirty thousand people had paid ninety-nine cents for the privilege, average age thirty-five. Those of us meaningfully older than the average do not need to be reminded, though Katie signed up anyway.

No routine reminders are necessary for one Denver hospice nurse who told us about a patient she became especially close to before he died. She asked him to send her a sign from the other side to let her know he was okay. A few days after he passed away, she was strolling down a random downtown sidewalk when a beautiful dragonfly, its translucent greens and blues sparkling in the sun, began buzzing around her purse. She thought it was odd, a dragonfly in the city. She gently tried to shoo it away, but it seemed intent on sticking around until it landed on the sidewalk just in front of her, forcing her to stop for fear of stepping on it. And then, the dragonfly flew away, revealing something etched into the sidewalk. She leaned down for a closer look and recognized the initials of her patient who in life had been a cement contractor. Even though it was against the rules, he had told her he always signed and dated the last concrete square he poured on any major project.

This hospice nurse embodies her mission to minister to the dying and believes she was where she was meant to be that day. She believes death is a transition, not an ending, to something else that allows for leaving a mark, or a clue. Being a constant witness to death must change you. In her case, it softens the hard edge between life and death, making her a spiritual seeker and an explorer of the in-between and the mystery beyond it.

Death is the great equalizer. There is no way out for any of us. Once death has come for someone you love, and you have had a front-row preview to its difficult possibilities—the gasping for air, the unrelenting pain, the bodies and minds no longer recognizable—it is not difficult to remember that we are all mortal and our time is limited. After the seeming finality of death, it is a gift when those who have passed away reach us with a message, a sign, or even a hug.

Katie describes her own experience with her father's untimely death at age fifty-four.

"At some point in the six short weeks after his cancer diagnosis, I remember my mother telling me that 'nothing prepares you' for the finality of it. She was right, of course. And, at the time, I was so black and white, dead and gone, which didn't help. Fortunately, I have evolved since then. I used to scoff at 'passing away' or 'lost,' and I now embrace the euphemisms. I realized eventually that he gave us a gift at the moment he left."

As Katie describes in *The Miracle Chase*, her father was in a coma, his eyes open and rolled back. For hours his breathing had not changed, a rhythmic, rattling gasp for air that made her want to run fast and far away.

"Each breath made me squirm and squeezed some hollow pit in my stomach into an ever-smaller space."

Suddenly, and for no reason, for her father's breathing had not changed, her mother leaned down to say a prayer over him, a traditional Catholic blessing for the dead. "May your soul and the souls of all the faithful departed, through the mercy of God, rest in peace." As her mother spoke, his eyes came down to meet hers with recognition and peace.

Katie continued, "I braced myself for another breath, but it never came. His death was truly a passing, 'out of one car and into another,' lost around a corner to those of us left behind."

Witnessing the untimely death of someone Katie loved had an effect much like suffocation. "The spirit of life was sucked out of me for a time. Years.

"I eventually came to see the gift in my father's dying, of seeing him there for one last moment to say a proper and loving goodbye to those of us gathered around him. I remarked recently to a friend that until that day I walked around like many people do with the unconscious and irrational notion that death and destruction are always something out there. It happens to other people. And in spite of being so sure that it won't happen to you, when it does, the effect can be profound."

Death is a hard lesson, and yet, the seeds of awakening can be found in acceptance of its inevitability. Because we have only so much time, and we don't know how much, we need to let those closest to us know how much we love them each day. Our best selves should start right now. The gift of the moment is often what we learn from the death of someone we love.

Cherishing the moment is all we have, yet each moment brings with it constant options. Kind of like multiple-choice test questions, some answers are sort of right, but one answer is the best fit. The whole exercise of living with the awareness that you are going to die is about choices.

Fred Rogers understood this: "You rarely have time for everything you want in this life, so you need to make choices. And hopefully your choices can come from a deep sense of who you are."[5] How do you spend your time? What is your job? Who are your friends? Who is your life partner? What do you have faith in? What are the choices that confront and define you every day? Not the mundane ones, like soup or salad, but the constant water-torture drip of the things you know you should be doing and are not. Sometimes choices involve things you shouldn't be doing but are, because they fill time and keep you from making any choice at all, the nonchoice default position of most of us.

"Don't forget, you're going to die." It has a ring to it.

Death is hard to contemplate, complete guesswork since none of us have experienced it, though there are plenty of accounts of near-death experiences (NDEs) that offer up some heavenly possibilities and leave us with a picture of what it is like for our loved ones who have passed. We've heard over and over from people we've met about signs they received from those who have died. One young woman approached us after a presentation we gave to her college alumni group. She asked a question at the end of our talk: "Can dreams really be miracles in disguise?" We responded that we thought so, especially since we have had more than one such experience ourselves. She seemed satisfied and afterward pulled us aside to ask if she could share her dream story. (This is like asking a chocolate lover if she would like a Hershey's Kiss.)

She shared that her beloved grandfather had died over the past summer of ALS (amyotrophic lateral sclerosis, or Lou Gehrig's disease). She visited him frequently while she was home from school and felt she was a spiritual listener for him. They had many deep conversations as his health continued to fail until he could no longer move or communicate, and finally, he slipped into a coma. On her last visit before she returned to school, she told him how much he meant to her, even though she believed he could not hear her. To her shock, he reached out and touched her hand. Hours after she left, he took his last breath.

She worried that she would not remember him the way he once had been and felt a constant anxiety about where he had gone and if he was okay. Months after he died, she had a dream. She was in a large outdoor plaza crowded with people and suddenly recognized her grandfather in the crowd at the opposite end of the plaza. He looked healthy and happy and was engaged in a lively conversation with others. She knew he did not know she was there and felt such relief and love as she observed him. But then, as if he had known all along, he slowly turned, found her across the crowd, and looked at her with unconditional love. The encounter startled her awake.

She did not need our blessing to know her grandfather was in a good place. And this young woman had done everything in her power to make her last days with her grandfather count. She had taken advantage of the moments they had left.

The mother of Katie's friend Andrea, the remarkable Mary Higgins, gave us another glimpse into life beyond. One evening just after finishing up her favorite meal, Mary suffered a stroke. Some fast action by Andrea and her husband, who had just come to town to help with a move, meant that Andrea's mother was treated rapidly, and her stroke did not appear to be life-threatening or debilitating in the long term. In fact, after a few days in the hospital, Mrs. Higgins planned to go home. Andrea and her husband left the hospital feeling relieved and excited that Mom could be released in a matter of days. It was good news that Andrea could share with her four siblings spread across the country.

Andrea was shocked when the next morning she received a call from the doctor saying that her mom was suddenly much worse. The medical staff now told them Mrs. Higgins was unresponsive and not going to make it. The siblings were called to come quickly and began to gather, saying prayers together at her bedside. They kept telling her to hold on, the others were on their way. Prior to their arrival, Mrs. Higgins was pronounced dead by the doctor and nurses in attendance. They told Andrea they were sorry for her loss as she, her one sister, and their niece began to cry by the bedside. Suddenly, Mrs. Higgins sat upright, took an enormous breath, and said, "I have been to the most amazing place! You have no idea how beautiful, peaceful, and colorful it all is. The sounds were so comforting, and it was like nothing I have ever experienced."

Mrs. Higgins explained that she asked the Lord if she could return because all her children were not there to say goodbye. She wanted to make sure they would be all right after her passing. The medical staff had no explanation for what had happened, and Mrs. Higgins was released from the hospital the next day. When she died after living for another year, all of her children were gathered around her.

What a gift to die with no regrets. A palliative care nurse from Australia, Bronnie Ware, realized in her eight years working with the terminally ill that death was a perfect tool for the living. Ironically enough, the dying hold the key to living well. "If only I had…" is the lament of so many of those whose time has run out. And almost every regret came down to a lack of courage. "The courage to live a life true to myself" was the number one regret Ms. Ware heard.[6] Busyness, addiction, working too hard all get in the way, suppressing the ability to make considered choices and find happiness. As poet J. Greenleaf Whittier wrote:

Of all sad words of tongue or pen,
The saddest are these: "it might have been!"[7]

Miracles, like death, have a way of shaking us out of our stupor. We can't help but see the world in a new way. Outside, the sun is still shining, the traffic is still moving, and you are not going to die; at least, likely not today. Slow down, look around, maybe go outside, and breathe in and out. It is the first day of the rest of your life.

TAKE A MIRACLE MOMENT

Life Saver: If you found out you had a week to live, what are the first three things you would do? When the reprieve comes, is there anything you would now change?

....

....

....

....

....

....

....

....

CHAPTER TWO
It Remains to Be Seen

*The universe is full of magical things patiently waiting
for our wits to grow sharper.*
—Eden Phillpotts, *A Shadow Passes*

Since today is the first day of the rest of your life, perhaps you would consider a different lens through which to view the people you encounter and the scenery and things that surround you. Try to see them as if for the first time. Consider anew the neighbor you run into at the grocery store, a co-worker you encounter every day, a loved one's voice telling you a story, or the tree that graces your front lawn or a nearby park. Yes, a tree. The one that provides shade on a hot summer day or bends to and fro in a cold winter wind. Simply notice the people, places, and things that are so familiar that they're often taken for granted.

The twenty-first-century default posture of many of us—head down, thumbs waggling, attention glued to a device in our hands—means we often miss what is happening all around us in the moment. Our addiction to gadgets has created a constant sense of urgency and availability that robs us of our freedom to *be*, of necessary downtime, and of being present in our relationships. Before phones became "smart," they could not distract us unless we were at home and within ten feet of a wall. Now, we check our phones an average of 110 times a day.[1] We miracle collectors are as guilty as everyone else, and yet, we remember the good old days, taking a walk when no one else was able to reach us other than whomever we were with face-to-face, or commuting to work with nothing but the radio, our thoughts, and our imagination available. Freedom!

Though all the technology and social media create a record for manic distraction, it is not a disease unique to the twenty-first century. After all, Tolstoy wrote over a century ago that the most important advice he could give is, "In the name of God, stop a moment, cease your work, look around you."[2] Perhaps it is the human condition to grab hold of something else because what is in front of you is tedious or expected or not enough. Stop and look. Notice. Listen. It should be simple, but we have made the simple complicated. We are immersed in a culture of busyness fueled by the gadgets at our fingertips. And yet, if we can simply focus differently, the sublime, the magical, and the miraculous become our reward.

Carolyn and her fiancé Michael were in the midst of packing up their car to make the trip from Denver to California for their upcoming wedding. Carolyn's mom had died suddenly the year before from a reaction to medication. "I just couldn't wrap my head around the fact that my mom wasn't going to be at my wedding ceremony," Carolyn said. She knew it would be too difficult emotionally to honor her mom by speaking about her at the wedding, so she and Michael decided they would place a vase of yellow roses, her mom's favorite flower and color, next to them on the altar.

Before finishing packing and beginning the long car trip, Michael decided to head out for a run. Upon his return, he was astonished to see a spectacular yellow rose in full bloom on the bright pink–colored rosebush in their front yard. It was too early in the season for roses to be blooming, and indeed, the rest of the rosebush was full of tightly closed, pink buds. He ran into the house to get Carolyn to show her the blessing from her mom that had been left on their rosebush. While Michael isn't known for noticing these kinds of things, Carolyn knew it was her mom's way of welcoming him into her life even though she had never met him. While they lived in the house for many more years, they never again saw anything but pink roses on that bush.

Of course, noticing rarely involves beautiful or unusual flowers shimmering in the sun. Sometimes, it is quite the opposite—simply finding solace at a difficult time in the appearance of a familiar face.

One woman we met was reeling from the effects of a bitter divorce since her husband had squandered their savings and she had lost nearly everything, including her business. Needing to begin anew, she decided to leave their East Coast home and move to the Monterey Peninsula, an idyllic spot on the Pacific Ocean where they had lived years before. The lengthy trip across the country with her dog in tow was not going well, when she decided to rest at a truck stop in Oklahoma City and exercise her dog. While she was watching her dog's joy at being out of the car, a woman came up to her, initially startling her. Her surprise gave way to relief when she realized it was a dear childhood friend. Her friend and husband were also exercising their dogs, having taken the same break on their own trip west to California. As the two old friends caught up with the myriad of life events that had occurred in the intervening years since they had last spoken to each other, her friend recognized the magnitude of insecurity she had about the trip. She decided to help by laying out the rest of the trip, including recommending places to stay that would be suitable for a pet. With her angst replaced by reassurance, knowing her friend was just ahead on the road, this woman felt far less alone, and the trip became less of a burden. When they arrived at the California fork in the road to complete their respective journeys, the long-lost friends waved to each other, grateful to know their bond was still strong.

Coincidence? This lovely woman thinks not. She knows her friend was an answer to a prayer. She saw their chance meeting as a miracle—that is how badly she needed someone to care about her. Her friend's presence and assistance changed her entire outlook. For her part, her friend, too, was changed as she accepted her role as a human compass.

One of the many hindrances in relaying a miracle story is that the repercussions from the experience itself, many times, can run far deeper than seeing our path forward in a welcome sign or the appearance of an old friend. Miracle experiences can often take place in the midst of trauma and are difficult to revisit. Sometimes they are relayed for the first time years after the fact.

This point is particularly poignant for Katie, since she told very few people about her own experience for the first twenty years after it occurred. And no matter how many times she has told her story since then, it never feels easy.

As Katie says, "The embarrassment about my own stupidity has gotten easier to take, but not the terror of thinking my life was over, or the evil made manifest on Ted Bundy's face."

Maybe this is why Katie started to get better at allowing a pregnant pause to hang in the air just long enough to make things uncomfortable, hoping someone might find the courage to tell his or her own difficult story. Sometimes noticing involves nuance, like catching someone's eye just as you are about to move on. This is exactly what happened at a cozy indie bookstore in Northern California, A Great Good Place for Books, when we were in the midst of a book event. After we shared our stories, Katie asked, "Does anyone have any questions or a story they would like to share?" After fielding a few book-related questions, Katie asked, "Anyone else?" She remembers allowing the question to hang in the air past her comfort zone. And in the midst of the silence, a woman decided to speak up.

"I have a story that reminds me a little of Katie's," a woman named Rebecca began. The story she shared occurred many years ago when Rebecca was a recent college graduate in the Washington, D.C., area and eager to find a job in film production. After making several contacts, Rebecca had been invited to two interviews, one on a Sunday evening at 6:30 and the other on Monday morning with a woman named Leslie at Yellow Cat Productions.

Her boyfriend, whom she eventually married, and her parents told her that they thought a Sunday-evening interview was odd and gave her a hard time about going. They were even more disconcerted when the gentleman who was going to interview her called to confirm and told her not to be late. Irritated with all of them for their seeming overreaction and lack of support when all she was trying to do was to find the perfect job, Rebecca kept the meeting place to herself. As she pulled up to the address, it turned out to be an out-of-the-way office complex of buildings looking quite deserted, given the day and the hour. After leaving her car in the parking lot of the designated building, she went inside and walked down a long corridor to the appropriate office suite and knocked.

A woman answered, let her in, and announced she was just leaving. "Are you sure you're okay?" It seemed an odd thing to say, but Rebecca saw other people milling about and said, "Sure, I'm fine." The woman directed Rebecca down a hallway to the office of the man who was going to be interviewing her. Upon entering, she saw photos and trophies and was impressed, thinking they must be film awards. Almost immediately, the interviewer suggested a tour of the facility.

As they began walking, Rebecca noticed the facility was now deserted. The man began to describe what he did to women who chose not to obey him. (With her fourteen-year-old daughter sitting in the audience, Rebecca left out some of the more graphic details, because the man had been overtly sexual and repulsive.) Rebecca decided pretty quickly the guy was dangerous and knew that if she were to survive, she would need to agree with everything he said. She continued to tell him she would obey his commands. As he walked her around for an hour or more and continued to terrorize her, she looked for any opportunity to escape. She was haunted by her decision not to tell anyone where she was going, not the name of the company, the address, or the person she was meeting.

Finally, with no escape having presented itself, they returned to his office. As they reentered, she realized the trophies were not for what she had assumed was film but were for martial arts instead. Just as she was certain that her life was over, his phone rang. He didn't pick up. It rang a second time and again he didn't pick up. The third time it rang, he picked up the phone in annoyance and answered.

Still desperate for an escape, Rebecca hung on his every word, and at some point in the conversation the man mentioned Yellow Cat Productions. *Oh my God, it is Yellow Cat Productions! The place where I have my interview tomorrow.* She was unsure if they were a subcontractor of his or what the connection was, but she knew she had found her way out. She yelled as loud as she could, "It's me, Rebecca! I have an interview with Yellow Cat Productions tomorrow!" She thought that this might save her. Now someone knew who she was, where she was, and who she was with.

When the man hung up the phone, he told her she was lucky, and he had decided to "let her out." He continued to threaten her, as he had throughout her ordeal, that she better show up and do as she agreed, and if she told anyone what he had said, he would ruin her life. He grabbed her by the arm, marched her down the long corridor to the door, and shoved her out of the building. She ran to her car, falling down and even losing her shoes in her haste, and sped the whole way to her parents' house, where they were anxiously waiting for her. She had been gone nearly three hours. They called the police and the man was located and arrested. He was a serial rapist who had been terrorizing the area for three years. The man was convicted and sent to prison, and Leslie at Yellow Cat Productions hired Rebecca, launching her successful career.

Neither Rebecca's best friend, nor Rebecca's daughter, who were both with her that night at the bookstore, had ever heard this story. Rebecca later shared how embarrassed and ashamed and vulnerable she felt at the time of the incident, believing that somehow it was her fault. She initially wanted to dismiss her experience but now sees that as a way of dismissing herself. At the time, she did not see the experience as miraculous but now she does. She said that night our presentation "woke something up" in her. It was a quiet reminder to treasure herself and recognize that she is sacred, body and soul.

In retrospect, she also sees that she saved herself. The coincidence of the Yellow Cat Productions connection was a means for her escape, but she had shown great presence in adopting an immediate strategy of reverse psychology. She had played that man's game in a fearless way, feigning naivety and being "into it" and committing to do whatever he wanted, and so she had managed to hold him off. This cunning and sadistic man seemed to hold all the power, and yet, she had found a way to empower herself. The strength and intuition required to survive in the moment is as much the miracle in her eyes as anything else.

For most of us, stopping to notice what is happening around us, difficult and out of practice though we may be, can be even more difficult when it is paying attention to what is happening within ourselves. Learning not to dismiss our own experiences and, rather, to recognize and honor the stories that define us is a key to staying in touch with who we are. As we revisit the familiar around us, why not look at ourselves with fresh eyes too? Are we squashing the "still, small voice" at the core of our being, a divine spark we all possess?

Nothing clears the static smothering that voice like a good romp in nature. Who among us has not felt renewed after watching a spectacular sunset or walking in the woods down a well-worn path smelling dirt and pine with the sun dappling and dancing up ahead? Finding the beauty in nature, wherever it is available to you, and welcoming these experiences to seep into your soul hold a key to reinforcing the importance of allowing yourself to simply *be*.

Ralph Waldo Emerson, the father of transcendentalism, a nineteenth-century movement that espoused an affinity with the natural world, wrote, "In the presence of nature, a quiet delight runs through [us]…in spite of real sorrows."[3] He reveled in the natural bounty at our fingertips and in nature's ability to soften and remedy the realities of life. He saw humanity as an integral part of nature's overarching presence. "Nothing is fair or good alone…Beauty through my senses stole; I yielded myself to the perfect whole."[4]

We cannot begin to notice the people, places, and things around us if we cannot quiet the constant chatter suffocating our own soul. It is like a fly buzzing around the room, a small nuisance that somehow takes up the entire space. Until we can release it out the door or window, there is no "yielding to the perfect whole."

In nature, miracles are available to all of us for the taking. To see nature's complexity as a manifestation of the Divine is to see its miraculous journey of evolution in every wise, old tree or shooting star, in every sandy ocean bottom, and in every wildflower on a mountainous expanse. "If we could see the miracle of a single flower clearly, our whole life would change," Buddha observed.

Connecting to nature is a spiritual exercise that also has profound health benefits both psychological and physical. One long-standing experiment concluded that patients who were recovering from surgery healed faster when they had a view of trees out their hospital window rather than a brick wall.[5]

There is a place in the midst of busy Central Park, at the top of the Shakespeare Garden, where Katie pauses during her morning walks and says a prayer or two. "Being in nature, however small the area, or however brief the encounter, fills me with a spiritual connection. I always leave that spot, surrounded by trees above and garden below, feeling renewed."

Each year Joan cross-country skis to the top of a hill in Aspen, Colorado, to visit her favorite pine tree whose trunk was split when it was young. "The divergent trunks grew from the same root system and the canopy they share forms a perfect heart. As I stop and catch my breath at the top of the hill, I always take the time to notice and appreciate the majesty that surrounds me and snap a picture of that heart tree to remind myself to be grateful for those I love."

The national evening news reported on a human-interest story of survival about a young hiker who had immersed herself in nature in order to regain her faith in humanity. Katharina, a young German tourist, had been hiking the entire 2,650 miles of the Pacific Crest Trail from Mexico to Canada. With less than 150 miles to go, she traveled alongside Nancy Abell, a seasoned hiker with a lifetime of experience on that section of the trail in Washington State. The mother in Nancy was doubtful about Katharina's preparedness to make it the last miles. She had no snowshoes, her supplies were dwindling, and Nancy knew the North Cascades' weather in October could turn wet and cold in an instant. Nancy tried to talk Katharina into holding off on her journey, but Katharina was determined. After coming so far, she only had a relatively short distance to go and wanted to finish what she had started. They parted ways after a couple of hours, but Nancy had trouble getting the young woman out of her mind.

A few days later, when Nancy saw snow in the forecast, she felt she had to act. She called 911 and convinced them that Katharina must be in trouble. Based on Nancy's insistence and her educated guess of the like-lihood of where Katharina might be, the dispatcher agreed to initiate a search-and-rescue mission by helicopter. As it turns out, Nancy's hunch was right. Katharina was frostbitten, stranded, her sleeping bag and clothes soaked, and the snow was still falling. Katharina had given up hope and had begun to write messages to her family, cursing her stupidity and trying to say goodbye. Despite the weather, the helicopter spotted her red coat near Glacier Peak. The rescuers said she had a day to live.[6] Being one with nature may have been a goal at the beginning of Katharina's journey, but it took the human connection, one person really seeing another and acting on her instinct, to restore her faith in humanity. It was an experience that saved her life in more ways than she could have imagined.

Of course, we humans are part of the natural continuum and the only living thing that can both follow our instincts and dial 911. We have the unique ability to notice one another and follow through to the next logical or intuitive step. While sometimes that next step is literally making a call, based on our own credibility and experience, other times, the step can be anonymous as well as mysterious.

Katie's daughter Allie left a party one night in New York City to find the downtown neighborhood eerily quiet, no cab or car in sight, even though 11 p.m. was hardly late by New York City standards. As she made her way toward the subway entrance several long blocks away, a group of drunken college-aged guys came up behind her and began to make crude remarks at her. She sped up. So did they. She crossed the street. They followed. No one else was around and she was frightened by the escalating comments and their aggressive pursuit. Suddenly, a cab came racing around the cor-ner, seemingly coming out of nowhere, and a young woman about Allie's age rolled down the cab window and asked her to get in. Allie agreed, and the cab dropped her at her destination, having left the boys far behind. But how had the young woman seen her? Or known she was in trouble? Was it as simple as noticing the scene unfold from elsewhere or was it something more?

These stories share a universal thread. Sometimes we are put in each other's path or are called on to help in ways that only we can at that particular moment. Perhaps it is a sign that some higher power has your back, be it a more traditional notion of God "by whatever name" or a sixth sense or energy at work in the universe that cannot be explained no matter how hard we try.

The effect of becoming aware of what is around us starts with the low-hanging fruit, and with practice we're able to observe the nuance of situations—the person who has something to say, signs of someone in trouble, the way a leaf moves on a still day if you watch it long enough. The more we become aware of what is all around, the clearer the path we cut to the soul within us.

We used to joke that if a miracle happens in the forest and there is no one around to notice it, is it still a miracle? As we find out in the next chapter, our answer is unequivocally yes. Noticed or not, it would still be a miracle, though encountering and recognizing a miracle has a way of snowballing. Once you stop and notice one, it begins to change the way you see the world.

TAKE A MIRACLE MOMENT

Full Stop: Take one minute to stop and look, sit on a nearby bench, find a favorite window view, or enjoy a sidewalk café. Are you surprised by what you see when you make the effort to notice?

CHAPTER THREE
More Than Meets the Eye

Change the way you look at things
and the things you look at change.
—Wayne Dyer, *How to Forgive Someone*
Who Has Hurt You In 15 Steps

What if a miracle happened in the forest and there *was* someone around to witness it? We might presuppose it would be easily discovered, recognized without a doubt, and celebrated for its grace and timing. Turns out there is something to the proverbial idea of not seeing the forest for the trees. Sometimes we are unable to sift through the barrage of images and activities all around us, and we miss what is right in our path.

Katie lives a few blocks away from the Metropolitan Museum of Art in Manhattan and rarely, if ever, passes by without admiring its façade. The giant columns and arched windows, the sweeping expanse of stairs, and the new fountains out front are especially dramatic when they are lit up at night. One morning, she noticed a crane reaching to the top and workmen walking along an upper ledge of the building. Four stacks of giant concrete blocks were piled on top of each of the double columns just below the roof-top. *Hmm, what could the concrete blocks be for and how did they get them up there?* she wondered. Intrigued, she took her husband Jim on an evening walk to point them out. He, too, was curious and unsure why they were there. Obviously for some construction purpose, but what could it be? After a few days, the crane and workmen were gone, but the blocks remained.

Several weeks later, while walking past a tour group across the street from the museum, she overheard the guide say, "Does anyone notice anything unusual about the front of the museum?" No one did, but Katie sauntered over, hoping to be enlightened about the mysterious concrete blocks. The guide continued, "If you look up, you will see piles of concrete blocks. Believe it or not, they have been there since this section of the museum opened in 1902."

In response to her shock at never having noticed the concrete blocks before, Katie's daughter Laura told her about an experiment called the Invisible Gorilla.[1] In a video that was presented to college students at Harvard, two teams of basketball players, one team in white T-shirts and one in black T-shirts, pass a basketball around. The students watching were asked to count how many times the basketball changed hands among those in white T-shirts. After watching the video and recording their answers, the students were asked specifically if they had seen anything unusual or unexpected. About halfway through the video, a gorilla, or rather a volunteer in a life-size gorilla costume, dances across the screen, stopping in the middle, thumping his chest, and moving on. The gorilla is in the midst of the players for nine seconds. Half the students never saw the gorilla.

Hidden in plain sight. It happens to all of us. We see the world through customized vision, colored by years of honing our particular experiences into assumptions about the way someone or something is or even what is possible. We bring this individualized worldview to bear in every situation we encounter. In short, we see what we expect to see. Becoming aware involves not just noticing what is around us but being open to the possibility that there may be something more to see.

Sometimes it is as simple as a change in perception. In the opening chapter of Stephen Covey's book *The 7 Habits of Highly Effective People*, he shares an iconic picture of a woman. Some people see an old woman, some see a young one. Most of us take a while to see both women embedded in the picture. In Katie's case, having read the book not long after college and ever the optimist, she could only see the young woman. No matter how hard she tried, she could not find the old woman anywhere, and yet, Mr. Covey insists that you cannot go on in the book until you see both.[2]

As a rule follower, Katie was stuck. Fortunately, there was a cheat sheet in the back to help her get through the impasse. The lesson had a profound effect on her. It is one thing to recognize that we each see the world through our own unique lens and quite another to experience it. For her, it was an epiphany, literally like walking in another's shoes. Seeing more than one side and the understanding this brings to any relationship, or even to a complicated concept like miracles, is important. Joan laughed when Katie shared this story. The picture was one of Joan's favorite images. She had no problem first seeing the old hag and then the beautiful young woman. It was never an either-or thing for her. Joan believes that nothing is as it seems at first and she is always reading into things. She told Katie it was probably from her years of searching for the hidden pictures in all those *Highlights* magazines she devoured in her childhood.

Differences in perception are not just about seeing two things in one or searching for hidden meaning. Perception colors our entire worldview. In fact, in our initial miracle-chase meetings, Meb and Joan enrolled Katie in the fictional miracle police force, because she insisted on acting like the gatekeeper for miracle stories—this one counts, that one doesn't. It was as if when a certain event was not enough of a miracle to her, it was deemed "miracle light," so to speak. Her limited view fueled her skepticism and she usually ended up in the same corner. Her narrowly prescribed view made it harder to believe a loving God was behind the action. This person is healed, that person is not; this person is rescued, and that person is not—so arbitrary and fickle and unfair. She was trapped in a conundrum believing in miracles but not being able to reconcile them (a real dilemma for a former banker).

What if miracles are available to all of us? Meaning that those thunderbolt miracles—inexplicable deathbed healings, or miracles at the center of the great religions, like the parting of the Red Sea, the resurrection of Jesus, or the escape from Mecca—are at one end of a whole continuum. At the other end is the idea that somehow a higher order has been achieved out of chaos and randomness: the ongoing gifts of Mother Nature, lucky happenstance in friendships, or life partners, work, and experiences that seem fated. These might not make the evening news but most of us have recognized at times we are riding a gentle wave that seems predestined. When we acknowledge that there can be more than meets the eye, we open ourselves up to a whole new world. Miracles are found when we are open to different interpretations of past experiences, when we look at something not head-on but out of the corner of our eye, producing aha moments when we realize something is different than we first believed or is more than what we saw before.

One woman we met said our talk made her rethink an experience she had years before. After suffering a late-stage miscarriage, an aide in the doctor's office literally harassed her to come in for an important follow-up test. She avoided the calls and did not want to go back to the doctor because the memories were just too painful. The aide was relentless and kept calling. While the woman thought the aide was insensitive, bordering on rude, she finally acquiesced and begrudgingly went in for the test. If nothing else, she thought it would at least get the aide to leave her alone. The test led to a diagnosis of early-stage uterine cancer. The timing and persistence of the aide saved her ability to have children, for which she is forever grateful.

Joan had one of those aha moments when out driving with her then five-year-old son, Gregory. "There's a white rainbow!" he exclaimed from the back seat. "No, buddy, that's just the vapor from a jet engine," she explained. At the time, we were early on in our miracle journey. But then she had her own epiphany: *Why can't a rainbow be white? It is time to shift my thinking. Perhaps there are rainbows all around us, but since we only see them a piece at a time, we mistake them for something else.* We think we know what we know, like the saying, "Never in doubt, often wrong." Changing perception is about acknowledging the possibility of a different interpretation.

"A miracle is often the willingness to see the common in an uncommon way,"[3] according to current-day poet and philosopher Noah benShea. We agree. One woman wrote to tell us about an experience she had that shed light on a challenging time in her life years before. As the founder and CEO of Guardian Nurses Healthcare Advocates, Betty had been asked to give an inspirational talk to the nursing team at the Cancer Treatment Centers of America in Philadelphia. She included in her talk the story of her own mom's four-month battle with and death from cancer when Betty was just twenty-three years old. The nurse who had cared for her mom was her inspiration to become a nurse herself, even though she was about to graduate from college with a degree in journalism. The memory of that time was especially fresh in her mind when she arrived at the hospital to give her talk.

As she walked down the hall to the auditorium, a frail woman walking ever so slowly and apparently dealing with some sort of cancer was approaching. She was being held and supported by a young woman, her daughter perhaps, who looked to be about the same age Betty was when her own mom was sick. The scene was so reminiscent of a different hospital corridor thirty years before that Betty had an immediate flashback. She had taken her mom for a second opinion and her mom had walked haltingly, using the support of a railing along the wall as well as her daughter's arm, until they got to the front door. Betty saw it as a sign, reassurance, and a blessing from her mom.

We love the notion of miracles as signs. Philosopher Soren Kierkegaard used a nautical marker to illustrate his point that a miracle is "a sign only for one who knows that it is a sign, and in the strictest sense only for one who knows what it signifies."[4] For someone who does not know what she is looking for, the blinking beacon in the harbor is just a pretty sight, instead of indicating to the sailor which side is safe and where the channel leads. Recognizing the signs we are given along the way is how miracles find us.

Rebecca W. recounted a sign that saved her life. Even though she was in her early fifties, she was not concerned that she had skipped having a mammogram for the past five years. A mother of four, she led a healthy lifestyle without alcohol or tobacco. She had let her health insurance lapse while she was doing contract work, and preventative screening was not a financial priority for her. One day, she decided to drive to work, even though she usually took the bus. She had the sudden urge to drive that day, thinking, *Maybe I'll do some errands on the way home.*

As she window-shopped after work, she noticed a woman about her age sitting on a bench and sobbing like her heart was breaking. Though it was a lovely day with plenty of people milling around, no one was paying any attention to her. Rebecca W. went over and asked if there was anything she could do. The woman explained that she had just had chemotherapy and the clinic told her there was a free bed at a shelter, but when she got there, the bed was no longer available. The woman had just walked the two miles back to the center of town and she was exhausted. As she continued to cry, with her chest heaving, Rebecca W. noticed the obvious space where one of her ample breasts should have been. Introducing herself, Rebecca W. learned that the woman's name was Sandy. Rebecca W. told Sandy that her church had a program called Room at the Inn and she could see if they had room for her there. Rebecca called and was able to secure Sandy a spot for the night.

Having a mammogram all of a sudden became a priority for Rebecca W. She had started a new job, but her health benefits were not yet effective. Immediately after her encounter with Sandy, she heard about the DeAngelo Williams Foundation, which provides fifty-three free mammograms a year, sponsored by former Carolina Panthers running back DeAngelo Williams in honor of his mother who had died of breast cancer at age fifty-three. When Rebecca W. called the foundation and left a message, someone called her right back and scheduled an appointment. After finding something suspicious on the mammogram, Rebecca W. was sent for follow-up testing and was diagnosed with breast cancer. Another charitable group was found at the exact right moment and paid for Rebecca W.'s treatment.

For the two years after her treatment was completed, Rebecca W. continued to look for Sandy in vain. Eventually, Rebecca W. went to the DeAngelo Williams Foundation website to send them a thank-you for what they had done for her. There, she saw a picture of DeAngelo's mom, who looked exactly like the woman she had met on the bench. DeAngelo's mother's name? Sandra.

That day on the bench, Rebecca W. gave Sandy a Snickers bar she had received as a store giveaway and all the cash she had, amounting to thirteen dollars. She asked if there was anything else she could do for her. Sandy told her that just the fact that she sat there with her was enough, because usually she felt invisible. In sharing her story, Rebecca W. believes, "We are all connected. And none of us knows enough to be a doubter. I do believe in miracles. I believe there is a life force in the universe."

Rebecca W.'s story illustrates the way miracles can be less than straightforward, meandering along a path that cannot be seen at first. We are not like drones, flying high with an aerial view, but are grounded with choices to make at each junction. As Rebecca W. cared for Sandy, she received a fateful nudge to care for herself as well. She had her own cancer diagnosed and treated through community resources in a roll-out-the-red-carpet, streamlined kind of way. That never happens: a miracle, no doubt.

The namesakes and look-alikes, Sandy and Sandra: Just a coincidence? Rebecca W. doesn't think so. Neither does DeAngelo Williams' wife, judging by the tears in her eyes when Rebecca W. shared the story with her. It reminds us of wisdom from the New Testament: "Be not forgetful to entertain strangers: for thereby some have entertained angels unawares" (Hebrews 13:2 KJV). And you never know what will unfold in the aftermath.

Entertaining angels unawares was at the core of an unusual story a woman named Jody shared with us. She and her husband were frustrated when, for years after building their new home, they found that they kept having to repaint the interior closet wall in the bedroom their two sons shared because the paint kept getting discolored. Finally, with the boys off to college, they decided to fix the problem once and for all and ripped down the wall. To their shock, they found that the furnace exhaust pipe had never been properly attached from the basement to the roof. Consequently, the furnace was not vented to the exterior of the house; instead, the condensation and deadly fumes funneled directly into the boys' bedroom. Attaching the vent was easy and the closet was repaired, though their embarrassment and fear about the tragedy that might have occurred prompted them to keep the whole experience to themselves.

After a conversation with a friend in which Jody confided her concerns about one of her children, her friend suggested that Jody make an appointment with a woman who had a spiritual practice that included communicating with angels. Perhaps, she thought, it could help relieve some of Jody's anxiety. When a skeptical Jody arrived at this woman's office, the woman immediately relayed an expression of relief from the angels that they could finally rest, having saved the boys for so long from the carbon monoxide that had threatened them for years. Jody was speechless. This woman had no way of knowing of the situation at their home, and yet she passed on the information as if communing with angels were an ordinary occurrence.

While we have all heard about angels and spirit guides, our friend Annie confided that she had actually pursued an experience with one by praying for her guardian angel to show herself. She prayed for this encounter each night for several nights and was finally rewarded when, one night, as she lay in bed with her eyes closed, something, or someone, touched her feet. She was frozen with fear and gripped her eyes shut when she felt the touch again. And then, whatever was there was gone. Beyond her fear of tapping into another dimension, she was aware of a profound and unconditional love she had never experienced before or since.

You might think this is a story of wishful thinking or that Annie was asleep and dreaming, or that guardian angels are the purview of children, like Santa Claus. But it takes courage to invite a spiritual being into your life. Seeing or feeling more than meets the eye can be confusing or frightening, as Annie discovered, but it can also be reassuring and enlightening, as Jody came to know. Talking about the experience is an act of bravery. No one we know is waving their hand to be called on in the classroom of odd tales. Including us. Sometimes we feel a bit like Moses, who supposedly had a speech impediment and wanted very much for someone else to be the spokesperson for the Israelites. But then, these miracle gifts landed in our laps.

Katie read an article from her alma mater about having an obligation to report such stories; Joan thinks we have an obligation to do everything. Initially, we became miracle chasers, finding out all we could about so-called miracles. Not exactly the career you dream about as a kid. But like Father

George in the movie *Saint Ralph* said, "If we're not chasing after miracles, what's the point, huh?" Ultimately, we morphed into miracle collectors as the power inherent in the miracle stories we heard caught up with our intellectual curiosity.

Jodi Parker of Idaho agrees that we have an obligation to tell others when a miracle touches our life. Her eight-year-old son, JT, had been helping his dad, Stephen, and seventeen-year-old brother, Mason, work on their Toyota Prius in the garage when Mason cut his hand and went back in the house. As Stephen worked on an axle, the car suddenly collapsed on him. Before passing out, he yelled for JT to jack the car back up. After adjusting the jack, JT began to jump on it and the car slowly began to move off his dad. He then ran into the house to have Mason call 911. Stephen was airlifted in critical condition with thirteen broken ribs but had no lasting internal injuries. Initially, it had taken all the strength of both Mason and Stephen together to jack up the car. So how had fifty-pound JT accomplished it on his own in an emergency? When he was asked, JT simply replied, "The angels helped me." When he tried to jack the car up again by jumping on the jack as he had before, the car didn't budge.[5]

This story begs the question, "What is the nature of reality?" Beyond perception and paradigm shifts, it turns out reality itself is a bit wobbly. As Deepak Chopra describes, naive realism, or the assumption that what you see is what you get, "hasn't been tenable for at least a century."[6] Einstein's theory of relativity proved a space-time continuum, or fourth dimension, which led to the quantum revolution and the understanding that there is definitely more than meets the eye. Uncertainty and mystery are beating at the heart of the universe.

Consider physicist Fritjof Capra, who saw direct parallels between modern physics and ancient Eastern wisdom traditions. Dr. Capra described his own mystical experience at the shore one afternoon when he "suddenly became aware of my whole environment as being engaged in a gigantic cosmic dance."[7] He felt the energy, rhythm, and sound of the universe and understood it to be the "dance of the Shiva," a reference to the divine energy flow and Hindu symbol of universal consciousness.[8]

He was not alone in noting these similarities. Many of the other great minds behind the quantum revolution agreed, including theoretical physicists Oppenheimer, Bohr, and Heisenberg. While subatomic particles can be both waves and particles, they are neither one nor the other, but instead are "probabilities of interconnections…and can only be understood in terms of the objects' interaction with the observer."[9] In the minds of the mystics, becoming "aware of the unity and interrelation of all things"[10] leads to enlightenment. Time suddenly exists in an eternal now. Christian apologist and writer C. S. Lewis spoke of God in an "eternal Now," reiterating that time is an illusion, as Einstein previously concluded. Lewis wrote, "It is probably that Nature is not really in Time and almost certain that God is not."[11]

With time not being what it seems, matter in its teensiest form being inexact, and all things in the universe being connected, there is plenty of room for miracles to grace our lives. Perhaps stumbling into peak awareness in the eternal now is what Annie experienced in the night and Capra felt at the shore. Our language limits the description of such transcendent experiences. We try with words like *energy, goodness, love,* and *divine.* It seems counterintuitive that physics provides us with a language for the mystical. Miracle stories offer us a more personalized and familiar way to transmit the mystery inherent in the universe.

"Help me, we're in here." All four officers heard it, the plea of a woman calling from a vehicle submerged in near-freezing water in a river below a bridge in Spanish Fork, Utah. The vehicle was hidden from the road, but a fisherman spotted it and notified the police. The woman's plea motivated the officers to risk their own lives in the freezing rapids to turn the heavy, waterlogged car on its side and get to its occupants. The only occupant they could save was an eighteen-month-old child, who was unconscious though still alive. The car had been submerged for fourteen hours overnight, and according to the coroner, the mother had been dead for some time in the front seat when they heard her call. One of the officers said he would not have believed this was possible except that his fellow officers heard the woman's voice as well.[12]

Where had the voice come from? Many faith traditions share the perspective that the soul, the divine essence of a person, lives on eternally and, hopefully, in heaven, nirvana, or paradise. Perhaps the love of a young mother can be so powerful as to defy gravity and delay the soul's departure. Perhaps she felt that heaven could wait a few more hours until her daughter was rescued.

The two of us believe a mother's love can, and does, transcend what we think we know of physical reality. It reminds us of Mary Higgins, who asked God to come back from her deathbed to spare her children the grief of not being there when she died. We certainly think the Divine could do the same for this mother to spare her daughter's life. And we hope the view of heaven that Mary Higgins described was visible to this young mother as she died.

Where does the physical world begin and end? Is there a spiritual spectrum, a staged departure from the physical world into the spiritual one? Richard Rohr, Franciscan friar and spiritual writer, talks about seeing with the third eye. Using a spectacular sunset as his prop, he describes the first way of seeing, the seeing that most of us do by noting the physical beauty, seeing what is right in front of you. The second way of seeing includes the enjoyment derived from placing the sunset within the context of what we know about the universe, the science behind the beauty. The third way of seeing includes the first two and, also, "remaining in awe before an underlying mystery, coherence and spaciousness that connects…with everything else."[13] The third eye is seeing with the soul.

Perhaps seeing with the soul is an ability we are born with and slowly lose over time, though it is always there to cultivate. Three-year-old Lindsay demonstrated her own ability to see more than is available to most of us. Her mother, Mellisa, shared that her father-in-law had recently died in his fifties. Three years before, they had buried his mother, Nanny, and Mellisa and her sister-in-law decided to pay Nanny's grave site a visit while they were back in the area. The cemetery was quite large and meandering, and with no one in the cemetery office to assist them, they drove around aimlessly for nearly thirty minutes, searching for Nanny's grave in vain. All the while, Lindsay was in the back seat, saying nonsensical things on repeat, as three-year-olds can do. "Wave to the lady." "That lady has a blue dress." "Wave to the lady." Finally, they tuned in as Lindsay said, "She says come here." Mellisa asked Lindsay where, and Lindsay directed them to the exact spot where Nanny was buried. The flat headstone would have been impossible to find without guidance. Before Nanny died, she had been excited about the birth of her great-granddaughter and had even purchased gifts for Lindsay that were found after her death. A connection somehow was forged between Nanny and Lindsay, as one life gave way and another life was born.

When we speak of the reality of dimensions beyond our own and the uncertainty inherent in the subatomic world, we must be open to the possibility that what we see is not always all there is. "A miracle is a change in perception, not a change in the rules," as Reverend Bill Tully suggests. As we embrace this practice of stopping to notice, of looking closer for longer, and of recognizing that we have just added ourselves to the equation, we create a unique recipe from which to experience the mystery of the universe. No doubt once you begin, you will be amazed as you see more than meets the eye.

TAKE A MIRACLE MOMENT

Hidden Pictures: Think about someone or something you encounter every day but take for granted. Find something new or different you had not noticed before. Are you surprised by what you see?

CHAPTER FOUR

Co-Incidental

There is no such thing as chance; and what to us seems
the merest accident springs from the deepest source of destiny.
—Friedrich Schiller, *The Death of Wallenstein*

"Surprise, surprise, surprise!" It was an exclamation of wonder from Gomer Pyle, USMC, in the 1960s homespun TV show of the same name. Surprise is what happens when you open yourself up to noticing what is around you and seeing the world in a new light. Even Pope Francis tells us, "God is a God of surprises."[1] Taking a change in perception one step further, we have all had instances in our lives where a coincidental event is just too outlandish for us to think life just happened that way. With Joan's son David, it took Katie and Meb urging her at the coffee shop to recognize that the series of events that conspired to save his life went beyond luck. Too many pieces had to fall into place for his fatal cardiac anomaly to be found, much less repaired. Sharing this experience together became the tipping point that began our miracle journey.

Many have introduced the notion that a coincidence is God's way of working a miracle anonymously. Still, not all coincidences are life-or-death events. In fact, many coincidences are simple and serve only to bring a knowing smile that calls to mind a forgotten joy or an unexpected, yet meaningful, message.

After the birth of Joan's first child, she was stunned by the number of floral bouquets that arrived, prompting her sister-in-law to share her own mantra that there is no such thing as too many flowers! Like Carolyn and Michael, Joan thinks flowers bring joy and connect us to nature and to each other in a way that goes outside of the ordinary, even more so when they are heaven sent.

Flowers are at the heart of a story Joan loves sharing about her friend Chris. Joan knew how devastated Chris was when her soul mate and husband died. On the first wedding anniversary after his death, Chris was alone in the home where they had raised their four children, pajama-clad and with an early-morning cup of coffee in hand, trying not to be overly maudlin. She was trying to focus on the love they shared and the time they had together. At 7:30 a.m. exactly, the doorbell of her house on the sleepy cul-de-sac where she lived shattered the silence. Someone must be in trouble was her first thought, since it was too early for visitors. She was shocked when she opened her front door and saw the huge bouquet of yellow roses being delivered as they had each anniversary for the previous forty-seven years. Clutching the precious bouquet to her heart, she returned to her chair, delighted that her children had remembered. After a while, she pulled out the card inserted amid the flowers, anticipating their names, and was surprised to discover she didn't recognize either the message or the signature. When she looked at the envelope, she saw the card was not even addressed to her. Same zip code, but the address was a street on the opposite side of town. She called the florist only to find it was still closed and left a message. When they called back, they couldn't understand the mix-up and returned to pick up the wayward roses. Regardless of the florist's confusion, Chris knew exactly where the flowers had come from.

Flowers are a symbol of eternal love connecting heaven and earth. Many pilgrimage sites honoring the Blessed Mother, including Guadalupe, Fatima, and Medjugorje, have been known to have an intense otherworldly aroma of roses associated with them. While researching what we came to call the "accoutrements of miracles," bizarre things that happened in inexplicable ways, we found the story of Saint Dorothy in the fourth century.[2] She chose martyrdom over marriage and was said to have delivered a fragrant bouquet of apples and roses to her intended after her tortured demise.

Sometimes, coincidences connect the dots left hanging after the death of a loved one. Other times, a series of coincidences can save a life or even a home. One young mother in San Diego was, by her own admission, a great cook but a lackadaisical housekeeper. That is, except, as she told us, on the day her first house cleaner was scheduled to arrive. She wanted to be sure that this new person would realize how pristine she wished her house to be kept and she had painstakingly cleaned it herself, down to the very last detail. She belabored this point, emphasizing more than once her particular dislike of ironing and the banishment of the dreaded iron to a far-off closet in the no-man's-land of the unused guest room in her home. Running out for a couple of last-minute errands before the housekeeper arrived, she had already put her two-year-old in the car seat when, once again, she reentered the house and went upstairs to be sure all was in perfect order. She was shocked to find the never-used iron plugged in, facedown on the floor. Somehow her son had discovered her hiding place. The rug, pad, and subfloor beneath had already been scorched. Her nudge to go back inside before leaving prevented the disaster that would certainly have occurred had she left when she initially intended.

How do we explain these moments? After all, we like things to be predictable: plant a seed, get a flower or a tree or a vegetable. Clean a house and expect it to stay clean, not burn down! We trust, by virtue of science, that what we expect will, in fact, occur. When events happen that are not generally connected, we may remark on the sheer coincidence. Where we find a deeper meaning, coincidence may be telling us something more; synchronicity is at play.

Synchronicity was the brainchild of the Swiss psychiatrist Carl Jung at the turn of the twentieth century, who described it as the "acausal connection of two or more psychic and physical phenomena."[3] In his role as a psychiatrist, he noticed coincidental events in the lives of his patients and realized that often these theoretically unrelated events had meaning, though they did not imply causality. He coined the term *synchronicity* to acknowledge circumstances where the manifestation of the universe is tied to our consciousness, the interconnection we talked about in the previous chapter. It is as if the San Diego mother had a sixth sense about something being amiss in her home. As Deepak Chopra explains, "Synchronicity says there's more in this world than you dream of!"[4] After decades of miracle exploration, we know he is right.

Many of us tell tales of meeting our spouse through a series of events we think are unusual or perhaps even eerily preordained. Sometimes, something occurs because normally unrelated events happen simultaneously or in concert to achieve an unexpected result. Who knows whether it is wishful thinking, hoping that seemingly random events have meaning, or whether they are, in fact, truly synchronistic? It is up to us, as individuals, to decide.

In the years before Jung died, he spent his leisure time in the garden of his home on the shores of Lake Zurich in Switzerland. His favorite spot in summer was in the shade of a magnificent old poplar tree. On the night he died, a storm erupted, and a bolt of lightning shattered the tree, splitting it in two. His friends wrote after his death, "This remarkable phenomenon has been viewed as a manifestation of the very principle of synchronicity that Jung had devoted so many years and so much energy…The magnitude and power of the event also pointed towards the titanic capabilities present within human consciousness."[5] In the case of Jung and his tree, the synchronicity seems fairly benign, though certainly some would argue it is a message from the other side that synchronicity is real. The opposing view, what is known as confirmation bias, proposes that we read significance into unrelated things, especially when we are looking for evidence to support what we already believe. The point is that we notice coincidences but hardly ever notice their absence.

In Joan's case, she knows if she had made a different choice six months earlier and had not said yes as a favor to a friend, she would not have been at school that fateful day and she would not have been present to see David's pain and near collapse herself. Instead of the series of coincidences that began to unfold months earlier that conspired to save his life, there is no doubt that she would have accepted the first doctor's simple explanation, a decision that could have turned out to be deadly. It is not always possible to know what event will become a miracle in our own life. It is as if the potential of a miracle in all things becomes a barrier to seeing a miracle in any one thing.

Such was also the case with Mary and the synchronistic events that occurred in her life. As the story unfolds, Mary was a thirty-year-old nurse, married with an eighteen-month-old child, when she discovered a lump in her breast. It was cancer, pure and simple. But at the time, nearly forty years ago, nothing about cancer was pure and simple. After surgery and radiation, she was one of the lucky ones who survived, though she never had another child. At ten years old, her daughter was diagnosed with a horrific parasite that was unresponsive to all but the most aggressive therapy. It is easy to imagine the disbelief of Mary and her husband when once their little girl was cured, the doctors explained that they had also found she had polycystic ovaries and when she grew up, she would likely not ever get pregnant.

Though they were devastated at the news, twenty years later, they rejoiced when their daughter did have a child. The joy their granddaughter brought was all the sweeter for its unexpectedness.

Remembering her own experience, eighteen months after the birth of her granddaughter, Mary insisted her daughter be tested for breast cancer. However, before approving the breast MRI, the insurance company required confirmation of whether Mary carried the BRCA gene mutation. Once the presence of the gene mutation was confirmed in Mary's genetic test, not only did her daughter have the MRI, but it was an opportunity for Mary's doctor to explain that Mary now had a 70 percent chance of developing ovarian cancer. Like so many other women in this situation, Mary chose to have her ovaries removed. There was good news on the day of surgery when the surgeon gave Mary's anxious husband a positive report. However, their relief was short-lived because two days later, the pathology report came back with a diagnosis of ovarian cancer. As the doctors laid out the difficult treatment options for her Stage III cancer, some might ask, Where is the miracle in that? The doctors explained if the surgery had been performed six months earlier, no cancer would have been found, and if it were six months later, she would have had no chance of survival.

As an acausal series of events that have meaning, Mary's story qualifies as synchronicity at its best. Whether a synchronistic event is a miracle or not, well, that is up to you to decide. It certainly felt miraculous to Mary and her family. These synchronistic events might well be able to be explained by the skeptical, but what we know for sure in traveling along in our own miracle journey is that miracles are not always recognized instantaneously, nor do they all need to be thunderbolts. In changing the course of any one life, when you are that one life, they are no less compelling than the parting of the seas, the raising of Lazarus, or the feeding of the masses with loaves and fishes.

The aha moment hits many of us at different times in different ways and we never know in advance what the tipping point will be. Miracles are no exception to the reality that things resonate with people in a variety of ways. As we know, a change in perception—being open and noticing the various possibilities around us—is central to the miracle discussion. It is like seeing the same play or movie but with different directors. The story is the same, but the interpretations are generally unique.

Back in the mid-1990s James Redfield wrote the popular book *The Celestine Prophecy*. In it, he postulates that life is a series of events, maybe even tests, where people or things come to us for a reason and stay until we learn the lesson they are meant to bring. This builds on the notion inherent in Jung's synchronicity where there is a "governing dynamic which underlies the whole of human experience and history—social, emotional, psychological and spiritual."[6] In acknowledging the interconnection of all things, and the observer at the center of it, Jung's philosophy was a different way of tying together aspects of relativity theory and quantum mechanics. This concept, picked up by Redfield, acknowledged, then reconciled, the paranormal. It was evidence of a unifying consciousness at play in the universe, creating physical manifestations of what is happening in our psyche.

One woman we met told us she had her dream job, the one she had worked hard for years to achieve in one of our many male-dominated professions. She appreciated that she was lucky. She had a great life with her husband, three children under the age of five, and a gratifying job, but it was also unsustainable. The pace was killing her, and she felt she would lose it all by trying to hang on. She even knew the solution. She needed to work part-time for a while to add balance to her life, but no one had ever done that at her company. Even worse, part-time work was frowned upon and she believed it was considered unrealistic in her senior position. Her resolve to make a change was frozen by her uncertainty and fear.

One sunny weekend day while driving down a busy Los Angeles freeway with the kids squawking in the back seat and too many errands crammed into too little time, she knew she was at the end of her rope. Frustrated, she sent up a prayer in desperation: "God, just give me a sign. Tell me what to do!" No sooner had the words come out of her mouth than she drove past a billboard advertisement for a Mexican brewery with a picture of Our Lady of Guadalupe (the special devotion to the Blessed Mary in Mexico) on the sign. Underneath the picture were two words in superlarge type: JUST ASK. She got the message. The next day she asked her boss for approval to work part-time. Not wanting to lose her, he said he had been waiting all along for her to "just ask."

While it might be nice if all miracles included literal signs and instructions to boot, usually events and the connection to their ultimate meaning are far murkier to discern until much later. Sometimes, it can take years to find clarity, as was the case with Katie and her rescue from serial killer Ted Bundy, and with the Lockerbie survivor. Sometimes, connected events can take years to unfold, as with Mary. Even when it comes later, it is the recognition of what has happened that is important, not the timing, in the evolution of a miracle.

Some people have stories of a recurring or lucky number that seems to be important, whether it is a birthday, an anniversary, or an apartment code, which gives credibility to random encounters or highlights the importance of someone or something. But even in these instances, often it is not an immediate case of playing the numbers like buying a lottery ticket; it usually takes a while to see the consistencies. Katie is one of these numbers people. She tells the story of the day she and her brother were choosing a cemetery plot for their dad. It was reassuring to have synchronicity at work, because truly how does one really pick out a cemetery plot? A nearby tree, a road, the place where the sunlight falls—who knows? In their case, they stood in the office at the cemetery, surreal in the moment, staring at a map on the wall as the office manager pointed at the available spots. When he got to one and said, "There is this one on the grassy slope," she and her brother turned to each other instantaneously and agreed that was the place. The manager consulted a sheet in his hand and said, "Good, fine, that's plot number forty-one." Given that was the number of the address where their parents lived, they understood that they had chosen correctly, and their dad would be at home.

Perhaps a coincidence is really an invitation. It is an opportunity to look with gratitude on the surface of the event, but by looking beyond, there is a deeper meaning to be found. Like all invitations, we can respond in different ways. Some can be dismissed quickly, like the group email blast that has no personal connection and is easily sidestepped. Other invitations can be accepted tentatively, akin to dropping in somewhere for a quick visit, then deciding whether to stay and invest the time connecting with those you know or meeting those you don't. Joan did this with her own set of synchronistic experiences. By testing the waters bit by bit, she became completely immersed in her personal miracle journey. And then, there are certain invitations that are accepted wholeheartedly from the very beginning. It is an "all-in" response, like one for a landmark birthday of a dear friend or the wedding of someone you care deeply about. Our LA freeway woman accepted her message right away. She was "all-in" instantly, and within twenty-four hours her problem was solved.

The jolt inherent in these experiences may be a reason some are wary of accepting the invitation to seek a deeper meaning. After Joan's father's death from the ravages of dementia, she decided to give him a job as a way of maintaining their close father-daughter relationship. In life, he always worried about her driving off to God knows where on her own. So, in death, she dubbed him her very own parking angel. Joan routinely drives to the front of any crowded venue and finds her parking space open and available. On the few times when her treasured space is filled, she concedes gracefully, glad her dad has merited a day off.

While Joan is not the only person we have encountered who connects with a parking angel of her own, others find this connection and the sense of a deeper meaning in the objects their loved ones leave behind especially for them. This was the situation for Angela, a senior administrator at a Catholic secondary school. Her mother had specifically left Angela her special gold rosary beads that Angela's dad had given her on their honeymoon trip. At the time, it was an acknowledgment of his welcoming her to the family and their traditions, though she was not Catholic. As the years went by, Angela's mother became an active member in the church and surprised the family with her own baptism concurrent with the baptism of her seventh child. Before she died, Angela's mother wrote notes to all her daughters sorting out the jewelry and gifts she wished to give each of them. As the note that accompanied Angela's gift said, her mother knew she was called upon to attend a number of funerals, and the opportunity to pray the rosary would be an ongoing one. Her mother thought the gift, though not as sparkly as some of the others, would hold more meaning for Angela. When we met her, Angela confided that it bothered her that outside of the small card in the box accompanying the gift, she had no idea how to say the rosary properly, and she wondered if perhaps something simpler, like a ring or necklace, might have been more appropriate.

A month after her mother's death, Angela had to travel some three thousand miles away from her home for work. So, instead of gathering with her family at the Mass commemorating her mother's death, she was far away, left to her sadness and shouldering her grief alone. Walking out of her hotel that morning, though she knew the upscale shopping area was to the right, she felt a nudge that sent her to the left. As she walked aimlessly, with thoughts of her mother consuming her mind, she realized she had crossed the railroad tracks and was now in a run-down industrial area that she normally would not have ventured into on her own. Suddenly, acknowledging her discomfort, she looked up and saw what she knew was a Catholic church situated upon a hill in the distance. With time to spare before her late-afternoon appointment, she decided to walk there and go inside. As she climbed up the numerous steps to the entry, she smiled at the church's name engraved on the lintel: OUR LADY OF THE ROSARY. Simultaneously, as she entered from the back of the church, the priest entered into the front altar and began the noontime Mass. Angela knew it was exactly when her mother's Mass would be starting three time zones away and decided to stay. She felt at peace, content to be experiencing the service at the same time as her family back home.

After Mass, there was a group that stayed to pray the rosary together. While she was still in her pew gathering her thoughts and recovering from the tears she had shed during Mass, one of the elderly women in the rosary group noticed that Angela was still there and asked if she would like help in learning how to say the rosary. Angela nodded and the woman gave her a plastic rosary with the same instruction card that had been included with her own rosary beads. As the older woman moved to sit next to Angela and take her hand, Angela felt the radiance and wisdom of a mother's touch. She knew she had been given the right gift, and now a reassuring message from her mother, knowing they would always be connected.

In telling her story, Angela expressed, "There were two lessons for me that day. One was that I had been given the most golden gift in my mother's rosary. For, what that gift did was that it led me to Our Lady of the Rosary. And, through the kindness of a stranger, an angel perhaps, I was able to feel true healing through this gift of prayer. Our Lady of the Rosary healed me in so many ways that day. Now, when I find myself wandering in life, I have Our Lady to turn to…the final gift from my mother."

We can all relate to stories where coincidence and synchronicity connect us to those we love. But stories like this abound in social media posts and the news as well. The twentieth-century urban legend of the Scottish farmer who saves a young city lad (Winston Churchill) whose family then pays for the education of the farmer's son (Alexander Fleming) who discovers penicillin, which in turn saves Churchill's life again when he was stricken with pneumonia, is but one example. The story is apparently untrue but there are plenty of real stories to go around.

One of these is the story of the San Francisco window washer who was in the process of clipping back into his safety harness when he lost his balance and plummeted eleven stories off the side of the building toward a busy intersection. On the street below, an unsuspecting technology specialist was trying to find his way to his next appointment when he was forced to slow down because his GPS lost its connection. Once the GPS picked up a new signal, he increased his speed, which placed his car in the exact perfect position to cushion the fall of the worker and to not be killed himself. A split-second difference in timing and the worker would have landed on the windshield instead of the roof, or even on the street itself. According to a spokesman with the California Department of Industrial Relations, "It seems pretty clear the cushioning of the car he fell onto kept him alive."[7] The driver of the totaled car said of the experience, "With all the changes in where I went and how I was going this morning, I think God wanted me to be there just at the moment that poor man fell. It was a miracle that he was able to fall on my car, and it was a miracle that I was OK."[8]

Not all coincidences are so traumatic. Some may just save worry. When Joan was in the throes of her cancer treatment years ago, worried about her young children and her prognosis, Meb constantly reached out to her recalling the message of Saint Julian of Norwich: Trust in God and all will be well.[9] Whenever she feels anxious, she tries to recall those words and take them to heart. Hence, the story of the apprehensive mother who had just left her youngest child at college for the first time and was worried about how he would adjust, who he would meet, and what the next four years would hold grabbed our attention. After dropping him off, this mother deliberately went on a silent retreat to a place without cell service or computer access so her son could be completely immersed, and she would use the silence to begin seeking meaning and direction in light of the empty nest she faced. Following nearly a week of no contact, she realized her approach was too rigorous and she really needed to know he was okay. As she walked on a beautiful trail through the California foothills, she gave up her worry to the "almighty spirit" and asked for a sign that all was well. After her walk, she returned to her cabin and started flipping through the free magazine she had absentmindedly picked up at the airport before she left town. As she turned the pages, she noticed numerous college ads listed among those for restaurants and housing. Looking at the ad for Boston College, where she had just left her son, she knew Someone had heard her plea. The advertisement in huge letters read, "Your Son Will Succeed Here." It was akin to, "In Boston, All Will Be Well." Even from three thousand miles away, her son probably heard her sigh of relief.

Her story recalls Saint Augustine's famous "tolle lege" message that, as Jung might say, is an example of using synchronicity to find the path we are meant to take. Saint Augustine was living a playboy's life but longed for more than the satisfaction of his lascivious behavior. Hearing what he thought was a neighbor's voice, he followed the instruction to "tolle lege" (take it and read). He knew the "it" to be the Bible, and when he randomly opened to a passage describing his own wanton life, the words shocked him as if they were a fourth-century defibrillator recalibrating his heart and piercing his soul.

Even after his experience, it took a while for Augustine to get on the miracle bandwagon. Initially, he believed that miracles were performed only to show Christ's divinity and no longer occurred, but over time he changed his mind. His view broadened, perhaps the murkiness surrounding his own synchronistic event cleared, and he came to believe "miracles are so numerous even in these times that we cannot know about all of them or enumerate those we know."[10]

Augustine's sentiment mirrors our own belief. In fact, we always sign our books with the inscriptions "Miracles abound," "Keep the faith," and "Celebrate the miracles in your life," reflecting our understanding that miracles continue in today's world if only we take a moment to appreciate their existence. In the words of newly canonized saint John Henry Cardinal Newman, "It is incomparably more difficult to believe the Divine Being should do one miracle and not more, than that he would do a thousand."[11] Whether through Augustine, Newman, or the Divine incognito of Kierkegaard, miracles are found in the daily occurrences of life. Some might be compared to fine wine, aged over time with the expectation of being savored, while others bring an instantaneous smile, the joy of recognition that someone is looking out for us. With this broader idea in mind, it becomes far easier to accept the possibility of each of our lives being touched by a miracle.

TAKE A MIRACLE MOMENT

Fate or Fortune: Think of a recent or memorable coincidence or circumstance that seemed fated and consider the possibility of deeper meaning. Has your interpretation of this experience changed over time?

CHAPTER FIVE
Let the Light Shine

You are as prone to love as the sun is to shine.
—Thomas Traherne, *Centuries of Meditations*

Saint Augustine's journey proves that it is not necessary to be a poster child for religion or spirituality for a miracle to occur. Take us, for example. We are hardly poster children for anything. Honest? Yes. Hardworking? Definitely. Fun? We hope so. Intelligent? Some days more than others. Self-aware? Now, there is a lifelong challenge, but we are working on it. Like most people, we never thought we were worthy of a miracle, much less that we'd actually receive one. Consequently, it was not the first thing we thought of when the miraculous found us. Now our view has changed. Our new mantra is, "If us, then anyone." We fully subscribe to the notion of miracles described by journalist and writer Kenneth Woodward: "To believe in miracles one must be able to accept gifts freely bestowed and altogether unmerited."[1] People share their stories with us because they sense we offer a safe haven for their vulnerability and we take seriously their questions about their own experiences. After all, we have firsthand knowledge about how hard it is to share these stories and reveal a delicate part of our inner selves in front of others.

Maybe it requires speaking up or speaking out, like the Lockerbie passenger who, upon hearing the collective gasp from her book group, finally acknowledged that her avoidance of tragic death was something more than sheer luck. The reaction of others can be just the wake-up call we need to see our lives in a new light. Psychologist Paul Tritschler explains, "Stories are part of the fabric of who we are, but only in sharing our life experience do we develop a sense of self."[2] Once we share our stories, our sense of self deepens, bringing us closer to who we are underneath our exterior façade.

This broadening sense of self often happens when a miracle experience is acknowledged. Like putting on glasses for the first time, the new connection forged to the Divine is illuminating, not only changing how we see the world but how we see ourselves as well. Sharing stories provides a buffer between the internal voice of self-doubt that supplies us with a running, though not always helpful, commentary and the response of others who recognize that something out of the realm of the expected has occurred.

Sometimes miracles are hard to identify. Perhaps we feel unworthy or that our need is too small, or too trivial, for personal attention from the Divine. We may feel overwhelmed by the world's troubles or are worried about a child or an aged parent or panicked by a terminal diagnosis in someone we love. When the problems surrounding us are so monumental that our own disappear in their shadow, we tend to burrow inward, afraid to state our own needs. It is difficult to feel empowered when there is bad news all around us consuming the spotlight. Smaller acts of generosity go unnoticed and uncelebrated. When a miracle does show up, whether we have asked for it or not, we may not even recognize it, as happened in this classic joke:

After a huge storm there is a man on the roof of his house because the floodwaters around him are rising fast. A group in a rowboat comes by and offers to take him with them, but the man replies,

"God will save me." A short while later a motorboat goes by and the captain offers assistance. Still, the man's response is unchanged: "God will save me." With the floodwaters nearly at the top of the roof, a helicopter arrives whose pilot begs him to get in. His response is the same: "God will save me." Needless to say, he drowns. When he gets to heaven, he is incredulous that he is dead. He questions God, "Why didn't you save me?" God's reply: "I sent a rowboat, a motorboat, and a helicopter…"

The truth is we never know the manner in which the response to our plea will come, nor is it likely that the world will look all rosy and perfect when it does. While it would be great if we could just sit down and say, "Okay, God, I'm ready for a miracle now," unless you are like the LA driver who happened upon the perfect sign, most times life, like the joke, does not work that way.

Sharing with others allows us to recognize when things are different than we first believed. Suddenly our vision is broadened by taking off our blinders and seeing a whole new range of possibilities. Expanding our outlook can lead to a change in perception. As Julian Fellowes wrote in the popular *Downton Abbey*, "A problem shared is a problem halved." The age-old sentiment remains a useful technique to change our view and move forward.

Hesitancy to share is a reason loneliness is on the rise and why public health experts have called isolation one of our most prevalent public health issues, even ahead of cancer and heart disease. By connecting with others, we increase our sense of value and of being good enough, and we become less isolated. Harvard's Dr. Robert Waldinger tells us, "Staying connected and involved is actually a form of taking care of yourself just like exercising and eating right."[3] This connection is a way to counteract the impact of social media, by which feelings of loneliness, depression, and anxiety can be exacerbated.

Even though socializing can be fun and is actually good for us, it still takes effort to get out or to invite others into our lives. Social interaction is one of the ways we experience a life worth living. As life experiences are shared, deeper bonds are formed, and connections are made. When we began our miracle exploration, it was like speed dating or a fast-track way of deepening connection. It is impossible to stay superficial when the defining moments of our lives are revealed to one another.

Joan had a powerful experience one evening when she Skyped into a book group a thousand miles away from her home. For one woman, the exchange that occurred after the miracle discussion in her long-established book group was freeing. She had grown up in California but had gone away to college in Seattle. As she drove back to school her senior year with her parents, her mom mentioned she had a headache. Between student teaching and finishing up her classes, she was busy but always made time to chat with her family, and she knew the headaches were continuing. Her dad reassured her not to worry: nothing bad was happening at home, her mother was seeing a new doctor, and all was well. But within three weeks, her mother was dead. In mid-October her brother called her in a panic at 3 a.m., telling her to come home quickly. While she was fortunate enough to arrive home to have some time alone in the hospital room with her comatose mother, it was not enough. She felt her mother was only partially there, a shell of her real self, and she had missed the opportunity for connection. At twenty-one, her heart was broken. Even though she thought it was crazy, over the years she would murmur a fleeting prayer that one day she would be able to say a real goodbye and tell her mother how much she loved her.

Years after her mother's death, she harbored an illogical worry that after she had moved from Seattle to different cities in the Midwest, her mom would never have any idea of where to find her. One night when her husband was out of town on a business trip and their four children were at home asleep, the doorbell rang at 3 a.m. Terrified at what she might find outside, she went downstairs and saw a woman motioning for her to open the door quickly. When she opened it, she realized it was her mother standing in front of her. Next to her mother was a young boy, his face obscured by a dark hoodie. The bizarre scene was made even more otherworldly by a large Colonel Sanders–looking man waiting under the streetlight as though watching for something.

She explained she was speechless trying to take in all that was before her as her brain processed, *How can this be?* Suddenly, she was enveloped in a warm hug, the one she had longed for, an expression of the deep love she felt for her mother and her mother's love for her. It was a hug she felt to the essence of her being. With her senses piqued, she suddenly noticed her mother was dressed in her favorite seventies long skirt and she smiled, realizing that her mother was no longer the fashion-forward maven she had been but instead was frozen in some fashionista time warp. The next thing she knew she found herself back in bed. Her first thought was that she must have been dreaming. She described that she was tingling with a feeling as if she were hovering over her bed. She explained she knew it was not a dream; she believed it was nothing less than an out-of-body, God-given experience.

Once she decided to tell her story, she did not want to leave anything out, even at the risk of what we might think of her. In addition to the peace that came with seeing her mother, she told us she knew that the faceless child was her first baby, the one she miscarried and prayed that he be sent to his grandmother for safekeeping. As she looked at the clock next to her bed and noted the time, she realized the date was ten years to the day of her mom's passing.

She often thinks about what God wanted to show her that night and believes that for her, it was an understanding of heaven and the certainty that God heard her prayer. Although professionally she is a public speaker and routinely stands up before large audiences, she kept her story hidden for years, even from those who knew her best. She admitted she was afraid to share her story for fear of being criticized, or worse, ostracized. Feeling embraced by her book group friends, who listened with openness, murmuring their wonderment and support, she knew she was in a safe environment where she could at last unleash her powerful story.

Our discussion of *The Miracle Chase* gave her newfound courage as she spoke openly for the first time about the hole her mother's death had left in her life and the gift that she felt rescued her soul. Finally, she felt truly complete, not only that she had been given the gift of the experience, but that she was at last able to share it. She knew what she needed—a goodbye and a chance to express her love. What she got was that and more: uncertainty transformed to grace.

The grace of that miracle moment swept over each of us present and inspired a new level of willingness to consider the miraculous in nontraditional ways. The book club member who had chosen the book and arranged for Joan to Skype in emailed her the next morning:

We ALL loved the evening…We all felt a tremendous connection! For our group, we shed some tears, broke through some defenses that were quite amazing, and really connected on a new plane. The conversation led to empowerment in our lives and our conversation lingered for another hour, and typically everyone is running home to kids and husbands after the last question of our discussion… A deepening awareness and resilience of the human spirit, and to begin to unravel and examine this in a short hour, on Skype no less, is quite powerful! Truly amazing and unbelievable, except that I witnessed it in my own living room!

Opening up a dialogue with others is one approach to navigate our path toward self-enlightenment and spiritual clarity. Sometimes, we have yet to uncover or even consider the beliefs we have adopted without question. While acknowledging a miracle may open new avenues to explore spiritually, it also creates additional questions. A defining moment is a call to action, requiring us to look beyond our complacency to consider our purpose: *Why am I here? Do I have a unique gift to share?*

Marianne Williamson recognizes the propensity we have to hide behind our insecurities and rationalizations and why sometimes it seems we cannot get past ourselves. In her book, *A Return to Love: Reflections on the Principles of "A Course in Miracles,"* she challenges all of us when she wrote, "There is nothing enlightened about shrinking so that other people won't feel insecure about you...your playing small does not serve the world...we are all meant to shine."[4] So much for the wallflowers among us who choose not to honor the light that is within them or are inclined to keep it burning low. The idea that we have a responsibility to put our light out there is not an exclusive concept developed solely as part of the New Age movement. It has been around for a long time. More than a hundred years ago, William James, the father of American psychology, said, "Believe that [your] life is worth living and your belief will create the fact."[5]

If we are each unique, a recipe of complex ingredients that experiences the world and the people in it in our own particular way, equipped with our own nugget of talent, then we each have something new to offer each other. It is, in fact, our uniqueness that powers the light within. The truer we are to our gifts, the brighter our light shines. If each of the billions of people in the world were given a blank canvas to paint on, with every possible color hue at their disposal, no two paintings would be alike. Since according to scientists the human eye is able to distinguish ten million different colors, imagine the magnificence of the art created by billions of people using their own color combinations. The world would be far richer.

Why do we hold back our biggest gift to the world, the gift that distinguishes us from everyone else? Do we see our offering as less than? Are we afraid it is unacceptable, unnecessary, or unwanted? Perhaps we think all that people will see is the mistake we made in the corner of the canvas, or the muted colors we chose in the wrong place. We compare it to other lives that we see as bigger, bolder, more colorful, or more complete than our own. Even though it may be daunting, voicing our opinion is important. We have more power to influence, comfort, and connect than we realize, and we need to use it.

Letting your own light shine begins by searching within yourself. When you close your eyes and focus your awareness just on yourself, whom do you encounter? Deep down, who are you? Can you see it, that thing that is unique to you and only you? Even when we think we are not ready, we must step up and let our light out into the world. As Matthew tells us in the New Testament, "Nor do people light a lamp and put it under a basket, but on a stand, and it gives light to all in the house. In the same way, let your light shine before others" (Matthew 5:15–16 ESV).

Even the famous and holy among us have had to battle their own demons of uncertainty. The sainted Mother Teresa is known to have doubted her own ability to feel the touch of God, though she accepted with her whole heart that God exists and was felt by others. Regardless of her sense of unworthiness or her feeling that God was hidden from her, she believed her work was her destiny and continued to allow her light to shine. She saw Christ in the people she served, and she prayed constantly that she would be worthy of God's presence to fill her soul.

As the Spanish mystic Saint John of the Cross described in his famous poem, "The Dark Night" ("La noche oscura"), this search for the presence of

God can be a metaphysical nightmare. The journey is called "the dark night" because darkness represents the fact that on some level the destination, God, is unknowable, and the path to God per se is unknowable as well. Mother Teresa internalized this unknowing in her personal dark night of the soul, patiently waiting four decades for God to speak again in her own life.

We felt this uncertainty ourselves in the process of exploring miracles. By career choice Katie was a banker and Joan a health-care executive—we were not philosophers or theologians. It would have been easy to "play small" and stay in the boxes we had previously chosen for ourselves. The challenge was to feel worthy enough to venture out into the world and tell our stories and to be open about our extraordinary experiences. Self-doubt and skepticism were slowly replaced by faith in ourselves.

We found the persistence to continue by recognizing the signs we were being given along the way. While some signs were clear, other signs we found were far more discreet and revealed through the coincidences we experienced. The year Joan needed to take her youngest child to visit colleges, they were getting a late start; but by child number three there is less incentive to consider much in the way of advance planning. Multitasking, a thing Joan does routinely, tied a trip to Colorado College with an overdue visit to her mother-in-law. Two days before her arrival, Joan finally went on the school's website to arrange a tour and visit.

On the top of Colorado College's home page, a banner listed new publications by their professors. The first one that came up was a book by Dr. David Weddle, professor of theology, entitled *Miracles: Wonder and Meaning in World Religions*. What were the chances! *Why not try to meet with him and engage in a conversation of miracles?* Joan thought as she sent an email requesting a meeting. Dr. Weddle answered quickly and while her son toured the college, she tested her miracle knowledge. We were about to embark on our first book tour and Joan had doubts about her layperson's analysis of the "wise guys"—the philosophers, theologians, and scientists she had written about. Professor Weddle had no idea what he was in for, but after pleasantries, they engaged in a lively discussion of the eighteenth-century miracle cynic David Hume. By the time their meeting was over, Joan not only had her confidence boosted, but she also agreed to head back to Colorado College the following spring as a guest lecturer in the class the professor was teaching that term. Dr. Weddle was excited about the idea, emailing, "A joint program would be terrific! We could put some of my classic stories next to your contemporary ones. That in itself would demonstrate how persistent is the hope for miracles."

In emphasizing the importance of advancing the accessibility of miracles beyond the ivory tower, Dr. Weddle offered us welcome encouragement to stay the course and helped us feel more secure in letting our own light shine. We knew we had information to share and hoped others would find it interesting, but, like most people who embark down an unfamiliar path, we had misgivings. Not knowing where the path would lead, all we could do was our best every day. As it turned out, we had no idea how continuing to expand the miracle discussion in new ways would surpass even our most optimistic dreams.

So, what is holding you back from feeling worthy enough to let your own light shine a little brighter, believe in yourself a little more, and share more of yourself with others? Or even asking for your very own miracle? One of our most humorous miracle moments occurred in the small town where we both once lived, when no sooner had we gotten into the car after our miracle presentation and discussion than we got an email from one of the attendees. She said while she knew it wasn't "really" a miracle, it would be a miracle to her if only she could find a pair of black sandals like the ones Joan was wearing. She needed them for a wedding the following weekend.

How great would it be if all miracle requests could be granted at a nearby department store? While we know all requests are not so simply fulfilled, asking for what we need in that moment is often inherent in miracles. Like the peace that comes with a proper goodbye as told by our book club raconteur and the comfort received by our Boston College mom, there are many other stories that reinforce this notion of asking the universe to consider our heartfelt request.

In one mother's case, a woman who was still grieving the loss of her young adult son, she explained that she was walking a trail in Maryland "talking" to her son about all the beautiful flowers of spring, when she ran into a fellow walker. The man's baseball cap was emblazoned with the logo of the law school her son had attended. It turned out he was a law professor there and they traded pleasantries. In an email sent to this professor after their encounter, she explained that she and her son "had lots of talks about an afterlife and he certainly wasn't a total believer…he was just trying to deal with the real possibility of his shortened life. But I asked him for a favor: One day he would give me a sign…that he was restored, healthy, and in a peaceful place." She went on to say that "when I saw and spoke with you, I was very convinced that he gave me that sign. I was pretty emotional after I left you and went home to tell my husband what had happened. I also wrote to one of my son's classmates and roommate…After writing to him and explaining our meeting, he told me you were their favorite Law professor…I am so thankful that I met you that day. I know that it was my son telling me that he is fine."

Whatever is your most important need *is* your most important need. It is vital that you treat it that way. No judgment or inner critic allowed. Letting our light shine requires that we accept our own validity and unique place in the world. We know that miracles, like answers to prayers, are not magic wands or genies hiding in bottles. We also know that not all prayers are answered in the way that we hope or expect. Meb's father prayed daily for the restoration of his granddaughter's eyesight, stolen when she was shaken nearly to death. While decades later Liz is still blind, she sees more than many of us, as she leads her life of service helping others who deal with fading vision.

Author Bangambiki Habyarimana tells us, "State what you want and go for it. Do not refuse yourself a request you did not make."[6] Many of us do just that. So, what if for one day, you chose not to play small? You let your light shine and your voice be heard. Would the world end? Or would you feel its warm embrace holding you as you embarked on a new journey?

TAKE A MIRACLE MOMENT

Let There Be Light: What would it look like to let your light shine brighter today? How might you ask the universe to assist you?

CHAPTER SIX

It's a Wonder-Full Life

The most beautiful thing we can experience is the mysterious…
Whoever does not know it and can no longer wonder,
no longer marvel, is as good as dead and his eyes are dimmed.
—Albert Einstein, *Ideas and Opinions*

Allowing our own light to shine can provide needed perspective in a troubling world. In order to feel truly alive, we must also embrace the beauty that exists around us. There is a unifying and connecting spirit found in feelings of wonder and awe that have been part of the human experience since the beginning. According to University of California, Berkeley, professor Dacher Keltner, "Awe is the feeling of being in the presence of something vast that transcends your understanding of the world."[1] Sounds a lot like miracles to us.

We often compare miracles to Russian matryoshka dolls—universally recognized, multilayered, and the closer you get to the inside, the more intriguing they become. As we peel back our own layers, becoming more aware by finding the time to stop and notice and consider that there is more behind the immediate scene, we can see that a synchronistic thread runs through our lives. When the spotlight of awareness highlights our own worthiness to let our light shine in our own unique way, we are ready to fully engage with the world around us. Cultivating a sense of wonder becomes second nature, once we are tuned into our surroundings and ourselves.

"It's a miracle!" The phrase is ubiquitous. We use it in our daily discourse to mean anything from the latest pop culture cure for thinning hair to finding a parking space outside a crowded store on Christmas Eve. The word *miracle* itself derives from the Latin *mirari*, which means to look in wonder. In the sense that a miracle evokes wonder and awe and that miracle stories abound in every religion and culture and language, miracles are a universal language we can all understand.

We recognized this universality as the world breathed a collective sigh of relief in October 2010 when one billion of us watched on live television as the first of thirty-three Chilean miners was rescued after sixty-nine days underground. Roughly 14 percent of all of humanity was riveted by an ordeal that had captivated the world. People who had been praying for their safety for two months in every language, religion, and culture sent messages of hope to Camp Esperanza, which was set up at the top of the mine. The trapped miners somehow survived a slab of tumbling rock weighing 770,000 tons that gave way on top of them and caused the collapse of the mine. One miner shared his epiphany that their survival from the very beginning carried with it "a hint of the divine" and took it upon himself every day to remind the miners that "God is with us." Some of the miners felt this presence through a "thirty-fourth miner."

With no electricity or access to outside air, the miners found they had provisions for twenty-five men for two days. A single peach or can of tuna was rationed into thirty-three equal parts and eventually they received only one cookie every three days. At mealtimes they always said a prayer, not to be rescued, but that the rescuers would keep trying. And even though there was constant disappointment as they heard the drills attempt, and fail, to reach them and the "monster of insanity" knocking at their door, they stayed united.

An American entrepreneur, Brandon Fisher, whose equipment and expertise finally broke through to the miners, admitted they had been more than lucky. "These tools should not have been able to bend and go around some of these curves. I mean, there's no question in my mind that the faith of God, and the faith of the world praying for these guys to get rescued was a huge factor."[2]

It was reassuring to see humanity care so much about the Chilean miners. Most of us can relate to the pain of their loved ones and the nightmare of the miners even though we have never experienced anything like it. Imagining the terrors of starvation, insanity, and the very real prospect of being buried alive, we wished for their rescue as if we were there ourselves. There was a level of "love thy neighbor" in the collective, universal prayers sent up that we rarely get to see in the news, highlighting our connection to each other, a divine thread running through our lives. And finally, somewhere deep down, we all hope or wish or pray, *If them, then why not me? If they can be saved, then maybe my faith is not in vain.*

In his book *Miracles*, Dr. Weddle wrote, "Belief in miracles is the confidence that, at rare and wondrous moments, grace may overcome fate."[3] This certainly seems the case with the Chilean miners. The 2018 rescue of the Thai soccer players provides a similar perspective.

Twelve players and their coach became trapped deep in underground caves for eighteen days when the monsoon rains came early and the cave entrance flooded. What started as a fun team-bonding experience of hiking and exploring turned into a disaster. Fortuitously, their coach was a Buddhist monk, who taught the young players mindfulness and meditation, a practice that focused their energy and helped ward off panic once they understood they were trapped. This preserved their energy and assisted in their deliverance. A British cave expert who had made a detailed map of the caves the previous year was only a few hours away, having planned to visit there the very next day. Based on his knowledge of the area, he was able to direct the rescuers to the only logical place the team could be trapped and still be alive.

Once the soccer team was located, highly skilled and specialized divers needed to make the trek through the tumultuous conditions multiple times a day to bring supplies and evaluate their options. The danger with each trip was underscored when one well-trained diver died in the process. The world, united, tuned in to pray and wondered how twelve unskilled youngsters and their coach who had to make the same treacherous journey would ever be retrieved.

At the site, volunteers from around the globe descended to offer assistance; villagers and family members kept their vigil from morning to night, acknowledging the spirit of the cave. When the decision was made to drain part of the cave, it caused flooding to the nearby farms and destroyed the livelihood of nineteen farmers for a year, yet none of them complained. The farmers said it was important to "do the right thing." All of humanity, it seemed, whether across the globe or in the backyard of the cave, was rooting for the Thai soccer players as if these twelve children were their own.

A global sense of community won out and the barriers that divide us came tumbling down. Maybe that is the miraculous point. Keeping vigil over the Chilean miners and the Thai soccer team brought out the best in us. After eighteen days, all thirteen made it out and the world breathed a collective sigh of relief. "The rescuers succeeded, or the cave relented, or maybe both happened at once. No one can say for certain, and perhaps it doesn't matter: It was a miracle either way."[4]

René Descartes wrote that wonder is "a sudden surprise of the soul,"[5] as compact a definition of miracle as there is. Perhaps a miracle comes as an epiphany about a past experience or knowing you have just met the love of your life or your new BFF. But it could also be the kind of experience available to us and repeatable every day, like a kaleidoscope of color after a seemingly endless winter, as you happen upon a garden in spring. Or it could be that feeling of oneness with the universe as you stare into the endless depths of the heavens, stars sparkling like precious jewels on a clear night. Wonder stops you in your tracks, prompting you to take in an air of appreciation and admiration, and momentarily expanding and questioning your place in the universe. Miracles relate to wonder in its many iterations, cultivating not just a sense of wonder, but the ability *to wonder*, to stay curious, to ask the question, "How can this be?"

Take the incomprehensible vastness of the universe: one hundred billion galaxies encapsulating so much that is beyond our current capability to understand, or perhaps ever understand. In 2019, the Event Horizon Telescope captured photographic evidence of a black hole billions of times more massive than our sun in a giant galaxy fifty-five million light-years away. Found in the constellation Virgo, the dark hole gobbles up anything that gets too close to its edge, sometimes called, ominously enough, the place of no return. Not even light can escape as the laws of physics apparently also collapse into this cavernous, mysterious, stellar-charged denseness. Truth is stranger than fiction, with one *New York Times* reporter describing it as "a smoke ring framing a one-way portal to eternity."[6]

This is connection and interconnection—all of life and matter and energy that exists in the cosmos. Joseph Campbell wrote, "The goal of life is to make your heartbeat match the beat of the universe, to match your nature with Nature."[7] Suddenly, we recognize that we exist not alone, but within a cocoon of a shared experience.

Socrates said that wonder is the beginning of wisdom. It means we acknowledge that we do not have all the answers and we remember to bow in appreciation of the universe's bounty, which has been laid at our door. We often walk right past it, not noticing the sound of wind in the trees, not seeing the common in an uncommon way. As an exercise in appreciation of wonder, we decided to ask ourselves the obvious question: What is the most "wonder-full" thing we've encountered?

"Recently?" Katie responded. "I'd have to say the Grand Canyon. Peering over the edge was like looking back through earth time at warp speed—the layers of sediment, how the canyons were carved by water over the course of five or six million years. We kept stopping at various points to peer over the edge and my stomach felt like it was going to drop over the cliff every time! The definition of taking your breath away!"

"Of course, you would come up with an actual wonder of the world," Joan said. "For me, it was when I broke all those vertebrae in my back and they assumed I had bone cancer or worse, three months after David was born. When the diagnosis turned out to be a mistake, that was pretty wonderful! I wouldn't have had a life. Would've been dead in my early thirties."

"Wait, I never knew that!" Katie said. "That's amazing. I am so happy you are still here. And I have another one I know you can relate to—the sound of a baby's or toddler's laugh. It's like the tinkling of a magical bell."

"I love that sound too. It makes everything better," Joan responded. "You can't harbor a negative thought when you hear a baby laugh. It is pure joy."

Between us, we have six grandsons four and under, so we each get to experience little bundles of wonder often. And it got us thinking. What about *senses* of wonder? Katie immediately went to the obvious, something we initially experience with our eyes. For Joan, it was a feeling of profound gratitude at getting to live her life. There is also music that can expose raw emotion in the depths of our soul or get us to dance like no one is watching.

A familiar and mesmerizing scent, like the smell of gardenias or lilacs, can also evoke beautiful memories as you recall a favorite path or maybe your wedding day.

Even a gentle touch can be a reminder that we are in this together, that we are loved and not alone. Katie knows that can be wonderful too.

"I had just gotten off the phone from a very difficult call with someone I loved, and I started to cry. Like really cry, which is kind of unheard of for me. I was sitting at my desk in the den near the door. Our dog, Molly, always sat just outside the door because the den was carpeted, and I had trained her not to come in. Given that the other members of the family allowed her to run amok, it landed on me to always be the tough one. Molly knew who was boss and understood our respective boundaries, but we had plenty of opportunity to bask in our mutual love for each other. As I began to cry like that, Molly got up, came in, and put her head in my lap and didn't move again until I had calmed down. Honestly? It still brings me to tears thinking about it."

If all humans could be more like dogs that respond from instincts of protection and goodness, the world would be a kinder place. Fortunately, especially in times of crisis, most humans do rise to the occasion.

Maryann is another survivor of what has become known as the Miracle on the Hudson, the plane that made an emergency landing on the Hudson River at 3:30 p.m., January 15, 2009. She believes it absolutely was a miracle and cites the many small things that resulted in everyone's survival. Imagine two minutes after takeoff, at only three thousand feet in the air, having both engines destroyed by a flock of very large birds and losing all power with 155 people on board. The pilot, "Sully" Sullenberger, said that his entire life—as an air force fighter pilot, a commercial pilot, and an aviation safety expert—had led him to that moment. His masterful gliding of the potentially doomed plane, his quick and thorough assessment of his options in the seconds he was given, and his perfect landing were just the beginning.

The plane had taken off from LaGuardia Airport forty-five minutes late, hardly an unusual occurrence, but the timing meant that the ferries were just firing up their engines for the 4 p.m. first commuter ride of the afternoon. Instead of clogging Sully's makeshift landing strip, the boats were poised and ready to assist in the rescue. Fourteen boats instantly headed to the plane as they saw it land in the water. Although it was a bitterly cold 20°F day, there was no wind. Consequently, there were no waves on the water, which assisted in the miraculous landing.

According to Maryann, none of the passengers panicked even though frigid water began to enter the plane immediately. She saw passengers literally giving the shirts off their backs to those who had gotten wet. She believes New York City was the only place the outcome could have been as successful, because after 9/11, helicopter pilots and first responders are so well trained in emergency preparedness that they descended on them in a matter of seconds.

This was not Maryann's first brush with potential tragedy. She had been in the World Trade Center when the 1993 bombing occurred, killing six people and injuring a thousand more. She felt the force of the bomb and smelled the smoke, and as the executive in charge, she was responsible for evacuating her company's employees. She has also survived a tsunami in Hawaii, a near miss with an avalanche in Colorado while skiing, and has flown through a hurricane to reach her sick father.

Even after Maryann experienced the Miracle on the Hudson, her most recent and hopefully last brush with disaster, she dismissed the experience and went about her life as usual. That is, until six weeks later when she read about a small plane that crashed and all aboard were killed. The reality of all that she had survived finally hit her hard. "This is how it's supposed to end when you are in a plane crash," she told her husband that morning and then was unable to sleep for a week. She gained a new perspective and it prompted her to change the way she lived.

"I won't let fear interfere with how I wanted to live my life and have learned to live in the moment," she said. An admitted workaholic, she recognized that the most important things in her life—her husband and two children—had not been the priorities they should have been. She stepped back from her high-powered job to do consulting, especially to empower other women in business. Maryann shared with us a sketch entitled "Wings on the Hudson" by Rex Babin of the *Sacramento Bee*. Giant hands cradle the crippled plane as it sits on the water, passengers and crew waiting on the wings. She believes God had a hand (or two) in their survival.

Maryann's story reminds us of the earlier joke about the drowning man who never accepted help from the rowboat, motorboat, or helicopter and ended up at the pearly gates in a conversation with God. In her case, she survived calamity after calamity and it wasn't until that fateful plane crash six weeks after the Miracle on the Hudson when she finally, and completely, changed her outlook on life. Perhaps it is no coincidence that Maryann has not been near a disaster since.

The survival of the Chilean miners, the Thai soccer team, and the passengers and crew of US Airways flight 1549 forces us to stop and wonder. As Alice Walker said in *The Color Purple*, "In wondering about the big things, you learn about the little ones." If we allow ourselves to be captivated by, and maybe even seek out, experiences of wonder, we cannot help but question our place in the universe. However trivial it may seem, it is imperative that we question and place ourselves in the midst of all that is. Only then can we begin to see how we are connected to each other and what lies beyond us. If we cannot see the bounty constantly around us, miracles of a subtler nature—someone who does not have time but makes time, giving or receiving the benefit of the doubt, a smile between strangers on a subway—these opportunities to feel the miraculous will surely be missed.

Having used the title of one of our favorite Christmas movies, *It's a Wonderful Life*, as a play on words in this chapter's title, we thought the connection would begin and end there. But in a cosmic twist, or synchronistic turn, as the case may be, that isn't what happened. As we were writing this chapter, Joan ran into a family friend she hadn't seen for years. She was a new mother to a one-and-a-half-year-old miracle baby. She shared with Joan that in vitro fertilization (IVF) had failed multiple times. The doctors told her she would never have a child naturally and, even worse, that if she got pregnant, it was unlikely she would carry the baby to term. Despite this bleak prognosis, she and her husband decided to try IVF one more time. She was ecstatic when she learned that she had conceived. A bit sheepishly, she confided that she had decided to ask Clarence, the fictional angel from her favorite movie, *It's a Wonderful Life*, to protect her baby and help her carry the baby to term. She even named the baby Clarence while still in utero, announcing proudly it was a boy. When she delivered a healthy baby, they shortened his name to Clark and will always cherish the miracle he is to them.

When we allow awareness to seep fully into our lives, wonder and wondering become part of who we are. If we live in the eternal now, we can even imagine that time could stop; for the birth of a child, the death of a loved one, the full gamut of the human experience both profound and subtle can lead to an open spirit and a changed worldview. Our preconceived notions about what can and cannot be true loosen their grip and perhaps even fall away.

Reverend Matthew Fox takes an intimate approach to wonder, with his view that "all awe renders us silent, and therefore all experiences of awe are this quick trip back to no sound, no words, to nothingness. And that's why they're so valuable, and we have to build our lives, our culture, our education, our spiritual lives, on the profound experiences that take us beyond."[8] So, take time to notice, be open to possibility, and cultivate a sense of wonder. It takes all three if we are to fully appreciate the gifts available to us, the connections to be made, and recognize they are all there for the taking.

TAKE A MIRACLE MOMENT

Awe-Some: Reflect back to your most recent experience of wonder. What could you do to capture that feeling more frequently? How do wisdom and wonder intersect?

PART TWO

Deepening Connection

Since you cannot do good to all, you are to pay special attention
to those who, by the accidents of time, or place, or circumstances,
are brought into closer connection with you.
—Saint Augustine of Hippo

CHAPTER SEVEN

The Secret Sauce

We are shaped by our thoughts; we become what we think.
When the mind is pure, joy follows like a shadow that never leaves.
—Buddha

Some of us remember the line item on our report cards that read, "Works well with others." We've been encouraged to share, to be kind, and to listen well at least since kindergarten. And sharing, kindness, and good listening are the key ingredients to generosity of spirit, the secret sauce that makes any relationship stronger. Somehow in this high-tech world of ours, we have lost some of these fundamental principles of living and working together. We tend to go a mile wide in our relationships where we can keep things superficial and nondescript. As we communicate more and more digitally, it is hard to go a mile deep instead. Texting has become synonymous with talking, and video conferencing often takes the place of in-person brainstorming. As a consequence, the dilemmas of daily life, once communicated over the water cooler or through an actual conversation, need to be replaced by newfound opportunities for sharing and connection.

For years, Joan has developed a special relationship with her California exercise friends. This diverse group first bonded over the necessity of exercise and now, years later, have deepened their relationships through their shared adventures and individual life experiences. As a result, they offer each other support and encouragement in times of challenge and celebration.

Finding a haven for deeper communication and camaraderie takes time and effort. The new virtual world order has altered our perception of time and, as a result, our perception of how we should connect with one another. We want to know what we want to know now and move on. There is not much room for listening, much less active listening to each other. The stories we might have told become lost, a casualty of our fast-living, hard-driving environment. As miracle collectors, we realized how important it was to tell our own stories and to listen to those of others. To be effective, we also had to develop new strategies to overcome what could, at times, be an emotionally charged topic. We wanted to allow room for differing opinions and discussion, but it was also important that we still be friends in the end. Learning how to disagree while maintaining respect and compassion for each other was no small feat. We had to discover how to listen without agenda or judgment, to recognize that our project was bigger than we were, all while allowing ourselves to be vulnerable. As we revisited life's defining moments, we added nuance and spice to the initial ingredients of our secret sauce. We learned that cultivating generosity of spirit is what sustained us and brought out the best in each other.

Generosity of spirit allows our relationships to deepen and our collaborations to flourish. Connecting the quality of being kind and generous with the spirit, the nonphysical part of a person where we find virtue and character, allows us to embrace all the positive possibilities that are available to us in our relationships. Generosity of spirit is also about being merciful, not only to others, but to ourselves.

In the Old Testament and the earliest commandments of the Torah, generosity is more commonly known as charity and refers to material giving. Jesus changed this interpretation to include "love thy neighbour as thyself" (Mark 12:31 KJV). In Buddhism, generosity is a spiritual practice, "the first of six 'perfections' or virtuous qualities one cultivates for spiritual awakening."[1] As we saw in the rescue of the soccer team, generosity is a commitment to compassion and to understanding the interdependence among all things. Combining generosity plus spirit results in a powerful force, a way of approaching life that keeps doors open and connects us with the best part of our being. In reality, generosity of spirit has been known to change the stars in miraculous ways.

Joan tells the story about an informal dinner she and Gene shared one evening with Bruce and his wife. After Bruce was reminded about the book Joan had co-written on miracles, he was willing to express his own bewilderment and sense of awe about an experience he was still in the midst of processing. He admitted he was not quite sure anyone else would see his experience as a miracle, but he viewed it as an inexplicable gift and decided to share what had happened.

A few weeks before his mother's death, he had a strange encounter. Even though his mother was not a young woman, the suddenness and the severity of her illness had taken the family by surprise. As the eldest, he knew his role was to speak with the medical staff at the enormous, world-renowned medical center where she was being treated and then to relay the information to his family. The responsibility was physically and emotionally exhausting. One evening, as his mother lay in the hospital, he and his extended and multigenerational relatives convened to share their concern and support over dinner in a restaurant close by. Looking around from his place at the head of the table to each of those he loved, Bruce's emotions threatened to overwhelm him, and he had to get up and leave. Stepping outside the restaurant and into a light rain, he began walking around the strip mall to clear his head and his heart of the pain he was feeling.

While he was in the throes of this angst, a homeless man pushing a shopping cart approached Bruce asking for money. Instead of his usual calm demeanor, Bruce was angry and blurted out, "Are you kidding me? My mother is dying, and you are asking me for cash? How dare you." Instead of reflecting back anger in return, the homeless man, whose name was Thomas, responded with empathy, acknowledging the great love Bruce must have for his mother and expressing sadness about her illness. Bruce was blown away by this response and felt something immediately shift inside him as a new view of humanity washed over him. Thomas' response allowed his anger to subside and his heartache to soften.

What happened next felt completely natural to Bruce. He and Thomas sat on a bench out of the rain and talked. After a few minutes, Thomas asked Bruce if he would like to pray. Bruce admitted that even though his mother raised him with religion, "I fell away, and I don't even think God hears my prayers anymore." Thomas immediately placed his hand on Bruce and reassured him, "God hears everybody." They prayed together, and Bruce was renewed. He felt stronger and suddenly able to go on to handle what he knew was to come.

Bruce conceded he made a friend that night. Though he did not fully understand what had happened, in his heart he knew it was important—a gift not to be taken lightly but to be savored. The emotion on his face as he shared the story was evidence of the depth of his feeling. He questioned whether Thomas was an angel sent from God or was even real. He knew it did not matter; that wasn't the point. What was important was to acknowledge the connection that was created as the right person with the right message at the right time became part of his life. That knowledge, and the certainty he felt about his renewed connection with the Divine, gave him an awareness that he was not alone. Thomas' affirmation that we are known by a God who reveals himself to us in ways we cannot anticipate, who is accessible at all times, and whose love for us is beyond understanding was exactly the message Bruce needed. He now understood that God does, in fact, "hear everybody."

Being entrusted with the stories of others is a gift. It takes courage to turn simple dinner conversation into the new territory opened up by Bruce. Moving from our tactile world to the supernatural one, where miracles abound, forces us to communicate in a new way. Sharing a miracle story is not always easy, as it often requires us to strip away the carefully constructed protective layers that shield us from additional hurt. Generosity of spirit allows us to listen openly and without judgment, to respond empathetically, and to find a deeper relationship with one another.

As we brought our own personal experiences into the light of day, we learned about the importance of responding with generosity of spirit. As miracle experts, we discovered it is not possible to talk honestly about miracles without also talking honestly about defining moments. When we confronted our own dark nights of the soul and came face-to-face with our own insecurities and fears, we learned that wisdom could result. Minister Chuck DeGroat notes, "Dark nights are not always problems, but opportunities."[2] While the experience of feeling confused and conflicted is not unique, with the help of others, we can emerge with a greater understanding and a renewed sense of purpose. Often, it is these connections that enhance and give the fullness of meaning to the defining moments of our lives.

In fact, whether the experience is traumatic or euphoric, we need a place that feels safe and to be with people we trust before we can share these stories. For some, there is no point in revisiting painful experiences. For others, staying superficial is the only way to feel emotionally safe. And yet, these defining moments make us who we are. When we close them off to others, it becomes impossible for anyone to truly know us.

Only when we allow ourselves to share these personal experiences can we begin to really connect with one another. It is a risk-reward proposition that is well worth the emotional effort and is a way to break down the barriers that close us in and keep us apart. Often, like in our prayers for the miners or the soccer team, we find we have much in common. As we led workshops around the country, we uncovered best friends who did not know key stories from each other's lives as well as complete strangers who discovered life-altering common threads, all by simply disclosing a defining moment in their lives. Imagine the new connections that would result and the relationships that would thrive if we did this as a matter of course.

To paraphrase Brené Brown, we humans are hardwired for connection,[3] and she is not talking about a gadget. Generosity of spirit provides us with an opportunity to see each other through a clear and authentic lens. While we "see" the downtrodden wandering among us, most of us never take the step of engaging in conversation. The generosity of spirit Bruce and Thomas shared that night enabled them to find their mutual humanity. They each found the gift of peace in a kindred spirit. No matter how that connection occurs, it is a boon to our existence.

Katie's response to Bruce's story was typical of our years working together. "Oh, what a great story. It reminds me a little bit about the story I told you of Elita's husband, David."

Katie had known David for over thirty years, since he is the husband of her best friend from college. She knew his mom had died young, but it was only recently that the rest of David's story unfolded one evening over dinner.

He was fourteen and the eldest of six children when his mother died of breast cancer. It became his job to help his dad care for his younger siblings, a weighty responsibility but one David shouldered willingly. His dad was a busy internist, still making house calls and often gone at all hours of the day or night. David was so integral to the family survival that his father was successful in petitioning the court to grant David a driver's license early, so he could shuttle his siblings around and take care of the routine family necessities.

Ten years after his mother's death, when David had completed one year of graduate school, his father died suddenly of a heart attack. While his last will and testament provided a monthly stipend for David's four siblings who were under eighteen and still in high school, their house had to be sold to satisfy other commitments. The court threatened to separate his youngest siblings and send them to live with family members they barely knew, spread across the country, unless a suitable alternative was found. David felt abandoned and afraid of what could happen. Planning to put his own education on hold since he no longer had money for his tuition, he got a call out of the blue that changed his life.

As David described what happened next, he found it difficult to go on. Max, the CEO of a large real estate corporation, heard about David's situation and called him into his office. David assumed it was to offer him a job, but instead Max stepped in to fill his father's shoes. Not only did he pay David's tuition, he helped make David feel that someone had his back and was watching out for him at a time when he felt bereft and alone. Boosted by Max's support, David found smaller, suitable housing and was able to keep his family together. When David went back five years later to pay his debt in full, Max ripped up the check. In a time before "pay it forward" was a thing, he asked David to help someone else if he ever had the opportunity. Max explained that as a poor young man himself, it was what someone years earlier had done for him.

David saw Max as his hero. Over time David became convinced that this man, who understood exactly what David needed to find the courage and strength to go on, was a miracle man on earth.

The death of or serious injury to a loved one is agonizing, a jab to the solar plexus that stops us in our tracks and leaves us reeling. Oftentimes, to reduce the pain, our defenses treat the situation more casually than it deserves, crossing the emotional minefield with stepping-stones that can be tread on lightly but never alighted upon for long. David and Bruce were braver than most—they were willing to face their pain head-on. David has been on the lookout his entire life to help others the way he was helped. Volunteering in his community, at his church, and professionally, he is always willing to lend a hand and share his talent, his time, and his treasure.

Over the years, we have learned a lot about how generosity of spirit develops and unfolds. First, we must learn to check our egos at the door and believe that our collective effort is more important than any individual goal. Seeing the end result as bigger than we are helps us act without jealousy or competition. Generosity of spirit is grace at its best, enhancing our capacity to actively listen and offer true empathy at the unveiling of each other's deepest fears and traumatic experiences. When we respond to each other, we need to echo this same generosity of spirit in return. And when someone misses the mark and delivers a response that is off course (we are human, after all), we need to give them the benefit of the doubt and appreciate that the underlying intention comes from a place of positive energy and thought. When we assume positive intent, most perceived slights can be deemed to be unintentional rather than personal. Building trust along the way makes navigating our emotional stories possible. In the end, generosity of spirit ignites an ever-expanding virtuous circle.

Working together provided opportunities to share experiences and delve deeper into our feelings and beliefs. Not surprisingly, as we exposed nerve after nerve, we encountered resistance and pushback, but we pressed on believing there was enlightenment around the next corner. We had to move cautiously to uncover our underlying aches in order to replace them with hope, forgiveness, or love. It was an opportunity for growth and for real connection to develop among us.

Former monk and psychotherapist Thomas Moore suggests, "It is precisely because we resist the darkness in ourselves that we miss the depths of the loveliness, beauty, brilliance, creativity, and joy that lie at our core."[4] Any dark night of the soul is a powerful experience that is unforgettable; it stays with us, becoming a part of who we are and how we view life. As co-authors, we sometimes had to take the lead to this internal place. We had one such moment years ago in a restaurant in downtown Carmel, California, when Katie had come to visit Joan for the weekend. Katie was still in her mindset of "Facts, ma'am, just the facts" about her encounter with Ted Bundy, and Joan knew it was her job to prod Katie into describing her feelings. Deliberately choosing a public place (and the wine we shared did not hurt either), Joan was able to urge Katie to dig deeper and be willing to expose the raw emotion at the heart of her experience.

It is hard enough to relive difficult experiences through sharing them, much less reimagining the anxiety and fear that lurk within these memories. If you are a Harry Potter fan like we are, you will recall the magical Pensieve, a font resting in the Hogwarts headmaster's office into which memories were placed and stored for safekeeping. Even under the watchful and loving eye of Albus Dumbledore, Harry could only take so much peering through the swirling sands into the past. We are the same. We need a guide, someone we trust, to stand by and help us through.

As Dumbledore knew, and now we realize, generosity of spirit is not only a force for good, but it is contagious. Once generosity of spirit is shared, whether inspired by David's Good Samaritan Max, the homeless Thomas, or in the circumstances that touch our own lives, we begin to recognize that grace can be found in the most unexpected places. Generosity of spirit is what allows us to show up for each other, whether it is in the wee hours of the morning before a medical procedure, on a cross-country trip after the death of a loved one, or with a warm meal served to someone in need. You do not even have to be in close physical contact for the effect of generosity of spirit to be felt.

We always enjoy our frequent telephone calls where we trade stories of the random acts of kindness we see or hear about. One winter morning Katie brightened Joan's day by sharing the story of Jim and his cab driver from the night before.

"It was stormy last evening [in NYC] and Jim was trying to hail a cab to get home, which is pretty much impossible at rush hour and in the rain it's even worse. But he eventually got lucky and a cab pulled over. The cabbie was in a foul mood and began complaining about the traffic, the surly passengers, and how exhausted he felt. Jim suggested they stop and offered to buy the driver a cup of coffee. You would have thought he had offered him the moon. The cabbie was flabbergasted. He would not accept Jim's offer, but his mood visibly lifted. It seemed like he just needed someone to care about him."

It was a sweet tale of city life, a reminder about the importance of supporting, rather than exploiting, the underdog. When Joan experienced her own version of Jim's story only a few months later, she couldn't wait to tell Katie.

"I was in Boston's Italian North End neighborhood and the cabbie that I scheduled in advance arrived fifteen minutes later than I had requested. The first thing he said to me was that he was desperate for an espresso. With less than an hour to catch my plane, and even though we were not far from the airport, I really should have convinced him to wait until later, but, because Jim's story was so fresh in my mind, I went along with his request.

"The cabbie was delighted and, yes, I was more nervous than usual as we drove to the airport, which as you know says a lot! I was rewarded with short lines, a rapid cruise through security, and arrived at the gate without breaking a sweat. It was so unusual for Boston."

Joan thought it might be karma and felt blessed, not only at having spread her own bit of generosity of spirit, but in making her flight without further hysterics or incident. It seems Joan and Jim are not the only ones who have found generosity of spirit in a cup of coffee. In Italy, there is a practice called *caffè sospese* where patrons can pay for a cup of coffee in advance as an anonymous act of generosity. When someone is in need of a cup but is low on cash, asks and is told a *sospese* is available, she is given one free of charge.

For generosity of spirit to thrive, we must be willing to put the needs of others ahead of our own. Sometimes this is easy, like switching the time to pick up or drop off a friend or adding additional groceries for someone else to our list while we are at the grocery store anyway. Other times, our flexibility and willingness to be open is tested. Perhaps because Joan travels so much, it was another taxi experience, this time in Chicago, where generosity of spirit transformed the hour-long ride to the airport from a necessary evil into the forging of a remarkable new bond.

It was one of our early-morning phone calls when Joan explained she had literally taken the high road on an elevated highway in Chicago. "I saw the cabbie while I was still standing on the curb, and frankly, he made me nervous right away. I was annoyed that even though he saw me struggling with my unwieldy suitcase, he did nothing to help and remained planted in his seat behind the wheel. 'Good Joan' wondered whether something was wrong with his back or leg. 'Not-so-good Joan' was silently cursing and wondering if another cab was nearby, so I could ditch the guy.

"Once inside the cab, our conversation went from monosyllabic instructions on my destination and route to one where we really connected. I don't remember exactly how the conversation began as I wasn't looking for a new friend or an intense discussion, but somehow the moment found us. He was fascinated when I told him of my exploration of miracles and said he was a walking miracle himself. The cabbie described the miracle of his survival on the south side of Chicago where he lived and where he had witnessed numerous drug deals, more than one of which had gone awry.

"He told me about the time he was lying on a hospital gurney after being shot, knowing the others he was with were dead, and he believed in his soul that it was divine intervention that saved him. He said this realization changed the trajectory of his life.

"He became more of a philosopher than a driver after that. He explained that it was the first time in his life that he found hope. Despite the odds, and without leaving the 'hood,' he went straight. He was convinced God helped.

"We talked about the change in perspective that usually accompanies a miracle. He told me that growing up as he had, hope was nonexistent. We talked about how hope provides the ability to look at life in a way that is outside of a bleak personal experience.

"Once we were stopped in traffic, I showed him that picture that you and I love of the illusion of the old and the young woman in the same image. He was stunned. He held my outstretched iPad like it was a foreign object and stared at the two faces blended into one. I never asked, and it didn't matter, which of the faces he saw, but it was as if a light bulb exploded as he came face-to-face with the idea that there was more than one way to view life. He recognized in his own aha moment that there was a whole new world to explore."

What started as an uncomfortable encounter became an interaction of the best kind. Being reminded of the importance of taking the time to acknowledge our differences and still making the effort to find common ground with each other is what allows connection to form. As the miles passed, generosity of spirit enabled their perspectives to change, resulting in goodwill and a new vision of what is possible. The hug Joan said they shared at O'Hare when the cabbie got out of his seat to retrieve her suitcase was spontaneous. As they parted, he thanked her, but in truth she was the grateful one.

Joan's experience with the cab driver stayed with her and reminded her of a story she had come across in her reading about Native American story-telling and customs. As one legend goes, a Cherokee grandfather explains to his grandson about the two wolves living within his soul. The good wolf, aka the "good Joan," is kind and generous and compassionate. It is the way we want to appear to the world. However, there is another side, the one we try to keep at bay but that occasionally comes out in times of confusion, impatience, or fear. This second wolf is the one who is cynical, irritated, or resentful. In response to the grandson's question about whether the good or the evil wolf is the strongest, the grandfather replies, "It is the one I feed."

We each face choices every day that put us in a position of choosing which of our "wolves" to feed. While in a perfect world we all would choose the good wolf, we know the world is far from perfect. It takes active inten-tion every day to feed the good wolf, especially in the face of growing polar-ization and misunderstanding. As Ferial Pearson, the woman who founded Secret Kindness Agents, says, "In feeding the kind wolf, we are building ourselves, [as well as] the person to whom we are kind, our community and our world. Kindness reverberates and expands."[5] This expansion of kind-ness has the same effect as Popeye eating his spinach; the generosity of spirit we share with each other gives us superpowers to be bigger than we ever thought we could be and better than we ever thought possible.

One of the most important elements at the core of successfully imple-menting generosity of spirit is the development of "extra" listening abilities. According to professional speaker Julian Treasure, "We spend roughly 60% of our communication time listening, but we are not very good at it. We retain just 25% of what we hear."[6] We know we need to get better at listen-ing: it takes intention and practice to be an empathetic listener.

One listening exercise we have used successfully with large audiences can also be initiated with a friend or family member. Take a minute to share an elevator story that describes a defining moment in your life and what came next. The listener is not to speak until you are done, and afterward, the listener takes one minute to repeat back what they heard you say. Then, reverse the process. Think about how it felt and whether you were surprised by what happened. We are often so eager to share our own stories that we forget to listen to one another. When someone genuinely hears us, we hear ourselves more clearly and sometimes even differently than we ever have before. Homing in on the true message we are trying to relay makes our implicit self more explicit, often both to ourselves as well as to others.

Mr. Treasure offers an acronym for this kind of empathic listening: RASA.[7] It is a Sanskrit word meaning essence, which, to any of us who have been misunderstood or have felt lost in the details, seems appropriate, kind of like missing that forest for the trees. The *R* stands for *receive*, which means paying attention to the person speaking. The *A* stands for *appreciate*—for example, making little noises like "hmm," "oh," or "okay." The *S* is for *summarize*, repeating back what we think we have been told and verifying that we have it right. This is a particularly important step, as often what we think we heard and what was said may be different. The final *A* reminds us to ask questions, to seek clarification. Taken together, these simple approaches work to validate the speaker as well as empower the listener.

Stephen Covey said, "Most people do not listen with the intent to understand; they listen with the intent to reply."[8] It is not the thought of the next question that is important; rather, it is the ability to hear what is really being said. And as we all know from experience, while it is important to attend to the words spoken, it is also necessary to listen for the nuance behind the words.

We must listen consciously to live fully. It is what connects us to nature and to each other. Listening and contemplation connect us to our spiritual being and are a common thread at the center of all spiritual paths. It is how we slow down our internal chatter, so we can hear the sound of connection, of the spirit in each of us, awakening to the soul of the universe.

Listening makes visible the words of Antoine de Saint-Exupéry about the secret of caring he describes in *The Little Prince*: "A very simple secret: it is only with the heart that one can see rightly; what is essential is invisible to the eye."[9] It is when we see with the heart that generosity of spirit thrives and makes anything, or perhaps it is everything, possible.

TAKE A MIRACLE MOMENT

All Heart: Find an opportunity to incorporate generosity of spirit today by being kind or giving someone the benefit of the doubt. Smile.

CHAPTER EIGHT

Telling Stories

Of all the gifts people can give to one another; the most meaningful
and long-lasting are strong but simple love and the gift of story.
—Clarissa Pinkola Estés, *The Gift of Story:*
A Wise Tale About What Is Enough

"Extra, extra! Read all about it!" We all love a good story. Some stories are front-page news, like the Miracle on the Hudson or the plummet of the San Francisco window washer. Other stories may not be breaking news but are miracle moments to be savored and celebrated nonetheless. The surest way to deepen connection with each other on this journey is to share our stories in a safe place where empathetic listening is practiced. When we express the emotions we all share—fear, hope, relief, sadness, or profound gratitude—we are connecting with each other on a foundational level. Allowing ourselves to be vulnerable in this way reveals who we really are.

Stories set the stage for generosity of spirit to help us hear the sound of connection. For Kendra and Roy, in-laws of Joan's sister, one such moment of connection had a spectacular setting on board the *Jewel of the Seas*, a cruise ship in the Caribbean. It was the middle of their first night on the ship when they opened their eyes in their top-floor cabin, smelled the salty air through their open door (though the rules said they were supposed to keep the door closed), and thought they heard something. Was the "Hey, hey, hey" a human call, the whistle of an unusual seabird, or something else? They had no idea. It was a scene out of the movie *Cast Away*, but Wilson the volleyball and Tom Hanks were nowhere in sight as they looked out over the dark water.

While they debated what to do, three men in an overturned motorboat were battling a nightmare in the open sea. What started out as a perfect weekend outing had gone disastrously wrong when the engines failed, and their boat filled with water and capsized—all within thirty seconds. The sun had set, and the three men were grateful for the three life jackets that floated up to them from their stowage below deck. As the dark hours passed, the men, shivering, thirsty, hungry, and bone-tired, felt their hope for rescue fade. After wishing on falling stars and sending up numerous prayers, they saw a large cruise ship on the horizon headed in their direction. Their boat was not on any normal route, and without signaling equipment, they knew the ship would pass them by. They believed they were too small to even be a radar blip. Even so, as the ship approached, they stood tall atop their upside-down, turtled boat, waved furiously, and shouted at the top of their lungs. As they anticipated, their yells were fruitless, and they watched as the boat slipped over the far horizon. After more than a half hour, with their hopes of rescue dashed, and a rainstorm now drenching them, a light emerged through the mist from the same direction where they had watched one fade. The ship had turned around! They knew this was no small feat for a huge ocean liner—the inconvenience alone to the guests and the loss of revenue to the cruise line would be huge. Turning around was not a part of any protocol, unless someone sensed disaster. Something unusual must have occurred.

The ship's brilliant spotlight turned on and scanned the water for whatever, if anything, was out there. At first the men were overjoyed, but the light was focused on the wrong side of the boat and then was turned off. Just as their hearts sank, the light reappeared on their side of the boat. After a few misses as the light trawled over the water through the sheets of rain, the beam finally found the distressed men and a boat was launched to recover them.

Kendra and Roy were not alone in thinking they heard something and had reported it to the ship's crew. As Myron Eshowsky says, "Listening requires we suspend judgment."[1] Sometimes, it is also a call to action. In spite of Roy and Kendra's second-guessing about other explanations for the sounds they heard, they were willing to force themselves awake and risk looking silly if someone's life was at stake. No strangers to ocean travel, Kendra and Roy had spent the time since they made their call to guest services wondering whether the boat would actually turn around and worrying about the people they now convinced themselves must be out there. The ship's movement was so subtle it wasn't until the spotlight turned on that they knew the boat had gone back. They hurried to the deck to watch as the ship's spotlight finally picked up the three men atop the overturned boat.

Suddenly, they had a story more meaningful than the great swimming, beaches, and entertainment they had enjoyed while on vacation. When they arrived home, they shared the email that came from one of the rescued men:

> As the Cruise Ship sailed by us, while we were floating in the ocean, hopeless as the ship sailed away, thinking no one heard our whistles and shouts, it turns out someone did…What we didn't know is that 4 guests in 4 different rooms heard our whistles and shouts and notified guest services and in turn the captain that they heard people in the water…all the while the ship was sailing away the guests were being the hero's [sic] that they are. It is actually hard for

me to write at this point as tears are welling my eyes just thinking of them...

It turns out that my boat had drifted 20 miles north and had gone up on the rocks, upside down; the boat is destroyed. It took the boat three days to get there and that would have been us...I love you all.

In the survivor's email, we see that sometimes it is not the actual telling of the story that is hard, but it is the emotion it evokes that is difficult to face. People can feel embarrassed about what happened or ashamed that they could have been so stupid, or they are not willing to relive the terror involved in the experience. We saw this with Rebecca, the woman who escaped the serial rapist. She had kept her story hidden from those who were closest to her. Over the years, she shielded its relevance even from herself.

Admittedly, it is easier to step back from sharing these defining moments in our lives with each other, rationalizing that it doesn't matter anyway. But ignoring a defining moment or miracle is not the solution. It is like the child who pulls up the blanket over his head and thinks no one is there. The person, like the experience, still exists and is a part of your life whether or not you acknowledge it.

We faced this reticence in our own budding friendship. We had known each other socially for a few years before Katie shared the story that put *Ted Bundy* and *hotel* together in the same sentence. Suddenly a light bulb went on for Joan. She understood why Katie was so adamant on the school field trips we supervised that hotel room doors were to be kept constantly locked and that the girls were not allowed to go up to their rooms alone. At the time, it had seemed a bit overly compulsive to be so skittish, but once Katie shared her story, it made perfect sense. In fact, on the occasions now when we travel together and share a hotel room, it is often Joan who locks the door first for her friend.

Telling stories is at the core of true connection. It provides a view into how we make sense of the world by what we choose to talk about, the way in which we share, what we emphasize or value, or perhaps, how we relate to others. As Kendra and Roy told their story, they became closer to those they helped save, and to those of us who heard the saga as well. Instead of an arm's length in-laws-of-a-sister relationship, they emerged in a new way for Joan. They were willing to go out on a limb even if others might think them crazy. In Joan's view of the world, that is a very big deal and she gained a new level of respect and admiration for both Kendra and Roy. We suspect the survivor's description of the events and the feelings he expressed in his lengthy email—from the beauty of the trip and the islands to the fear of the unknown, the relief at being found, and the gratefulness he now feels toward strangers—cast him in a new light for his family and friends as well. He allowed the essence of his soul to shine through in the wonder and gratitude he conveyed, becoming more real and multidimensional than before.

Of course, we all tell stories. When we first meet someone, telling stories is a way to find common ground. What changes over time are the stories we tell. As we evolve in wisdom and openness, we are willing to allow our stories to reveal more about ourselves. Sharing the significant stories of our lives connects us to each other beyond superficial commonality and drives us to be able to go beyond the surface of any interaction.

Like the matryoshka dolls we love to talk about, we peel back our protective layers in a willingness to allow our vulnerabilities to show. But it also takes time for us to fully grasp and appreciate the meaning inherent in the stories of our lives. Joan's story with her son would have stayed superficial, "just random, bizarre coincidence," if not for Katie's prompting to go deeper. Katie thought no one would believe her if she told her terrifying tale. For years, she "wouldn't go there" and was in good company with Joan, who just wanted to "move on." As author Kate Swoboda says, "We make meaning out of our experiences by telling stories…your stories have everything to do with how you see yourself and the world—whether you are a victim or a survivor, whether an experience is dangerous or an opportunity, and whether you have the capacity to develop more courage or you are just 'not very brave.'"[2] This is why sharing is a crucial element of "making meaning." Left to our own devices, the movies we create in our heads can take us down a path very different from the one we are meant to be on.

Not long after Katie relocated from the West Coast to New York City, she was obliged to go deeper in a new relationship, faster than she might have done otherwise. This can be an occupational hazard if you are a miracle collector! She had known Lee for nearly a year when they met a new friend, Andrea, and decided to get together for a lunch date to get better acquainted.

No sooner had they ordered than Lee announced, "Katie is writing a book about miracles and it will be published later this year! Katie, tell Andrea your story."

Katie was looking forward to knowing Andrea better, but she had no idea it meant baring her soul in their first casual lunch together. Launching into a miracle story felt out of place.

"I felt like I'd been asked to serve someone a meal before first inviting them over to dine," Katie explained.

She felt she needed to at least give a bit of a lead-in first and began with the background that Lee already knew. How we three friends discovered we each had experiences some people might call miracles; how we wanted to find out what a miracle really is from the great faith traditions and thousands of years of philosophers, theologians, and saints; and how real life got in our way: a potentially fatal heart condition called the widow maker, invasive breast cancer, and the implosion of a marriage. How different and personal the topic of miracles became once our backs were against the wall. And finally, Katie told Andrea about her encounter with serial killer Ted Bundy and her miraculous escape.

"Andrea was momentarily speechless after I finished my story. She might have asked me some questions. I don't remember those details exactly, but I do remember what happened next, because shortly, she began to tell her own story."

"At the end of my dad's life, right before he slipped into a coma," Andrea began, "he became anxious because he had not had a chance to thank his nephew, Jim, a Lutheran minister who had gotten his congregation to pray for him throughout his illness. On the day my dad died, Jim was jostled awake from an afternoon nap by my dad, who told him, 'I am in the hands of the Lord.' Dad continued to explain to Jim, 'I said to the Lord, I have some unfinished business; please may I thank Jim for the prayers that meant so much to me? And the Lord said yes.' After seeing my dad, Jim immediately called his own father, who confirmed that, indeed, his brother had just died.

"My mom and I prayed by my dad's bedside when we thought the end might be near. Just as we finished our prayer, my dad smiled peacefully, and he was gone. Right then, we saw a white light and a glow—I don't know how else to explain it.

"My dad was a deeply religious man, a lifelong practicing Catholic who loved the rosary. He had always said what an honor it would be to be 'going home' on the Lord's day. He died on a Sunday. One of my sisters didn't make it to the hospital in time, so we gave her Dad's rosary, which had the same strange glow to it when we handed it to her."

Andrea finished her story, sat back, and acknowledged, "Wow, I don't think I've ever told that story before." Once begun, the words just toppled out, unstoppable. That is the way it goes with miracle stories.

"You give people permission," Andrea later told Katie. She also explained how reticent she was for her stories to see the light of day, worried that people would think she was crazy. Certainly, this is something we have experienced ourselves. Now Andrea is more comfortable sharing her stories with others, and to her surprise, it seems she has become a magnet for miracle stories in return.

Through this sharing of our personal stories, we find a new depth of connection; it is a way to find empathy with, and for, one another. But empathy is one of those words in our vernacular that is not always clear. As a consequence, sometimes when we think we are being empathetic and have the best intentions, we still lack true understanding. Empathy is a powerful and complex tool that means a penetration of feeling from one to another and, in practice, allows us to walk in someone else's shoes.

Empathy gives us the ability to understand, appreciate, and relate to someone else's emotions. While we all aspire to be empathetic, empathy is found in the space between—not always seen but felt in the close proximity and constant association we have with each other. It is what happened at Katie's lunch that day and at so many other times when miracle experiences are shared. Empathetic listening, inherent in generosity of spirit, is how true connection ignites and flourishes.

Researcher Theresa Wiseman identified the four important attributes that need to take place in order for an empathetic response to occur. The first is to be able to see the world as someone else sees it. She uses the readily understandable example of going into a warm room and noticing someone wearing a sweater. Many might ask, "How can you possibly be wearing that? Aren't you hot?" Because it is a part of our human nature to step out of an empathetic response, our guard must be up at all times to try to create an environment of understanding. This is why the second of her attributes is being nonjudgmental. While we may not have used derogatory language verbally, we still may have silently wondered what could possibly be "wrong" with the sweater person. Somehow, if they are not in the same temperature-sensitive mindset as we are, it must be "their" problem. The third aspect of empathy requires us to understand someone else's feelings by focusing on that person and not on ourselves. Perhaps we need to ask if they are okay or deal with the situation by offering a blanket, a seat in the sun, or helping them move away from the air conditioner. Lastly, she suggests we need to communicate our understanding of the other's reality. It is a way to express a connection in difficult circumstances in times of discomfort, stress, or uncertainty. Empathy provides a road to understanding and compassion and is a way to unearth solutions.[3] How many times have we experienced this in our own lives when we share a problem or a concern and suddenly the solution comes into view?

In fact, when was the last time you sat around with your friends talking about the miracles you have heard or felt yourself? As a rule, we are conditioned not to go there. We tend not to unburden ourselves in social gatherings or public places unless it is an environment where we believe our openness will be met with respect and compassion. When we communicate by texting or through social media, instead of through in-person conversations where the inflection and nuance of the words used can be heard in our voice and seen in our expressions, real connection can be lost.

While the miracle stories we hear do not always consist of life-and-death moments, the power they convey is universal. Often these stories include initial uncertainty and questions of "How could...? What if...? Why me?" Sometimes the stories are events that actually transpired in the physical world; other times they are stories like the young college student who found reassurance about her grandfather while she was in a dream state. We actually heard a number of dream stories and even had a few ourselves, but one of our favorites stands out because it had been hidden for over half a century. It was only after our miracle discussion one evening that the story was brought to light.

Mary, a lovely woman in her eighties, is a respected stalwart in the church group where we had been asked to speak as part of a Lenten reflection series. While others in the audience had stayed seated as they asked their questions or told their stories, Mary got out of her chair and stood up to her full five-foot height as if to underscore the importance of what she had to say.

As she addressed the gathering of women, she asked if any of us had ever heard of something called a "healing dream." In spite of our blank stares, but perhaps knowing we were a receptive audience, she began sharing her story from so many years before. She said, "I guess he [God] wants me to tell it, but I don't even know what it is! I haven't told many people, but I think I should now.

"I had a problem with my knee with a lot of pain and had an operation, but there was worse pain afterward. I had a lot to take care of with a husband and seven kids and now even my husband thought I needed another operation.

"I was asleep and in my sleep on the side of my knee was a little, shiny silver button. And a man's voice that sounded very nice, but very firm, said, 'Press it.' I had my finger hovering over the button and wanted to press it, but I didn't dare. I got a little angry at the voice and asked, 'Where did the button come from? That wasn't there before. The doctor didn't put it there.' The voice again said, 'Press it.'

"I kept my finger waiting there, not knowing what to do, and the third time the voice, this time speaking more loudly, said, 'Press it,' I did. And then, *whoosh*, a strange feeling came over me and I could feel the pain leave. I said, 'Thank you, God.' I woke up my husband and said, 'Dear, I'm cured. My knee is fine.' That is my story!"

While none of us had heard of a healing dream before, we were unanimous in wishing we had. Just like Andrea, Mary had been afraid to bring up the dream for fear people might think differently of her. In fact, when we surveyed numerous audiences, the single biggest reason given for why many had not shared their miracle stories was their fear of being ridiculed. But all these years later, still walking solidly on her own, she knew it was time to share what she believed was a God-given experience.

The women in the audience who had worked with Mary for years began a whole new dialogue, sharing their own stories that took them deeper into the mysteries of the Divine. When the two of us left the church hall, the women were still talking, deeply touched by what they had heard that night. While they had anticipated an evening of community and breaking bread in a Lenten soup tradition, they got much more: an experience where sharing stories not only made the ordinary extraordinary, it made the extraordinary real.

TAKE A MIRACLE MOMENT

Inside Scoop: Everyone loves a good story. Practice empathic listening. See what it takes to uncover a story you have never heard before.

CHAPTER NINE

Beyond the Beyond

A miracle is when the whole is greater than the sum of its parts...
when one plus one equals a thousand.
—Frederick Buechner, *The Alphabet of Grace*

The stories we tell illustrate a lot about ourselves—who we are and how we got here. When we look deeper, we realize stories also connect us to something larger than ourselves. In combination with generosity of spirit, we lay the foundation for others to be open and authentic with us, offering up a canvas to color in the stories of their lives, and deepening connection with each other along the way. Breaking down the barriers that separate us allows us to begin to develop empathy. Only then do we gain an understanding beyond our own view of the world and cultivate a sense of compassion outside it. With miracle stories, we are also acknowledging the Divine, overcoming the "what will people think" in favor of the sacred, the spiritual, and the inherent mystery that surround us. Miracle stories give voice to the spark of divine light that takes hold when life gains new meaning.

A brush with a miracle does give one cause to pause. Not all lives that are saved or all miracles that are received require us to live life differently, or to reassess some of the big questions like, "Why am I here?" Yet, if we are not here to live in a vacuum, and developing empathy with each other is key, then making the effort to live life with a greater good or higher purpose in mind takes that connection one step further to something beyond ourselves. Women's empowerment expert Kathryn Ford explains it this way: "Remembering our higher purpose and actively helping others allows us to connect, or dial in, to the feeling that we are a part of something larger than ourselves."[1] When we practice empathy by volunteering or imagining someone else's plight, when we draw on higher ideals—honesty, integrity, kindness, and love—or when we acknowledge a higher power through prayer or meditation, the whole becomes greater than the sum of its parts. We become conduits for connecting the dots of the universe. The result is an expansion of the soul and a perpetuation of the cycle of connection.

A spirit of giving to those less fortunate or who live on the margins of our communities was ingrained in us from a young age. We both went to Jesuit universities whose core values include "men and women for others." In the New Testament, there is the famous verse from Luke 12:48: "From everyone who has been given much, much will be required" (NASB). While the message is meant to be universal, we have always felt compelled to devote time to issues that are near to our hearts, including the education of children, women's health, and the well-being of families. It is why we set up the MiracleWorks Foundation from the proceeds of our first book.

Fortunately, we are not alone in our desire to contribute to the good of the world. Many have found the rewards of volunteering in everything from keeping their nearby park beautiful to staffing a soup kitchen when they are able. There are many ways to contribute to the greater good by serving nature and each other. When we volunteer our time, we find out that those we seek to help, help us in return. Touching the life experience of another broadens our conception of the communities where we live. We develop empathy and exercise compassion in a way that has applications far beyond the serving of a meal or the coaching of a child.

Recognizing the plight of another becomes miraculous when it changes the outcome of a stranger's life, as occurred with David and Max. Sometimes, it begins by simply stopping to notice. That is how a miracle began to unfold in a West Chicago neighborhood, when Joel Cervantes stopped to buy fifty dollars' worth of Popsicles from a bent, aged man who looked like he could use a helping hand as he struggled to push his paleta (Popsicle) cart. Mr. Cervantes snapped a photo of the man, then posted it to social media. Through this picture, his friends saw what he saw: the sad resignation of a man who had worked too hard for too long. The photo touched so many people that Mr. Cervantes and a friend decided to start a GoFundMe campaign. They discovered the eighty-nine-year-old man, Mr. Sanchez, had recently lost his daughter and that his wife was ill. Their campaign to raise $3,000 attracted more than seventeen thousand contributions and raised more than $384,000. As Mr. Cervantes wrote, "This is a true example of people showing love for one another and how we can together accomplish something beautiful and greater than ourselves."[2]

We do not always know when or how a kind gesture will turn someone's world around, or whether we are one of many doing our part to change the stars for someone. It is simply important that we do it, that we recognize the opportunity when it has our name on it. Author Kent Nerburn observed, "Our lives are lived in the quiet corners of the ordinary. We build tiny hearth fires, sometimes barely strong enough to give off warmth. But to the person lost in the darkness, our tiny flame may be the road to safety, the path to salvation."[3] In the case of the man with the paleta cart, people from around the world speaking the universal language of compassion each sent out a little light in mostly five- and ten- and twenty-dollar increments.

From selfie obsession to self-promotion, we live in a culture of "Look at me!" This is the reality of the twenty-first century. If you want to utilize the compounding effects of social media, you have to hop on board. But it is important to keep that reality in perspective. Ironically, it is when we use these tools for good, to shine the spotlight on someone or something else, that our own self-worth is magnified. It turns out that participation, and the connection that results in contributing to the greater good, brings with it a type of happiness that was first proposed by Aristotle, who called it eudaemonic happiness.

Viktor Frankl wrote, "For success, like happiness, cannot be pursued; it must ensue, and it only does so as the unintended side effect of one's personal dedication to a cause greater than oneself."[4] Focusing our attention on someone else, on a cause we believe in, or offering an extra pair of hands in a crisis, exercises the muscles of connection and compassion. Mothers understand this as if by instinct. You lose yourself for periods of time in your children, but you can find your soul. Keeping in mind the greater good or higher purpose is the antidote for "Look at me!" The ego dissolves into the collective working together to accomplish the same outcome. In the case of the Chilean miners and the Thai soccer team, we have no doubt the outcomes were affected by this degree of mutual cooperation to achieve the safest and speediest result.

Of course, it is important we do not lose ourselves completely in the process; it is a balancing act. Most times when we are confronted with a situation that may benefit from our help, it is because of who we are and the specific gifts and talents we bring to the circumstances. We are the right person in the right place at the right time. The sentiment of Rabbi Hillel centuries ago still challenges us: "If not me, who? If not now, when?"

Rose Mapendo understood what the rabbi meant. Katie met Rose on a shuttle bus ride during the Texas Conference for Women. Glancing at the seating options as she got on the bus, Katie noted all of the women were sitting by themselves, heads down, engrossed in their cell phones, except for one. Rose was simply staring out the window, looking a little lost, and Katie decided to sit next to her and introduce herself.

"Are you speaking at the conference?" Katie asked her.

Rose began to tell Katie her story. She is a Tutsi from the Democratic Republic of the Congo (DRC) where the Tutsis suffered the same despicable fate in 1998 as they had in Rwanda a few years before. Rose's husband of eighteen years was tortured, then murdered, and she and her seven children were sent to a death camp. There, she discovered she was pregnant. When she gave birth to premature twin boys, she had survived near starvation and unrelenting disease. The children were born on the cement floor of Rose's prison cell where she had to cut the umbilical cords herself with a piece of wood. While in labor, she had to keep quiet for fear of discovery. She was certain they would have taken her to the hospital, a place from which no one had ever returned.

Katie asked Rose, "Did you name one of your sons after your husband?"

"No, I named them after the commanders who murdered my husband," Rose said.

Katie was certain she must have misunderstood and asked again, "I'm sorry, Rose, I didn't understand. *Who* did you name them after?"

"The two commanders that murdered my husband," Rose repeated.

"Why?!" Katie wanted to know.

"Three things," she said. "First, in my culture, if you name a child for someone, they cannot be your enemy. Two, this was the only way I could forgive. If I am not their enemy, they are not my enemy either. Three, I wanted my sons to *survive*."

Tears welled up in Katie's eyes as she and Rose made their way inside. The evening welcome party had a forced festivity about it, worlds away from a death camp in the DRC. The next day, Katie saw Rose highlighted on the cover of the women's conference program. Rose had been named Humanitarian of the Year by the United Nations, was a CNN Hero, and was honored at the White House for her commitment to "educate the global audience about the effect of war on women and children."

While the power of forgiveness lies at the center of this story, Katie later thought about something else Rose had told her. "I go back. I go back to tell the women they do not have to be victims. They can help me bring peace and forgiveness."

War, in particular, can bring out the worst in some, but it can create opportunities to bring out the best in others. The ultimate commitment to a higher purpose is when someone is willing to risk her own life for another. Elisabeth Eidenbenz was a Swiss nurse who saved pregnant refugees escaping the Spanish Civil War, and later, those escaping the Nazis. Those fleeing Spain were held in camps in the south of France, not far from the Spanish border. The conditions were deplorable; food was scarce and there was no shelter or medicine available. Ninety percent of the babies born there died at birth. Their mothers did not fare much better. Ms. Eidenbenz helped set up a maternity hospital in the south of France where she was allowed to bring pregnant women from the camps to give birth. As World War II got underway, the refugees she saved included Jews whose identity she concealed, ignoring the law that prohibited it. In order to keep the maternity house open, she continued to defy the Nazi police and the Vichy government in France. As she explained, "We welcome women of all nationalities. Neither misery nor unhappiness have a homeland."[5]

Ms. Eidenbenz is credited with saving six hundred children and as many mothers as she could find new identities and jobs for until 1944, when the Nazis commandeered the house for their own use. After the war, the maternity home was lost to history and decay until some of the children she saved resurrected her memory. When a visiting professor from the United States went to visit the recently restored site, he reported that it had an "incredible aura," an aura of good.[6]

Most of us do not go searching for an opportunity to stand up to tyranny. Some individuals, like Rose and Elisabeth, are thrown into situations not of their choosing and rise to the occasion, recognizing a cause greater than themselves. Most of us will never be forced to take the higher moral ground in life-or-death situations, which should make us grateful but not diminish the forays we do make into helping others. Mother Teresa once told someone who wanted to help her, "Find your own Calcutta." And whatever it is, big or small, she stressed the importance of doing it with great love.

One way to harness the power of love is to pray for a cause or an individual. When those prayers involve all the languages and religions of the world, they stir up a universal energy that reminds us we belong to each other. Prayer is an easy way for one plus one to equal a thousand. Great minds like Soren Kierkegaard and C. S. Lewis understood that prayer was not about changing God but about changing ourselves. As individuals in crisis, we may pray for what we desperately need, but in naming that need, we also recognize the value in gaining peace of mind, courage, or strength instead.

Mahatma Gandhi said, "Prayer is not asking. It is a longing in the soul…better in prayer to have a heart without words than words without a heart."[7] Prayer is opening a dialogue and sometimes finding the answer in the silence that follows. We pray because we have hope. There are also plenty of reasons to pray outside of foxholes if we can get into the practice of prayer. We pray to send out a blessing to someone or some cause, to thank God for the abundance in our lives, to live up to our best selves. Corrie ten Boom, who became a concentration camp survivor after sheltering Jews as a member of the Dutch resistance, asked, "Is prayer your steering wheel or your spare tire?"

When you grow up as we did, steeped in Catholic tradition, prayer was learned and exercised from the time we could talk—prayers before bed, prayers before dinner, prayers on Sunday. A favorite prayer in Katie's family was the prayer of Saint Francis: "Make me an instrument of your peace; where there is hatred, let me sow love...where there is darkness, light..." It is the quintessential philosophy of her youth that combined the virtues inherent in a generosity of spirit with those of giving back and paying it forward.

Saint Francis was radical in the sense that he came from wealth and privilege and gave it all up. While he recognized corruption in the church, he went about his life going back to the basic tenets of Jesus' great commandments: love God with all your heart and all your soul, and love your neighbor as yourself. Saint Francis may have added one more in his mystical relationship with nature, showing us how to be stewards of creation and to appreciate the majesty it has to offer us. At a time when it was considered revolutionary, he extended his love to Muslims and brought their Islamic prayers back from Egypt during the Fifth Crusade.[8] Peace and love were his mission wherever he went—simple to say and pray for, radical to embody and live.

"I love this prayer; it covers the gamut of what we can aspire to and it's an easy prayer in the sense that it focuses prayer in the right direction—in this case, a request to be our best possible selves for the sake of those around us. We always had a statue of Saint Francis in our yard. My parents hid the extra key to the front door under the statue. Maybe that's how I connected Saint Francis so directly with the key to a good life!" Katie explained.

"That's pretty funny," Joan responded. "I'm a big fan of Saint Francis, too, and his challenge to 'start by doing what's necessary; then do what's possible, and suddenly you are doing the impossible.'

"But the most common prayer in my family had nothing to do with communing in nature like Saint Francis. When you are raised in an Italian family like I was, food is the centerpiece of conversation. Dinner is an occasion to share the day's events, engage in political commentary, and discuss upcoming plans—none of which occur until the obligatory grace is said. We were constantly reminded that we are the recipients of God's bounty every day. It was expected that we give thanks for the blessings that come our way both in food and in life."

It was a lesson Joan absorbed early, before gratitude journals became a New Age accoutrement. Being grateful is good to remember, a way to focus on something and someone other than ourselves.

In addition to counting one's blessings and to remember to love your neighbor as yourself, prayer can also be a powerful tool of healing and forgiveness, as Katie's friend Paul relays. Having befriended a Rwandan priest, Father Ubald, Paul has made several trips to Rwanda to better understand the truth and the reconciliation efforts rebuilding the country. They traveled to Kibeho where a massacre occurred in the spring of 1994 at the Catholic church there. Thousands of Tutsis were murdered, some outside the church as they tried to defend the lives of those who, in fear, had barricaded themselves within the church walls. Eventually, the perpetrators bombed their way into the church and massacred everyone inside.

On one of Paul's trips to the restored church, Father Ubald conducted an exorcism, a series of prayers to override the evil that could be felt inside. On the day of the exorcism, Paul and the group he was with arrived at the church, and he noted the beautiful blue sky outside. "The lighting was magical," he said, but inside the church was a different story. "Darkness had moved in." When Father Ubald and a fellow priest began their prayers, a hailstorm began pounding on the temporary metal roof. The ruckus combined with the sense of evil overwhelmed Paul. He was so terrified he began to scream the Lord's Prayer at the top of his lungs: "...For thine is the kingdom, the power, and the glory..." Suddenly, the hail stopped, the evil dissipated, and a gentle rain began to fall. When Paul went outside, he saw that the storm and the cleansing rain had fallen only on the church property. Beyond it, everything was dry.

Paul asked Father Ubald why he never speaks of that day that was so powerful to him. Father Ubald explained it is an ordinary occurrence for him to sense and dispense with evil. Father Ubald continues to seek peace and forgiveness between victims and perpetrators through the Center for the Secret of Peace. He acknowledges that the evil and the good continue to coexist, but he is optimistic. "The good wins out," he says.

Katie finds the whole conversation about evil disturbing. "I find it difficult to acknowledge this level of evil, much less confront it. Even though, for one minute of my life, I was in its grasp. There must be something redeeming in recognizing that evil exists and that we are all susceptible. It is incumbent upon each of us to grab what grace and goodness we can and fling it out into the world so that, as Father Ubald says, we ensure that 'good wins out.'"

Joan faces evil in her own way. "I believe it arises from an absence of hope and the temptation to despair. Evil has a need to feed on all that is good because it has no power of its own. It exists from the power we give it. Like the story of the good wolf and the bad, we all harbor both within us—it is the choice we make between acting from a place of love or from a position of fear that becomes our daily challenge."

Meditation works to change how we relate to the world in the same sense that prayer does. As the Native Americans might say, it is a way to keep us in balance with the universe; it is about laying bare the struggles of the human condition and striving to connect with a higher power. Each of us has discovered meditation as a method to awareness and connection.

Joan initially began to meditate because she is always wearing her Sherlock Holmes hat—*Hmm, what is this all about?* She became intrigued with Eastern religions as part of our miracle journey and has practiced yoga for decades. It is not a surprise that she keeps accepting Oprah and Deepak's 21-Day Meditation challenges, hoping one day to actually be still long enough to fully participate in the whole twenty-minute exercise. Katie's reasons are more fundamental. Meditation is a practice that soothes her lifelong struggle with anxiety and has introduced a path to serenity. Both of us agree that meditation quiets the constant mental chatter, that annoying fly buzzing around, creating needed space in our brains for awareness and connection to thrive.

In the beginning of her foray into Eastern thought, Joan met with a college friend of her husband's. Mike worked at her husband's alma mater, but Joan never knew that he had been meditating since the 1970s. He has been steady in his practice even as the art of meditation has come and gone and come back again.

In their conversation, Mike shared an experience about the power of meditation that continues to reinforce his practice even today. He explained that the Dalai Lama had come to the college three times. While Mike was inspired each time he saw him, Mike was particularly interested in the topic of the third visit where the Dalai Lama was leading a conference on Christianity and Buddhism. Before the conference concluded, the press corps had been invited to a question-and-answer session.

Mike was disheartened to hear the members of the press ask political question after political question relating to the Dalai Lama's exiled status from Tibet and the suppression of the Tibetan people by China. No one was asking about the topic of the conference and the purpose of the Dalai Lama's visit in the first place: the universal connections between Christianity and Buddhism. This was the question Mike wanted to ask and was disappointed that no one had broached the subject. As he formed the question in his mind, he repeated his personal mantra out of habit, calming himself and assuaging his frustration.

As the question-and-answer session wrapped up with Mike's question still unasked, the Dalai Lama got out of his chair and, turning around, looked out into the crowd and pointed directly at Mike, who was standing in the back of the room surrounded by numerous attendees. "This man has a question," he said.

Stepping forward, Mike said, "Yes, Your Holiness, I do. What can Christians learn from Buddhism?"

The response from the Dalai Lama was instantaneous. "Tolerance," came the one-word answer.

Not only did he know Mike had a question, but it seemed the Dalai Lama even knew what that question would be. To connect on such a deep level with the world around him and achieve oneness with the thoughts and desires of others is miraculous. His is clearly a higher realm of consciousness, a perfection of mindfulness and awareness, achieved by a man who has devoted his life to peace and who believes our purpose on earth is to help others. Our fledgling entry into meditation and mindfulness, even if we practice and persist, will not bring us close to the Dalai Lama's wisdom and prescience, but we can move in the direction of deeper connection to the world around us. We can aspire to his words: "If you want to be happy, practice compassion."9

TAKE A MIRACLE MOMENT:

The Sky's the Limit: Consider what the greater good or the purpose of life means to you. What steps could you take to share your own gifts and talents with a cause or purpose that is bigger than you are?

CHAPTER TEN

Let the Spirit Move You

We are not human beings having a spiritual experience,
we are spiritual beings having a human experience.
—Pierre Teilhard de Chardin, Quoted in
The Seven Storey Mountain by Thomas Merton

Meditation is not only about finding our inner calm, but about finding our inner being, our soul. It is the beginning of the answer to another one of the big questions: "Who are you?" And not the "you" of the ego, but the "you" of connection. This connection goes beyond one another to a higher purpose, connecting each of us to the center of all that is and expanding the notion of who we are, both individually and collectively. The practice of yoga goes beyond its physical benefits as it unites the "individual consciousness or soul with the broader Universal Consciousness or Spirit," according to practitioner Bianca Alexander.[1] *Namaste*, the word that is spoken reverently at the end of yoga practice, conveys this bond, where the light in me honors the light in you. It is an acknowledgment of the spiritual essence we all possess. When we honor one another's light or spirit, we are connecting to each other *and* to the great beyond, the Divine, or, God.

As physical beings we are adept at keeping our spiritual "beingness" under wraps. When we change course and consider ourselves to be "spiritual beings having a human experience," and not the other way around, then we become part of the universe's tapestry, no longer tethered solely to the earth. Our soul, our spiritual core, becomes the essence of who we are, not our bodies, or our titles, or our bank accounts. While most of us might agree that we have this spiritual core that propels us to act with kindness, integrity, honesty, and love, it is not something we routinely identify. Often, miracles, like our spirituality, are on the "don't ask, don't tell" list, keeping us from offending the sensibilities of someone else. But this view holds us back. We never get to portray who we really are or what we really think. In our own foray into chasing miracles, we employed tools that spring from that spiritual core and are the hallmark of good friendships. The generosity of spirit we talk about includes collaboration and understanding, active listening, assuming positive intent, bringing out the best in each other, and living up to one another's high expectations. The result? We became far more than friends; we became soul sisters too.

But what, or where, is the soul? Depending upon your cultural or religious mindset, this question is answered in different ways. Carl Jung found the soul in what he called *The Spirit of the Depths*, beyond ego or time and place, discovered by most of us the hard way, after we have experienced a jolt from a difficult experience, maybe even a tragedy. Like the archetypal hero's journey, where through life's vicissitudes, the hero is forced to "learn something from the depths of his soul that will infuse the rest of his life with meaning,"[2] he emerges from the dark night of the soul to the light of day. The hero is now ready to share his newfound wisdom, in spite of knowing only some will be willing to listen.

Carl Jung's journey included encounters with what he considered the collective unconscious, an inheritance from our human ancestors, not shaped by individual experience. Just before the onset of the Great War (World War I), he had a series of horrific dreams where he saw Europe covered in a sea of blood. The collective unconscious is part of *The Spirit of the Depths*, where dreams are a vehicle to all that came before and, in this case, foretell the future.[3]

In *The Alchemist*, Paulo Coelho describes how contributing and merging with the "Soul of the World" is only achievable once we have discovered our Personal Legend.[4] This is another portrayal of the hero's journey, the path to find our own soul or spirit. Like Buechner, Coelho also recognizes that the sum, the Soul of the World, is greater than the individual parts. Our life's journey is tied to a greater good and a higher purpose, which in turn becomes our contribution to all there is.

Perhaps this notion of the collective unconscious explains a prescient dream Joan had that spared a young child from certain harm. It is a dream she has a hard time sharing because it was too real, too intense, and, in the end, too true. As she lay in a state of transition, half-awake, half-asleep, a scene began to unfold in her mind. A little blond boy, maybe five years old, was sitting on a skateboard, rolling down a familiar sidewalk on a gentle hill in the town near her home. His dad was a few yards behind him pushing a baby in a stroller and had stopped to talk to a woman on the corner. Engrossed in his conversation, the dad was unaware that his son kept going down the hill. It was obvious to Joan that the child was not going to stop when he got to the next corner. She realized the oncoming cars wouldn't be able to see him; he was so small as he sat on his little skateboard and the cross traffic didn't have a stop sign to slow them down. She was startled awake when he got to the busy intersection by what she knew was about to happen.

The experience was so terrifyingly real that Joan went through a quick mental checklist. Were her own children, now grown, where they were supposed to be? Yes. Did she even know a little blond child like him? No. Too wound up to sleep, she obsessed about what the meaning of this surreal vision could be, or whether it was just her already active imagination working overtime.

The next day en route back from an uncharacteristic early-afternoon errand to the grocery store, Joan was driving down the same street that appeared in her mind the night before. Suddenly, she saw a little blond boy rolling down the sidewalk on his skateboard. The father has stopped at the corner to chat, hands full with baby and stroller and oblivious to his son, who just keeps on going, picking up speed as he heads for the intersection.

"Time stood still as I watched in horrified anticipation of what would be an inevitable disaster," Joan recalled.

She had to act fast. In her car, Joan is able to beat him to the intersection, ignoring her own stop sign and blocking the traffic with her vehicle. Horn blaring and with a screech of brakes, the oncoming car stops just in time as the boy flies past in front of his bumper.

"It was one of the most powerful experiences I have ever had. I was filled with mixed and conflicting emotions that shook me to my core. I was terrified at what might have been, embarrassed to tell anyone about such a vivid premonition, and confused about whether this was a once-in-a-lifetime thing or would continue to occur," Joan explained.

Joan could completely understand Annie's anxiety after inviting her guardian angel in when she experienced such a mix of emotions, feeling both a spirit of overwhelming love but tempered by fear of the unknown at the same time. Crossing the demarcation line into realms we do not yet understand can be uncomfortable. According to Brené Brown, "Spirituality is recognizing and celebrating that we are all inextricably connected to each other by a power greater than all of us, and that our connection to that power and to one another is grounded in love and compassion."[5] Perhaps spirituality in its purest form is the love Annie felt, and the compassion Joan exhibited.

If we are indeed primarily spiritual beings, then the soul is a powerful force. It gives us the ability to see more than meets the eye in each other, gives us perspective about our connection beyond ourselves, and is our passport to the Soul of the World. And, based on the many stories we have heard, the soul gives the dearly departed a bridge to "Earth Central," once our bodies have died.

Barbara was proud of her dad, George, a World War II Army Air Force B-17 bomber captain who flew the maximum number of missions allowed over enemy territory. Though they lost planes to his right and left and even on occasion lost the planes that took his position in the squadron on the days he had off, he managed to survive the war. "Now, how do you account for that?" he asked his family.

George was an avid golfer, a sport Barbara also embraced with zeal, though with less skill. One day, not long after her father had died, Barbara and her husband took advantage of a round of golf they won at a charity auction and played at a well-known club in the Hamptons. Barbara was particularly self-conscious because of the club's lofty reputation and worried she would not play well. Instead, she had the best round of her life! After playing, as she changed in the ladies' locker room, the Air Force anthem began to blast from a few yards away. "Off we go into the wild blue yonder, climbing high into the sun…" Even though her phone was on silent and was not even connected to her playlist, somehow the theme song from her dad's life was serenading her from her purse. Suddenly, she understood what was behind her amazing round of golf—a gift from her dad.

If we are, in fact, spiritual beings, then at our death our spiritual essence lives on and can continue to touch others in unexpected ways. It is also not surprising that the transition from one form of consciousness to another may occur with some degree of fanfare. While we have talked before about the spark of divine light, even we were surprised to hear a story that ignited that spark literally.

Debbie was the kid in religion class who just did not get it, acknowledging she was not a believer or religious in any sense. Debbie had a brother, twelve years her junior with whom she never had much of a relationship, given their age difference. She always found this sad, but by the time she had time to resurrect their relationship, it was too late. Her brother struggled throughout his life with mental illness and stayed in Georgia where they grew up, while she moved west.

One night, while she was at her home in Idaho, the phone rang at 3 a.m. Coincidentally, Debbie's husband had just gotten up and walked downstairs. If he hadn't been up, they never would have gotten the call, because the phone in their room on the second floor was being repaired and they wouldn't have heard the phone on the first floor ring. It was her father calling to tell Debbie that her brother was on life support, ready to be pronounced dead and have the plug to his respirator pulled. Two doctors had already given their consent, but in accordance with Georgia law at the time, they were waiting on a third doctor to give approval. As Debbie threw clothes into a suitcase, her husband found the one seat that was left on a flight from Spokane, which she could make if they left right then in the darkness.

By the time she landed in Atlanta, the third physician had been found, but he agreed to wait until Debbie arrived at the hospital. Once at her brother's bedside, Debbie was able to tell him all she had never expressed about her feelings and her regret at their unfinished relationship. With her family members in the room, Debbie laid her hand over her brother's as the nurse who was watching the monitor said, "He's going now." Just then, Debbie felt a powerful electric charge of energy flow from his hand, piercing through her own, and heading upward to the sky. She saw prisms of the color spectrum reflected above her. She exclaimed to the nurse, "Did you see that?" The nurse was not at all surprised by Debbie's description and responded that she frequently saw amazing things as people left this world. The experience was so powerful that Debbie changed her view and now not only believes that there is a hereafter, but she is intrigued about what it will be like.

Years later, while caring for her terminally ill husband, Debbie described lying next to him one night holding his hand. Exhausted from caregiving and stress, she fell asleep. She had hoped to experience the same closeness to the Divine she felt with her brother when her husband's time came. That night she slept soundly until the final tingle of his departed spirit passed through her hand, waking her up and leaving behind a bit of heaven on earth.

Near-death experiences (NDEs) look at these spiritual connections from the other side. According to consistent reports, an NDE takes the soul on a journey where it is surrounded by the unconditional love of spiritual beings, including the Divine Being, incomprehensible beauty in colors and sounds, and where the wisdom of the ages is absorbed almost by osmosis.

In one such experience described by Anita Moorjani in her book *Dying to Be Me*, she concludes, "The mind is more about *doing*, and the soul is more about *being*. The infinite self is our essence. It's who we truly are."[6] Ms. Moorjani had these experiences while in a coma, as her organs began to shut down in what were thought to be the last days of Stage IV cancer. She emerged from her NDE on her way to an inexplicable cure, astonishing her family, her doctors, and herself. Ms. Moorjani now lives her life sharing the message she learned while she was "dead"—we are love incarnate and we are connected to all things in the universe.

While most of us have at least wondered about an *after*life, few of us think about the "*before*life." Katie shared an experience about her daughter Allie, which got her thinking about it for the first time.

"I was driving down Highway 80 near Berkeley [California] one day with Allie, who was three years old and in the back seat of the car. I pointed out an unusual and beautiful cloud formation out the window. 'That's where Papa Dickie is,' she responded. It seemed an odd thing to say, so I asked her what she meant. She said, 'He's in the clouds and I talk to him there. I talk to him all the time.' Her comment sent shivers down my arms. My father died years before she was born, and his death, or even the concept of death in general, was not something I discussed with my toddler, though, of course, she had seen his photo and knew his name."

Katie took Allie at her word, that she had some unearthly connection to her grandfather—perhaps she had met him another way and he continued to be part of her life. Allie is not the only child who has felt this connection. In 2016, a four-year-old child fell from a second-story window in San Diego County. The paramedics who responded marveled at how seemingly unhurt the child was. The boy explained that his grandfather, who had recently died, held him in his arms and cushioned his fall to the ground.[7] This recalls three-year-old Lindsay's story when the lady in the blue dress directed them to Nanny's grave.

William Wordsworth's poem "Intimations of Immortality" from the nineteenth century offers further enlightenment:

> *Our birth is but a sleep and a forgetting:*
> *The Soul that rises with us, our life's Star,*
> *Hath had elsewhere its setting,*
> *And cometh from afar.*[8]

As we age, we soon forget our connection. Wonder fades, children become adults who get bogged down in the human experience. "Full soon thy Soul shall have her earthly freight,"[9] as Wordsworth so eloquently continued. Our physical experience manages to smother our most essential treasure, our spiritual self, the secret weapon available to all of us to help navigate this life with wisdom and grace. The superficial self is nurtured through our acquisition of things and reliance on projecting a controlled image to the world around us. It will never lead us to the richer, deeper life of the spirit, the part of us searching for, and with any hope of finding, meaning.

Miracle stories offer a beam of light illuminating a path between the human and the spiritual experience. It is true—we miracle collectors see miracles as inextricably linked to the Divine, but there is also truth in seeing them as evidence of mystery out there somewhere, adding texture to what we cannot see and a sense of uncertainty in the vast cosmos. Humankind is plopped haphazardly, it sometimes seems, into this teeming, chaotic soup, and a miracle story can be seen as a peaceful respite and a reminder that there may be a method to the madness after all.

Regardless of whether your beliefs take you closer to the faith traditions of the East or the West, the presence of the Divine, a power larger than us, is acknowledged and celebrated through stories of the miraculous in each of these cultures. Acknowledging our spiritual essence raises our spiritual intelligence, helping us become more aware, more open, and better able to distinguish spiritual traits in others and achieve our own spiritual connection through meditation and prayer.

Sally Kempton, writer and meditation guru, describes spiritual intelligence in three parts. The first is an "ability to sense and connect to the presence of spirit/love/God in yourself, in others, and in the physical world." Second, spirituality facilitates "access to feelings of compassion, peace and insightful awareness." And finally, it is "a recognition of the interconnectedness of all life, and the realization that other's lives have the same value as your own."[10]

Patricia was introduced to Katie by her friend Andrea, and told Katie about her father, who was born in Italy and was definitely controlling where his six kids were concerned. He owned a construction company and when Patricia was sixteen, long before the age of technology, he outfitted her car with a two-way radio so he could always reach her. When her sister's son, TJ, was born with a life-threatening cardiac anomaly—the valve between the heart and lung was too short and baby TJ turned blue whenever he cried—the parents had to prevent him from crying until the doctors could figure out what to do. A cardiologist in Chicago where her sister lived said TJ required surgery, and soon. Her dad insisted they come to New York to get a second opinion. The cardiologist in New York City concurred, and they went back to Chicago and scheduled the surgery. Less than a week after her return, but before the surgery took place, her father suffered a massive stroke and died at age fifty-seven. TJ's surgery had to be delayed so the family could attend the funeral. When they returned to Chicago, the cardiologist performed another exam and the anomaly had inexplicably disappeared! While he probably had not planned on such an early death, Patricia's dad clearly had an agenda when he got to the pearly gates.

We seem to have attracted a lot of father-daughter miracle stories. Perhaps it is because we were both fortunate to have our father's unconditional love and share in the confidence it bestows. In prior generations, with mothers in charge on the home front, we joke that perhaps dads left their most important child-protecting to the hereafter.

It was the birthday of Katie's sister Mary, and a long-held tradition in their family was for their father to write each of his five children a special letter to mark the occasion. Mary was nineteen and a sophomore in college when their father died, and this particular birthday without him was hitting her hard. She regretted that she had not been the best steward of those letters, and as she sat watching her baby daughter, Carolyn, crawl around the family room floor, Mary began to cry, thinking what she would give to have one of his letters now. Just then, Carolyn began pulling books off the lowest shelf of a bookcase. A Bible that had been given as a wedding gift fell out and opened to the page where long ago a letter had been tucked inside, as if for safekeeping, but then forgotten.

As Mary explained, "The reason my birthday was hitting me so hard was because he would never meet my daughter, which is what I was thinking as I watched her crawl around the floor. Christmas music is playing in the background, which made the tears fall harder, and then she flops open the Bible and there's his letter. What in the world! It was like God winking and telling me Dad does know her, and, by the way, happy birthday."

The letter was the one her dad had written for Mary's seventeenth birthday. "You are a breath of fresh air in a much confused world," it read in part. It is true that love, like the written word, lives on. For both to be delivered at a particular moment of longing is a testament to the spirit-to-spirit connection that is possible.

Mary had forgotten the incident until she and Katie had a conversation about other stories we had heard while we were touring the country and it jarred her memory. It is as if sometimes miracle stories cause temporary, or even permanent, amnesia. These are certainly events you would think people would remember, but there seems to be something unique about miracle memories. Maybe it is because they are not easily stored—there does not seem to be a "box" to put them in. Maybe miracles are marks left on our soul and not on our brains—a different experience altogether, one not recalled in the same way. Or maybe miracles do not fit our own preconceived notions about how the world behaves. They become a wrinkle in an otherwise neat and tidy view, stored in a mind hardwired for predictable outcomes.

Miracles push the boundaries of possibility, which presents an inconvenient choice about whether to bother with delving into a new paradigm or not. They poke at our false sense of control when the ground beneath our feet shifts. Ignoring them is less uncomfortable; we just want to regain our balance. Or we simply forget them after a while, as C. S. Lewis recognized: "That soft, tidal return of your habitual outlook…and the familiar noises from the street reassert themselves."[11] Life goes on. It was "just" a coincidence. Recognizing our own spiritual core, as part of all the spiritual energy that exists, requires a willingness to be open and off balance.

But what if when our life is in disarray, the universal soul comes looking for us? Katie's college friend Johanna tells the story about the day she had to bring her beloved dog Emma to be put to sleep. At a time in her life when she had felt especially alone, Emma had been her constant companion, providing the unconditional love and instinctive protection that she needed. Emma was her only comfort, because she had not shared with anyone the depth of her sadness. Johanna knew Emma was in pain and beyond hope, and the vet told her it was time. After putting her phone and wallet in the car, her heart feeling like it would break, Johanna went to retrieve Emma and bring her out to the car. As she did, she heard what she thought was the car radio, which made no sense since she hadn't yet started the engine. As she got into the driver's seat, she realized it was her phone that was playing music. Initially it annoyed her, because she wanted these last moments with Emma to be without interruption. Then she recognized the song, a beautiful lullaby she had played when her son was a little boy, "The Golden Day Is Dying," by the musical group Hem.

"It was as if someone was speaking to me that things will be okay and I felt warmth and love and an acknowledgment of a special bond," Johanna wrote. At one time she had the song on a CD but had not downloaded it to the iTunes list tied into her phone. When the song repeated on the way to the animal hospital, it was more than music to her ears.

As spiritual beings, we are connected to all there is. We are connected to the earth as we listen to the wind rustle in the trees and marvel at the ocean as it creates a unique imprint with each wave. We are connected to the stars as we imagine them light-years outside our vision and to the gift of the sun we get to experience every day. And we are connected to each other as we weave the divine thread among us. When we are able to see with the eyes of the soul, we see how we are included in the cosmic dance with the Divine Being and universal consciousness that holds all that is together.

TAKE A MIRACLE MOMENT

Soul Mate: What does it mean to you to be spiritual? Do you have spiritual traits or spiritual states? How would you nurture that part of yourself?

CHAPTER ELEVEN

The 90 Percent Rule

The secret of life is not about knowing what to say or do...
The secret is simply to show up.
—Glennon Doyle, *May We Help You*

How many times do we talk ourselves out of going to an event or a gathering, believing that our presence doesn't matter, that no one will notice, that there is somewhere else we would rather be or something else we would rather be doing? The excuses we use range from the mundane ("I have nothing to wear") to the honest ("I'm too tired"). We rationalize, procrastinate, or justify our decision, and sometimes, even when we do show up, our attitude can be closed-minded, distracted, or even resentful.

To discount the importance of showing up when we say we will is another way of subjugating our spiritual side, thinking it is only our physical presence that will be missed. Certainly, it is true that in today's busy world of commitments, both real and imagined, we can face conflicts about where we need to be at any given time. Until we learn to be in more than one place at once, like the Catholic saint Padre Pio and the Buddhist Yogis, we are forced to assign priorities and make choices. When we do show up with an open spirit, many times we are gifted with a surprise story or gain a more complete understanding of a friend's situation. It is really hard to know if you are where you are supposed to be if you never venture out or consider what else you are called to do.

Life is not just about showing up; it is also about how we show up and about testing the range of possibilities before us. We discovered the power of friendship by showing up for each other. Each of us is called to pay attention to the opportunities that surround us and to show up and be who we are, regardless of whether we think it will matter. Many times, our presence makes a difference in someone's life in ways we never could anticipate.

We can walk through life by going through the motions, or we can be present and let our light shine. As one ninety-three-year-old New York physician said when asked why she continued to show up for work, "Someone may need what I have to offer."[1] This was certainly the case for Cynthia, a nurse in Boston who, upon her encounter with a concerned and worried patient in the middle of the night, offered the actual care that was needed. Gayle was sick, anxious, alone, and needed an MRI. The thought of being placed in the narrow tube with a cage over her face and head to ensure she didn't move terrified her. While checking her vital signs, Cynthia asked Gayle about the rosary beads in her hand. Suddenly the moment was transformed into a reassuring conversation about spirituality and faith instead of IVs, test results, and why Gayle had to leave her rosary beads behind. When, at long last, it was Gayle's turn for the exam, Cynthia saw the worry in Gayle's eyes. Ignoring hospital rules, Cynthia pressed an object into Gayle's hand. It was a rosary ring that she carried with her, a sign of her own faith. Because it was nonmagnetic, Cynthia knew Gayle could wear it in the machine. "My fear dissolved. I felt a light in my soul and knew I was completely safe. Cynthia was an angel," said Gayle, who has yet to remove the ring and passed on her rosary beads to Cynthia in thanks.

Uniting compassion with connection, showing up and being all in, transformed a moment of fear into an experience of peace. Being wholly present creates opportunities for miracles to unfold in unexpected situations. This is why we have lived the mantra that)0 percent of life is just showing up.

Each story we hear reminds us to appreciate the mystery inherent in the world we inhabit. We know from our own experience that miracle stories are not relegated solely to places of worship and are not the purview of a privileged, holy few. Since we are spiritual beings, miracles are available to all of us. Sometimes, these stories found us in unexpected places, like the interaction between Katie and her hair stylist, Melyssa, when the subject of miracles came up.

Katie: "Do you believe in miracles?"

Melyssa: "Sure, yes."

Katie: "Have you ever experienced one, or know anyone who has?"

Melyssa: "Hmm, wow, I've never thought about that before…Hmm [long pause]…I'll have to think about that. That's a really hard question… I guess that depends on what you mean by *miracle*."

Katie: "I think miracles encompass everything from a beautiful sunset to an unexplained healing and everything in between. So, I guess I think we all have opportunities to experience a miracle."

Melyssa: "Did I tell you I was getting divorced?"

Katie: "No, but I wondered since I know you're moving and haven't talked at all about your husband."

Melyssa: "Well, anyway, we are, and we had been going to counseling and it was really weighing on me. A while back I was in Thailand with a group, and I walked a bit away from them, when this woman came up to me and asked, 'Did you know Thailand was built on crystals and that many people have emotional responses to being here?' And then, I did. I had this epiphany, literally—a voice told me to 'let it go' and I knew it meant my marriage. I came home at peace and moved forward with what for me has been the right thing and really freeing. I also subsequently met an amazing man…I guess I always felt that someone or something was watching out for me."

Then Melyssa turned to a woman who was sweeping the hair off the floor. "Hey, Louise, you seem like someone who has had a miracle. Have you?"

Louise: "Oh yes, I have a miracle baby. When I was six months pregnant, I was at work and got this weird premonition that something was terribly wrong. I went to my boss, who said, 'Go to the doctor and get checked,' so I did but they checked me and said everything was fine. So, I went home. Just after the cab left, I started to bleed and went quickly to the emergency room where they saw that my baby's umbilical cord was around his neck and he was dying. They didn't even have time to give me anesthesia—they did the C-section that fast. He survived and is a perfect eight-year-old now."

Katie: "Would you call that a miracle?"

Louise: "Definitely!"

In a similar vein to Katie's encounter at the hair salon, Joan was invited to join a new friend for an open house at her backyard pool. Even though she had other commitments on that beautiful summer afternoon, it was a simple choice. Because this new friend made the effort to include her, Joan thought she should manage to make time to squeeze in at least a quick hello. After greeting a number of people, Joan began talking to a woman she had never met before. As they were chatting and watching the youngsters in the pool, the woman suddenly pointed to her daughter. When Joan commented on how much fun the little girl seemed to be having, the woman shared the story of her child's tumultuous first days.

She explained she had gone into labor with twins two months early. Fortunately, one of her newborn twins was healthy and just needed time to grow. However, her other newborn daughter was in crisis and was considered terminal. This baby was born with a rare and deadly condition that was expected to take her life within forty-eight hours. In shock, the mom needed to escape, to run away briefly from the madness overwhelming her. There was just so much wrong. Even the hospital where she delivered the babies was not the one she had planned on going to; it had been the closest one where the ambulance felt it was safe to take her. As it turned out, the hospital was across the street from where she had gone to high school years earlier.

She explained to Joan that her sister, who had been with her throughout the months leading to the babies' birth, realized her frantic state of mind and proposed a brief field trip across the street to their alma mater. Her sister hoped that a combination of the fresh air and being out of the stifling confines of the hospital might renew her strength. A few minutes later, they found themselves in the school's gym, the site of years of their shared athletic prowess and success. Surrounded by their old team pictures on the wall, they recognized the simplicity of those years and mindlessly batted around a tetherball. They returned to reality abruptly when a groundskeeper confronted them and threatened to throw them out of the building. They explained they weren't meaning to trespass; they were just alums looking for calm in a place that had brought them comfort in years past, searching for an uncomplicated respite from the life-and-death decisions that awaited them across the street.

As it turned out, the groundskeeper was a Reiki practitioner and instructor. She heard their pain and asked if she could pray with them. Forming a circle, they focused their request to ask for salvation for this helpless child and called upon the energy of the universe and the Divine to assist them. As they held hands, eyes closed, each alone with their unified plea, they were interrupted by a phone call from the hospital. The nurse on the line told this young mother that while the staff had no medical explanation, moments earlier the little girl had reversed her deadly course and now had an operable condition with a curable diagnosis.

Hearing this story at a pool party Joan had been invited to at the eleventh hour reminded her of why she hardly ever says no to anything. Truth be told, Joan's FOMO (fear of missing out) is part of the answer, but the inspiring interactions that also occur reinforce the importance of keeping up with the 90 percent rule. She is always glad she makes the effort because of the people she meets and the conversations that occur. It is what keeps her up at night finishing her work, so she can accept invitations with old and new friends during the day, even when the honest answer may be, "No, I'm too tired or too busy."

A few years back Joan was asked to give the commencement address at her alma mater, St. Mary's High School in Lynn, Massachusetts. Trying to inspire these young graduates to find their place in the world, she ended with the words of Mother Teresa:

> Life is an opportunity, benefit from it…
> Life is a challenge, meet it…
> Life is love, enjoy it…
> Life is a struggle, accept it.
> Life is an adventure, dare it…[2]

The full poem encourages us to see beauty and appreciate laughter, to take on difficulties and gain perspective around our sorrows. Mother Teresa dares us to show up for life itself, to become more aware of the opportunities in the life we have, and to deepen our understanding of each other, as fellow travelers on parallel journeys.

In fact, we think Mother Teresa would have appreciated the special connection that was made at a book-signing event one spectacular Sunday afternoon in Southern California. It was the kind of day in which you just want to be outside enjoying the warm sunshine instead of inside a dark chapel filled with people. After our *Miracle Chase* talk to the mothers and daughters at an all-girls high school, a woman, Mary, approached us to buy our book and announced that she really did not want to be there that day. We completely understood as any time indoors seemed a sacrifice on such a gorgeous day. But still, it struck us as a little odd that she would be so forthright about her feelings.

Apparently, it was not missing out on the beautiful weather that bothered her. Mary explained there was another commitment she had wanted to attend. In truth, she said she really resented having to be present at the annual mother-daughter function where we were speaking. She had reluctantly agreed to come because she knew her daughter was counting on her to attend, and having graduated years earlier from the school herself, she knew how important it was for the mothers to accompany their daughters. She was hoping to leave early to get to the other event before it was over, so she was particularly disappointed to find out there were speakers at the Mass who would further delay her departure. When she heard the story of Meb's daughter who was shaken and blinded by the babysitter, and her use of a guide dog, she was shocked. The place she had wanted to be was the graduation of a guide dog that a close friend had raised. Suddenly she did not feel so sorry about missing out, and putting aside her impatience, she began to really listen to our talk.

Mary said Joan's story of her son's heart surgery resonated with her personally because she knew she once had a brother who died shortly after birth from some kind of cardiac problem. It was something her family never would discuss, and she had so many unanswered questions. As Mary lingered talking to us, not only did she buy a book for herself, but she bought one for her mother as well. It was nearly Mother's Day and she thought it would be a welcome gift.

The next day Mary sent us an email describing her feelings when we started speaking. She was "speechless...I realized I was where I was supposed to be and hearing what I was supposed to hear. When I told my mother where I had been and what I had heard...She told me the whole story I had never known about the baby she had lost at five days and how Mary [the mother of Jesus] had come to her and let her hold the baby one more time." After receiving her email, we spoke to Mary again and she told us that she and her mom had shared a moment of closeness that was a God-given gift she never could have anticipated. She came to realize that "it's amazing what comes to those who really need it." Willa Cather finds just the right words when no other explanation will do: "Where there is great love, there are always miracles."[3] It is a motto we have taken to heart.

Sometimes we tend to skate through life, checking things off our to-do list, making appearances where we want, or, like Mary, initially resenting the demands others place upon us. There is a price we pay for this myopic approach to the world. Getting out and being with others is vital to our health and well-being, as we came to appreciate more than ever as a result of the COVID-19 pandemic. In fact, the eudaemonic happiness Aristotle described is correlated with advantages to our physical health.

Consider the 2015 study at Brigham Young University that found there are 3.5 million Americans who are at risk of premature death at a rate 26 to 32 percent higher than normal because of loneliness and isolation.[4] While we have seen how feelings of unworthiness may contribute to social isolation, once we come to the realization that we are, in fact, worthy, we now have an invitation to show up and let our light shine. Involvement in service initiatives contributing to the greater good of humanity is one way to restore the human contact that has been lost in the workplace. Even exercising in groups, as Joan has found, supports the role of personal interaction and has been shown to provide a greater health benefit than exercising on one's own.

Problems of loneliness and isolation are the plague of the twenty-first century. According to former US surgeon general Dr. Vivek Murthy, "Over 40% of adults in America report feeling lonely."[5] Regardless of whether feelings of loneliness and isolation are due to self-absorption or insecurity, he notes this epidemic is as dangerous as smoking fifteen cigarettes a day![6] Recognizing that not all of us are extroverts or comfortable in crowds, Dr. Murthy also appreciates the value each of us brings our community, be it joining colleagues for a social hour after work or volunteering with our faith community at a nearby soup kitchen. In his personal attempt to stem the tide of isolation and its increased health risks, he instituted a five-minute exercise[7] he dubbed "Inside Scoop" at his Public Health Service meetings, encouraging the staff to share personal and meaningful stories and photos to facilitate interpersonal connections. Not only is telling stories a prescription for a healthy life, but showing up and getting out into the world and connecting with each other is good for our souls as well.

Laura, Katie's daughter, realized the significance of showing up and being where you are supposed to be when she accepted a party invitation one Sunday night. Once there, she was put in charge of baking cookies. Daniel, a roommate in the apartment where many such parties were held, had decided it was not a party he needed to attend, this being the third party in a row during a three-day weekend. Instead, he was relaxing on his own in his room rather than joining in the festivities. "There's no one there I want to talk to tonight," he told his roommates—his now famous words of all time. Eventually, a roommate convinced him to join the party. In the kitchen, Daniel ran into Laura, who wondered if he could help with a broken oven door. All of a sudden, he decided staying at the party was a good idea. After all, who can resist a warm chocolate chip cookie? The rest is history as their marriage two years later and their two sons can now attest.

The lesson of getting out there was not a one-time thing for Laura. She got Katie to go out one frigid January evening to hear Father James Martin, who was speaking down the street from Katie's apartment. While Joan had brought the event to Katie's attention, encouraging her to see what the man Stephen Colbert refers to as the "Chaplain of Colbert Nation" had to say, Laura was the one who actually got her to go by agreeing to accompany her. Katie readily acknowledged she "just didn't feel like going." It was no wonder she was reticent about attending—she was in the midst of an unexpected health crisis. We all know how hard it is to muster the energy to do one more thing when our strength is lagging. Not only did she have to travel to Denver for a host of speaking engagements the next day, but she was scheduled for major surgery upon her return.

That evening, Father Martin talked about the problem of becoming too focused on any one thing. When she heard his words, Katie knew that was exactly what she was doing. She was so focused on her health and upcoming surgery it got in the way of everything else she wanted to do. At Laura's urging, Katie prayed that night. "I asked God to help me with the anxiety and the obsessive focus...I got through the next several weeks without feeling anxious...completely uncharacteristic."

Father Martin went on to talk about the importance of "allowing yourself to be where you are supposed to be" and posed the question, "What would your best self do?"

It was a question Katie acknowledges she needed to hear right then because she really did know the answer. What was essential was to "calmly and with gratitude for feeling well enough, get on that plane and get to Denver." Needless to say, Katie did show up and the multitude of stories that came our way was our ideal reward.

Assistant editor at Guideposts' magazine, *Mysterious Ways*, Daniel Hoffman admitted he was no stranger to miracles.[8] He was intrigued by the question of why some people seem to attract more miracles than others. Recognizing that miracles are available to each of us and no one religion or culture has a corner on the miracle market, he wanted to know whether those who report miracles are more aware of them than he is, or whether they show up differently in their everyday lives. It was an issue that bothered him because he felt that he was missing out; miracles seemed to be passing him by, even though he wanted more than anything to experience one. About ready to give up, he met a woman whom he described as seeming to "have an inordinate amount of divine good fortune."[9] Over the next few years they became friends. Bemoaning his fate upon hearing of another of her miraculous encounters, she explained he was "a miracle conduit."[10] It was an epiphany. Suddenly, he realized that "maybe all the would-be miracles I'd experienced lately would reveal their meaning in due time...it did seem as if there were something larger at work, something I simply didn't yet understand."[11] As Thomas Merton said, "You do not need to know precisely what is happening, or exactly where it is all going. What you need is to recognize the possibilities and challenges offered by the present moment, and to embrace them with courage, faith and hope. Our job is not to despair over our lack of comprehension of the vagaries of life, but to acknowledge, to share, and to celebrate that which we do know."[12]

Somehow, we think we get to understand everything right away all the time, but in the case of miracles, that is not always what happens. For Tina, a woman Joan met at a book gathering in Monterey, California, a random encounter had a big impact. Tina had come to the bookshop that evening because she did not want to be alone after the diagnosis of mental illness her fifteen-year-old son had been given that day. While her son was out with his father, she showed up at our discussion. There, Tina met Debbie, the woman who shared her miracle story about her brother's mental illness, the path they had taken as a family, and the electrical charge she had experienced upon his death. As a result, Tina summoned the courage to share her own internal battle. Sitting next to Debbie at our impromptu dinner after the event, Debbie was able to offer practical advice and support to Tina in her renewed commitment to her son. Sharing our vulnerability and offering support is what make us, and keeps us, human and connected with each other. Oprah describes exactly what occurred that evening: "The impact someone we don't even know can have on us is incredible—no matter how brief the interaction. A nugget of wisdom shared in passing, a word of encouragement when we need it most."[13]

Joan also had an experience of being the right person at the right time on one of her many cross-country flights when she had to change planes in Denver. As Joan explains, "There I was, sandwiched between two men as we sat on the tarmac for over an hour in the middle of a blizzard, when a story—a miracle moment, really—evolved. The gentleman to my left seemed unapproachable, thick book in hand, strong glasses perched on his nose, and I was sure a pocket protector in his houndstooth jacket. As I climbed over him to put away my bag, he asked about my trip. 'Business or pleasure?' he inquired."

"Both," was Joan's reply; a book event in her hometown of Boston provided the dual opportunity of book marketing and a visit with friends and family.

"Congratulations," he said. "I want to write a book one day." While Joan refrained from rolling her eyes, she could only imagine what type of book it might be.

After the plane took off, they settled into silence since it was once again "safe to turn on your electronic devices…" Some five hours later, as they began their approach into Boston, Joan returned to her good humor and was feeling more outgoing in anticipation of landing on terra firma (dread of flying is one more thing the two of us share in common). She smiled and asked what kind of book he would write. "Management style and its impact on business efficiency," was his immediate response. She was hardly surprised, having already labeled him as a bit straitlaced.

Before Joan could reply, he asked about our book: was it "*Miracle Chasers*"?

"No," Joan said, using our favorite rejoinder to that question, "that would be the 'bar drink!' Our book is simply *The Miracle Chase*," and she gave him the "elevator" version of our journey.

He paused, grew thoughtful, and a hint of sadness crept into his eyes. "Would it be a good book for a twenty-one-year-old struggling with a cancer diagnosis and in treatment?"

Feeling humbled, Joan admitted what she usually doesn't share with strangers on airplanes. "I am a cancer survivor myself, and yes, the message is hopeful and perhaps could help someone even through the sometimes difficult days of treatment."

"It is my son. And he is facing a reoccurrence of non-Hodgkin's lymphoma. He told me, 'Dad, last year we said we would be the best we could be to get through it…if that was our best, what do we do now?'"

The gentleman told Joan his family had faith and was pursuing aggressive treatment, but the look she saw in his eyes said so much more. He was worried, really worried, afraid for his son and the road ahead of him. The gentleman told Joan he would buy our book.

"It seems like a message we need to hear," he explained.

It seemed a lot more sincere than a random or idle promise, and Joan believed him.

Joan wished him well as he exited the plane ahead of her. A few minutes later, she saw him off to the side of the long corridor leading to the baggage claim area, putting on his winter coat. Nervously, she stopped.

"This is the only copy of the book I have and it's the dog-eared one I use at book readings," she told him. "I don't want to weigh you down and I know you are traveling all week, but I'd be honored for you to have it, if you would like."

He smiled and nodded, and as she tried to hand him the book, he pressed a pen into her hand. "His name is James. Please write something special for him."

As Joan apologized for how long it took her to complete her inscription, this dad stood watching, and in her heart, Joan knew he was praying for a miracle. When she finally handed back the book and pen, this man whom she had taken to be meticulously proper had a final request. "Can I have a hug?"

Joan always gets teary when she reaches this part of the story, because we both know that in that hug, this father's love was so great for his son he would do anything to spare him. Hugging a stranger in the middle of the bustling Logan airport with people everywhere was hardly the place he would have chosen for a personal connection, and yet when the connection found him, he responded with openness and hope.

We have spent the years since this encounter praying that this nameless gentleman, emblematic for us of those we have met on our journey of sharing, truly receives the miracle he craves for his son's recovery. As we wrote in *The Miracle Chase*, "It is through fully living our experience that gives the miraculous the power to change lives far beyond our own."[14] The reality is that in order to fully live our experiences, first, we have to show up.

TAKE A MIRACLE MOMENT

Be There or Be Square: Consider the last time you showed up for someone or something you were tempted to skip. Were you all in? Did anything unexpected happen?

_____

_____

_____

_____

_____

_____

_____

_____

_____

_____

_____

_____

_____

_____

CHAPTER TWELVE

Forgiveness' Sake

*We must develop and maintain the capacity to forgive…He who is
devoid of the power to forgive is devoid of the power to love.*
—Martin Luther King Jr., *Strength to Love*

The connection between forgiveness and love is one that does not come easily to most of us. We recognize the love of James' father and the hope that he
has of a cure for his son, but comprehending a connection between love and
forgiveness, demonstrated in Rose Mapendo's story, can take a greater leap
of faith. Forgiveness of her captors in the midst of such evil was grounded
in her belief that it was the only way to save her children. Unfathomable in
its horror, and yet, hers was not the only story we heard that reminded us
of the capacity for grace of the human spirit. We were on another multistop
speaking trip, when just before we began our presentation and discussion,
Joan was called over to join two women who were talking softly together.
One of the women was the person who had arranged our event; the other
woman, Leticia, was someone she had specifically invited to attend, and
she wanted to be sure we met her. With the introductions made, the orga-
nizer said Leticia was a survivor of the California Christmas massacre
in 2008.[1]

The events that Christmas Eve would change Leticia's life forever. While her holiday started out like so many others, with family reveling in the season, it evolved into a nightmare there was no waking up from. Leticia knew that her ex-brother-in-law was disturbed about his recent divorce from her sister. It is impossible to really know what he was thinking; perhaps he thought he would show them, or maybe he was just too ill himself to acknowledge any responsibility. Whatever the reason, he set out for revenge. Dressed in a Santa Claus suit, he rang the bell of the home where he knew the family would be gathered for their traditional Christmas Eve dinner. Leticia's eight-year-old daughter answered the door, and for the honor of letting Santa in, she was shot in the face. Within minutes, nine family members were dead, and the home was a burning carnage. The commotion attracted the attention of the neighbors, who called 911 for help. A local manhunt tracked him down; he had been injured and burned in the destruction he wrought, and his escape was not as rapid as he had planned. Once he realized he was cornered, he took his own life.

While Katie was engaged with our other attendees, she knew something serious was happening across the room when she saw Joan sit down in the middle of a conversation. Leticia explained that her daughter had survived, and, with numerous surgeries planned to repair her face, she was hopeful that one day her daughter would be able to appear in public without embarrassment. Leticia was trying hard to forgive this man who killed her parents, her sister, and her cousins because she knew how dangerous it was to allow ill will to fester.

Leticia had been convinced to come to our event because she acknowledged that miracles have a foundation in love and that love is the basis of forgiveness. She hoped to find a nugget she could hold on to that would help her on her journey. While her presence was a powerful reminder of how much the human heart can seek to forgive, it was also evidence of how much the human soul strives to be at peace. Joan told Katie in the car later, "It was just too horrific to take in the magnitude of the tragedy; I couldn't even trust myself to stay standing upright."

Robert Enright, the scientist *TIME* magazine called a "forgiveness trailblazer," explains, "When we overcome suffering, we gain a more mature understanding of what it means to be humble, courageous and living in the world."[2] We may be moved to "help others who've been harmed overcome their suffering, or to protect our communities from a cycle of hatred and violence."[3] The arc of forgiveness begun by Leticia is far-reaching, and now her beautiful teenage daughter is using her own voice and experience as a powerful spokesperson against gun violence.[4] Instead of hiding or wallowing in the magnitude of this tragedy, forgiveness has empowered Leticia's family to go outside themselves to help others. It is an exquisite example of connection to a higher purpose.

Navigating our way to forgiveness can be confusing. Once we entrench ourselves in an untenable position, it becomes harder to let go, even when the facts say otherwise. Sometimes we may think the universe is conspiring against us. And yet, accepting the reality that none of us is perfect means that sometimes the person we most need to forgive is ourselves. The common expressions "shooting ourselves in the foot" or "cutting off our nose to spite our face" are the result of eons of behavior patterns that do not serve us but are so ingrained that they are difficult to change. The ability to forgive ourselves can be one of the most difficult aspects of forgiveness. While we can easily see the wrongs of others, we can be blind to what we most need to change.

Sometimes this blindness stems from our perceived lack of worthiness. With a front-row seat to our own wrongdoing, it is challenging to get past feeling ashamed. According to Kathryn Ford, "When the dark night of the soul…appears in our lives, we are given an opportunity to strengthen our sense of value and self-worth…So much of the outcome depends on the level of forgiveness we allow ourselves to give and receive."[5] Errors in judgment, unkind words, or even anger—we are all capable of mistakes big and small. Actions as simple as posting pictures where someone is obviously excluded or not at their best are not rooted in love or grace and can often cause pain. While it is important to recognize our errors and forgive the errors of others, it is also important we move past berating ourselves for what we have done and for what others have done to us. Lest we forget, Buddha reminds us, "You yourself, as much as anybody in the entire universe, deserve your love and affection."

Forgiveness is the key to starting over. It begins to provide a path that guides us away from anger and devastation toward inner peace. Once we forgive, we free ourselves from the angst of a poor choice in the past. Only then can we appreciate and connect to the bounty that surrounds us.

A fellow Boston College graduate like Joan, Kathleen shared a moment of connection that snuck up on her, causing her to rethink her own view of forgiveness. Five years previously, while crossing the street in a crosswalk in her small hometown, she was hit by a truck that came out of nowhere. As a result of the accident, Kathleen had a traumatic brain injury that took a year out of her life and lots of hard work to overcome. She thought she had moved past her ordeal when she decided to attend a ladies' membership coffee for a group she had little interest in joining but thought she should check out anyway. Just as Kathleen was making her exit, she was approached by Rose, a woman who said she had been waiting a very long time to meet her.

Rose was clearly nervous, even shaking a bit, and Kathleen thought Rose might want to ask for job advice. Instead, Rose stunned Kathleen by telling her that she had been in the truck that hit her that day five years before. "Rose kept saying how sorry she was and so I hugged her (primarily to stop the shaking) and told her that I only had love in my heart for her and there was no need for forgiveness," Kathleen told us.

The other women at the meeting were now staring at Kathleen and Rose seemingly swept up in the moment. At that instant Kathleen had an epiphany, a message she felt was sent directly from the Holy Spirit. "The accident was not all about me and my recovery over the last five years. In fact, it was about all of us impacted by an event."

Kathleen asked Rose to forgive her for not realizing how upsetting the experience must have been for her and her family and for not reaching out to them. They hugged one last time, and in spite of herself, Kathleen decided to join that group where she has seen Rose once again. "I now smile and wave as if I am seeing a longtime friend, although we were simply two people whose lives crossed very briefly one fateful night."

There is a sense of completeness in this story, a rare opportunity to see differing vantage points, to find closure from two directions. There was courage from Rose to approach Kathleen and grace from Kathleen in return. Grace is a key part of forgiveness, allowing us to see choices that encompass more than the obvious. Sometimes when we think we may have moved on, as Kathleen so valiantly did, there is more to do.

The story of miracle man Artie Boyle is another account with more to uncover. We interviewed Artie for our first *Miracle Chase* book and were struck by his faith as much as by his miraculous healing from Stage IV cancer. At the time, we did not fully grasp the degree to which he tied forgiveness to his healing. While he tells the whole story in his book, *Six Months to Live: Three Guys on the Ultimate Quest for a Miracle*,[6] he acknowledges that even after going twice to confession (the way of receiving forgiveness for perceived transgressions in the Catholic faith), it was only after he finally forgave his parents for their separation decades earlier that he felt completely unburdened and truly believed that the cancer had exited his body.

Forgiveness comes in many forms, but ultimately it is a tool that allows us to move forward in a new way. Archbishop Desmond Tutu saw an abundance of evil in the years of South Africa's apartheid. As chairman of the country's Truth and Reconciliation Commission after apartheid ended, Tutu was instrumental in bringing both sides together to seek forgiveness for the tragedies that occurred and finding grace in the process. He understood Agathon's words from the fifth century BCE that "even God cannot change the past" and bravely looked to the future, preaching, "Forgiveness says you are ready to make a new beginning."[7]

Some, like Rose, Leticia, and Archbishop Tutu, are wise enough to know that our ability to thrive is contingent upon our ability to forgive. Forgiveness unlocks the door to finding acceptance and joy. As difficult as forgiving others can be, sometimes our anger is directed at God, or at circumstances beyond our control. Often the answer to coping and finding forgiveness relies on the passage of time. Whether you use the fifteen steps of forgiveness[8] of Dr. Wayne Dyer, the eight of Robert Enright,[9] or any other approach, in order to move on, we must be willing to create, and then travel, a road to forgiveness that may be filled with unexpected twists and turns.

Dave was brought up in Detroit as a member of Michigan's oldest Jewish congregation. His was a traditional upbringing with religion playing a significant role. That is, until his dad suffered a massive heart attack and died unexpectedly at age forty-nine. Dave blamed God. In anger, he turned his back on his faith.

Years later in California, he met his wife, who was raised Methodist, though admittedly, she was not very religious. They moved back to the Midwest and explored different faiths, searching for a church or temple where they could be comfortable. A friend told them about a nondenominational Christian church, and after visiting they decided they would attend regularly and begin to become involved. At first, Dave was reluctant about joining a Christian church, but he started listening to the sermons and singing in the choir. He chose not to receive Communion, but he felt he was beginning to build back his relationship with God and that faith was growing in him.

As he pulled into his driveway after work one day, Dave felt numb on his right side. He went inside, took off his suit jacket and hung it up, except it kept falling off the hanger. *Weird*, he thought. He went to his desk and thought he would do a little work and hoped the funny feeling would pass because basically he believed he was feeling "fine." Yet, when he went to write, proper words would not form on the paper in front of him. He knew it was time to get to the hospital and started talking out loud to himself. When he heard the words, he realized he was speaking gibberish. Now he was scared. He rationalized it would be best if he drove himself to the nearby hospital because if he called an ambulance, he feared they wouldn't understand him. Not long after he left his driveway, he was totally lost. As he weaved all over the road with car horns blasting at him, he began to talk to God. "Forgive me for being an idiot. I promise to join the church as a full member."

Though he had already passed by the hospital in his confused state, the car somehow seemed to revert to autopilot and he arrived at the door of the emergency department. A nurse approached him and when he spoke to her in gibberish, he was brought immediately back to see a physician. The nurses found his wallet, called his wife, and explained her husband was in serious condition and she needed to get to the hospital immediately.

The neurologist explained that Dave had suffered a severe stroke, and shortly, he would likely be a vegetable (this was pre-tPA, the drug used today to treat stroke victims). He went on to say that he was testing a new drug and though it could kill Dave, it could also make him better.

Not knowing what to do, Dave's wife called her brother-in-law, a physician in Detroit. He told her she had no choice; she needed to authorize the drug. They both knew Dave would not want to live in a vegetative state. She gave her okay and the drug was administered.

The next morning Dave woke up as though nothing had ever happened. The nurses told them they had never seen anything like it; he had been way too severe to have recovered this quickly. A month later, the neurologist insisted that it was remarkable that he had no residual problems. When Dave jokingly asked whether he should buy the drug company's stock, the doctor's answer was a resounding "YES!"

Dave made good on his promise to God, releasing his anger, and immersing himself in his new faith. Three years later, the pastor asked if he would share his story about the presence of God in his life. His first reaction was to say no; but Dave promised to think about it, and in the end he agreed. His talk was scheduled for Easter Sunday. Since the Easter service is typically longer and more complicated than usual, Dave had to go to a rehearsal so everything would be perfect. On his way home after practice, he stopped at his mailbox to pick up the mail. He was surprised to see a letter from the drug company. It was the first letter he ever received from them, and while it thanked Dave for his support in testing the drug, it also indicated, "Unfortunately, the drug [you received] wasn't suitable for stroke victims because it doesn't work...[Oh, and by the way,] you got the placebo."

Dave told us the letter should have been postmarked from heaven and said, "Hey, guy, guess Who?" Dave's explanation was simple. "I gave up being pigheaded and just prayed. It was as if God knew I loved being in control and put me in the situation in the hospital I feared most." The story of Dave's recovery was rooted in forgiveness with an added touch of God's hand shining through. It is an example of letting go, of acceptance, and of redemption. It even has a happy ending—our favorite kind. When he went to visit family in Detroit, his brother actually checked Dave's driver's license and told him he had changed. In the course of forgiveness, something inside Dave had fundamentally shifted; he had found his heart.

Growing a heart reminds us of *How the Grinch Stole Christmas*. The Grinch's conniving, miserable existence gives way when he hears the joyful song of the Whos, their generosity of spirit in full display in spite of their stolen presents and feast. He is overcome when he witnesses the Whos' sense of community and care for each other. Perhaps he recognizes forgiveness as part of their goodwill, and as a result, he is finally able to forgive himself. His heart triples in size. This is what forgiveness does. It takes us from being stuck in the past and entrenched in our positions to forging a hopeful future and deeper connections with those we are now able to invite into our lives.

Forgiveness, like generosity of spirit, can be contagious. One heartfelt apology can often lead to another; all of a sudden it doesn't feel as difficult to consider an apology yourself. The story Annette shared with us about her cousin in postwar, post-Communist Poland takes forgiveness even further—not where there was any wrongdoing on the part of her cousin Zygmunt, but a pay-it-forward, do-the-right-thing, generosity-of-spirit form of reparation.

Zygmunt lived in the small town of Rzeszów in eastern Poland near the Ukraine. There was a lively family restaurant there that was owned by a local Jewish family. Everything changed after the invasion of the Nazis in 1939. Whether as prisoners or refugees, the Jewish family was forced to abandon their home and their livelihood.

In the aftermath of World War II, the Russians took over that part of

Poland and all property was seized by the state. Poverty, the kind that the vanquished always seem to experience, was rampant for the next forty years. Being a non-Jew, Zygmunt managed to survive this postwar period eking out a mere sustenance by doing odd jobs.

Things improved in Poland in the 1980s with the country's gradual rise out of Communism, and in the late 1990s the new Polish government sold off the once prosperous Jewish restaurant property to Zygmunt. As he worked to renovate the establishment, he considered the family who had owned it back in the halcyon days before the war. Zygmunt went to speak to the local rabbi about finding the family, but he was told it was useless. There were no records because multiple bombings during the war had destroyed the town's municipal and community buildings, including the temple. The prior owners were like so many others—tragic and nameless victims of a war that claimed the lives of 90 percent of Polish Jews.

When Annette brought her family to Poland to retrace her ancestral roots, Zygmunt explained to them that he felt a link with his kindred restaurateur. As a means of respect and tribute for all they had endured, Zygmunt kept the name of the original restaurant and brought a check in equal amount of his purchase to the rabbi to be used in building the new synagogue. He was proud of this accomplishment and with gratitude and forgiveness in his heart served Annette and her family one of their most memorable meals, nourishing both body and soul.

Sadly, injustice is not limited to wartime; it exists all around us. When we feel our self-importance rise by putting others down, we need to seek forgiveness. It is crucial that we realize the impact of our actions on others. "Let there be peace on earth and let it begin with me" are not merely words from the 1955 song written by Jill Jackson-Miller and Sy Miller and performed by numerous artists over the years; they are a way to approach life, an attitude embraced by Zygmunt, Reverend King Jr., and so many others.

Like any big change we want to see on the face of the earth, it must begin within ourselves.

Synchronicity was at work the spring day Joan spoke at Colorado College, as agreed, with Dr. Weddle's class on miracles. Hours after the discussion, we received a message from a young woman who was no stranger to the consequences of injustice. She had been a sophomore in high school when she was attacked by a group of men. Her friends said it was a miracle that she wasn't raped or killed, because her friend came out of the party and scared off her attackers. In the hospital with a concussion and a broken nose, pelvis, arm, and collarbone, and four broken ribs, she told us, "It did not feel like a miracle to me…My miracle would have been my life ending in that hospital."

In time, she told us, she became happy again and stopped praying for her life to be taken from her—that is, until her junior year of college, when she was again attacked by a group of drunken guys. She explained that it put her over the edge, and she plummeted into a deep depression. When she admitted to her friends what had happened, they backed away, further contributing to her isolation and despair. We know how important it is to be open and vulnerable, but there is always risk involved. When we go deeper, some people will turn away, but others often lean in and offer assistance. We were relieved when she told us she had overcome her depression and was finally happy again.

After sharing her story, she posed a question we had not been asked before: "Can one person's miracle be another's greatest pain?" We know that many times miracles and painful experiences go hand in hand; it is one of the reasons people hesitate to revisit certain miraculous events in their lives. She explained that at first she thought that her "miracle would have been to have quietly passed [died] after my first assault. But it would have been my parent's [sic] tragedy." Since then she has come to believe, "Maybe my miracle wasn't that my friend found me in 'the nick of time,' maybe it is surviving to live another day. Every day. Maybe my miracle is that I choose to live and keep moving on. Maybe my miracle is not having my prayers answered."

What a remarkable young woman! As we told her in our response, "It takes courage to survive such abuse and trauma and still wake up the next day and make yourself take the next step, moving ahead, going to class, making new friends, thinking about miracles." It is easy to be a victim in these situations, holding on to the pain. Yet submitting to victimhood gives away our power, letting others exhibit their control over us. It was the lesson Rebecca learned in her own harrowing experience.

Forgiveness is not about forgetting. It is about moving forward rather than being immobilized by past hurts. Dorinda is a woman of faith whom we encountered through our online blog and who shared her personal journey of forgiveness. After her mother's death when Dorinda was nine, she had to overcome years of sadness and mistreatment by her father and his new wife. In a moment of clarity, as she was undergoing neurosurgery, she heard the fateful words, "Father, forgive him for he knows not what he does." Releasing the resentment she felt for decades toward her dad, a "peaceful, calm feeling with no anger, worry or negative feelings took its place." Just days after her surgery, she was able to tell him herself, "Dad, I love you and forgive you."

Making the effort to live wholeheartedly, even in choices we feel forced to make, rather than harboring resentment or doubts has its own compensation. Maintaining ill will or bitterness gets in the way of our happiness. While poor treatment by others is unacceptable, it is important to find a way through to forgiveness. Life is too short and too precious to be bogged down in animosity toward others and especially toward ourselves. Joan's dad's typical response to her childhood transgressions was his trademark line, "We only reach perfection in heaven." He knew he was not always perfect either, but what all of us can do, and what is important, is to forgive and to work at being better next time.

As you revisit difficult situations from the past, give yourself a gift that only you can give—forgive yourself and others by letting go. As Dr. Phil says, "Forgiveness allows you to unlock the bonds of hostility and set yourself free."[10] It is a necessary step on the path to finding personal meaning.

TAKE A MIRACLE MOMENT

Woe Is Me: Begin the process of forgiving someone today; it can even be yourself.

PART THREE

Finding Meaning

What is the meaning of life?…The great revelation
had never come…Instead, there were little daily miracles,
illuminations, matches struck unexpectedly in the dark.
—Virginia Woolf, *To the Lighthouse*

CHAPTER THIRTEEN

Be the Miracle

*Lighthouses don't go running all over an island looking
for boats to save; they just stand there shining.*
—Anne Lamott, *Bird by Bird*

Once we practice the art of noticing, cultivate deeper connection with each
other through shared experience, and acknowledge our spiritual essence,
we can shine our light down a clearer path. Perhaps it is a matter of small
degrees, like the three-way light bulb—the shadows keep getting smaller.
Or maybe an epiphany is involved as happened with the two of us. Either
way, or in between, clarity brings most of us right to the heart of where we
already are, with the relationships we are already in, in the geographic place
we call home. Like T. S. Eliot said, we will "know the place for the first
time,"[1] and that is everything.

We are each born with a unique set of blueprints from which to build
our lives. The raw material we come into the world with melds together
with the circumstances of our birth to give us the building blocks to structure our future. We slowly gain freedom to have a say in our own destiny
and, if we are lucky, to seek and find our purpose and passion in life. We
hold a place that no one else does. Relationships, experiences, profession,
gender, generation, and geography all combine to create a unique lens from

which to view the people and situations around us. In the miracle business, we like to say that everybody has a job and only you know what that job is.

This kind of job has no description and it is not a line item on a to-do list. Knowing your job takes advantage of all we have talked about so far. You know your job because you are the only person with your unique set of time, place, passion, and experience that can do the next right thing.

It is about stopping to notice a friend or colleague whom you know well enough to see she is at a vulnerable point in her life and could use some extra TLC. Or about seeing something begin to unfold and realize you are the best, or only, person to take action, as Meb did in her quest to protect children from abusive caregivers. We all have opportunities at work and in our communities as we simply go about our business as usual every day, where we are confronted with choices of how to respond and whether or not to become involved. It is hard to be the contrary voice when everyone else has the same opinion. Yet speaking up when you are in possession of certain facts or experience can change an outcome. We turn the concept of miracles inside out from those hoping for a yes from God to requiring us to say yes instead. It is a view where the Divine or the universal consciousness uses us as part of the plan, where we are responsible for transmitting the power behind the miracle.

Katie's daughter Allie was bullied throughout sixth grade. She understood all too well what it felt like to be an outcast, to spend recess alone, to have her lunch thrown in the garbage, and to be lured back to the group only so they could exclude her from the next get-together to her face. It was a devastating, depressing, long nine months. By seventh grade a new group of friends developed, and things began to improve. One day, when Katie was exasperated with Allie for her seeming lack of care—she was a thirteen-year-old, after all—she asked, "When was the last time you did something nice for someone else?" Allie told her mom about a classmate who had been ostracized for her weight, among other things. Allie explained, "I wait outside of the one class we have together and make it a point to say hi and sit next to her. I just want her to have one person be nice to her every day." That is knowing what your job is and choosing to say yes.

Science tells us that one flap of a butterfly's wings can cause unpredictable and large-scale weather events on the other side of the world.[2] It is the same with one small gesture of kindness. In many cases, these small gestures will pay a dividend later on for some other random stranger. There is always the added advantage that our simple gesture is contagious, prompting another kindness, and another, and so on, like allowing someone to go in front of you in a traffic jam or helping the mom with a crying baby in a long line at the grocery store. It is not just good for the soul and our connection to the people that cross our path; it is good for our bodies also. According to clinical studies, "Endorphins are released whether we are the givers, the receivers or the witnesses of random acts of kindness."[3] We hold the power to light a spark for goodness' sake. That is a lot of power at our fingertips.

Edward was introduced to us in the course of our miracle collecting. He remembers clearly an incident from his childhood when his family became the beneficiary of an act of care and goodwill. His parents were divorced, and he and his younger brother spent every weekend with their dad. This required a drop-off at his grandparents' home, halfway between Clinton, North Carolina, where they lived with their mom, and Topsail, North Carolina, two hours away at the coast, where their dad lived. Edward remembers his father's distinct car, a maroon Pontiac Bonneville, and his fondness for listening to classical music on the drives.

In those days, the route was on remote back roads where hours could go by without seeing another vehicle. One day, in the middle of nowhere, his dad started to drive erratically, and Edward asked if he was okay. His dad said he was not and was trying to stop the car, but he was unable to move his foot off the accelerator. Edward leaned down and pushed his dad's foot off, and somehow his dad was able to press on the brake and stop the car. His dad told the boys to flag down help. Soon, a beat-up and rusted blue truck stopped with a couple inside. The man that got out, big, burly, and disheveled, asked if they needed help. His wife instructed the boys to get back in their car and out of the road. The man moved his dad to the passenger seat and took the wheel. While he drove their father's car back to their grandparents' house, the man's wife followed behind them in the truck. Edward remembers sitting in the back seat with his brother feeling scared for his dad and uncomfortable with the unruly looks of the man. When they reached their grandparents', their dad was whisked into a car, off to a doctor, and eventually to the hospital.

Their grandmother asked for the couple's phone number, hoping to find a way to thank them. A few days after they left, she called the number they had reluctantly divulged, only to discover it was no longer in service. She was so confused by this she later called the telephone company and learned that the number had never been in service. Edward's grandmother decided the couple must have been angels. Edward is not so sure but doesn't think it matters. "They were clearly down on their luck, had just gone two hours out of their way, and my grandmother wanted to express her gratitude." He believes they did it simply out of the goodness of their hearts and wanted nothing in return.

His dad was always on the lookout to help others. He even organized anonymous donors to put money in people's bank accounts when he knew they were in need. One woman, a widow whose World War II veteran husband had died prematurely, could no longer make her mortgage payments, but somehow every month the required amount kept showing up in her account. While she asked around for clues in finding the earthly angels who helped her, the bank stayed mum.

We all have heard the phrase "one good turn deserves another"; it seems the help Edward's dad got that day on a remote road was paid back several times over. He understood what it meant to be the miracle. Regina Brett, who literally wrote the book *Be the Miracle*, explains, "If you want to change the world in a big way, you do your small assignments with greater love, greater attention, greater passion. Simply embrace…the task you have been given."[4]

A lesser-reported story from 9/11 illustrates the impact of this point. As the first tower fell, those who had begun to flee Lower Manhattan took off, running for their lives. Many had no choice but to run south toward the water's edge where eventually 500,000 civilians gathered in desperation as the terror continued to unfold before them. Covered in dust and in white-out conditions, they went as far as they could. It must have felt like the end of the world in more ways than one. Some even made the ill-advised move to jump into the water and try to swim their way out of the city.

On the water, a miracle began to evolve, without coordination or communication. Despite the threat of more attacks, vessels of every type, ferry-boats, tugboats, party boats, and sightseeing boats, all began to turn toward Lower Manhattan. Independent of each other, they saw the black smoke and raced to the scene, confronting the mass of humanity.

Eventually, the Coast Guard called on all boats in the area to assist, and they did, filling every available slip over and over again. It would become the largest maritime evacuation in history. At Dunkirk during World War II, nearly 350,000 Allied troops were rescued from the shore over the course of nine days. On 9/11, 500,000 civilians were rescued within nine hours.[5] "That day, a series of lifesaving, selfless acts performed by everyday people transformed New York into a place of hope and wonder."[6]

Ordinary human beings going about their day jobs, joining forces to do what they could to alleviate suffering, consequences be damned. The whole is greater than the sum of its parts, which is how big shoes like Hope and Wonder get filled in the midst of catastrophe and despair. It is how we become an instrument for good and make miracles happen.

Most of us will face opportunities to be the miracle for someone else. We can make the choice to act or to listen, not knowing whether anyone else is coming to the rescue. Katie's husband, Jim, had one such experience when he was a recent college graduate on his first job assignment living in Phoenix, Arizona. On his way home after dinner with friends, he was behind a driver going too slowly who then ran over the curb when they stopped at a light. When the light turned green, the driver did not go. Jim flashed his lights to get him to move, which he did, but his driving was clearly erratic and so Jim flashed his lights again, hoping to get the car to pull off the road. The driver understood and pulled into a car wash where Jim followed. Jim went up to the car window and told the man he shouldn't be driving and asked him where he was going. Fortunately, the driver was drunk enough to be compliant, got out of his car as requested, and into Jim's car. When he finally told Jim where he was heading, it was twenty minutes in the opposite direction from the one they had been traveling! Jim drove the man home and put his keys and a note in his pocket with the address of where to find his car. The man pleaded with Jim to come in and explain his situation to his wife. Being the miracle is one thing, but that is where Jim drew the line, leaving the man to contend with his wife on his own.

Jim often wonders what this gentleman thought the next day when he realized some Good Samaritan delivered him safely home in his drunken stupor. Maybe it helped to lessen the hangover and soften his wife's anger. Maybe, even, he thought Jim was an angel. Whatever the case, we hope he ultimately made peace with his wife and his drinking.

Helen Keller said, "When we do the best we can, we never know what miracle is wrought in our life, or in the life of another."[7] The story that

Cindy shared on our visit to Denver during one of our book events was one she hesitated to mention because she was not sure anyone else would understand it as a miracle. Her cousin, Lucille, was bedridden with a serious and complicated foot injury. Knowing how much Lucille loves reading and books helped Cindy and her mom choose how they could make her next months more bearable. They decided they would send her an original story, ten chapters in length, one sent for each week of her confinement, accompanied by a gift related to that installment.

Cindy and her mom would normally not have attempted such a thing without at least an outline, but they decided to just jump in and write and were surprised how the ideas and story flowed out of them. They developed the main character around her cousin's attributes, called her Lady Lucille, and had the story take place in a castle near Paris. Each chapter revolved around a different character based on a relative they knew Lucille would recognize, even when disguised as a bird or animal, like the colorful uncle who loved to sing or the flashy cousin who taught dancing in Hollywood. In their big family, there seemed to be no end to the characters they could imagine.

The only original character they created was a young chambermaid who made her way throughout the chapters caring for the main character, Lady Lucille, who was bedridden within her castle walls. The chambermaid reminds Lady Lucille, "Your family is always with you." In one scene, the chambermaid is taught to dance and twirls so fast that a beaded necklace she is wearing unravels and beads fly off in all directions.

Each Monday, the real Lucille received the next installment. When Cindy and her mom finished, they went back to the beginning and realized that the chambermaid was the personification of Lucille's daughter Katherine, who died at age nineteen in a car accident. Lucille understood from the beginning that the chambermaid was Katherine in disguise and by Lady Lucille's side throughout her ordeal. Cindy later saw a picture of Katherine at Lucille's house and was reminded that Katherine always wore a strand of pearls around her neck, recalling the chambermaid's dancing scene from the fictional book.

Why had it not occurred to them to put Katherine in the book in the first place? She was surely the most obvious choice. Cindy believed the story flowed so easily because they had help from elsewhere. As Cindy told us, "Katherine helped me. It took a lot to go into that realm. Makes you more open to it, believing, seeking this out and dwelling there." At first, the realization frightened her, like Joan felt when she had her premonition about the little boy on the skateboard, and Annie with the guardian angel who touched her feet. It gives one pause when the spiritual dimension brushes up against you, but once we have the experience, we become more open to its existence.

There are many examples of stories that involve someone who has died pulling strings for those of us on the workman's side of the tapestry. It seems that even Katherine knew what her job was, giving an assist to those trying to entertain her mother through a tough convalescence.

Sometimes knowing what your job is and choosing to act on it becomes obvious over time as happened with Cindy and her mother. Other times, it is in front of your nose right this minute, now or never, as happened with Jim, and still other times, it is an ongoing "job" like occurred with Allie. Being the miracle for someone else can also happen when we find ourselves in the middle of a crisis that requires us to think clearly and act quickly.

Katie B. is a young woman who moved to New York City from North Carolina after graduating from college two years before. She was out one evening celebrating her birthday at a bar with friends when she ran into the roommate of her ex-boyfriend. It was so out of the ordinary that even though it was late, she was prompted to call a friend to tell her about it as she walked home to her apartment. She continued her conversation as she stopped for a quick errand and then walked to her building. As she put her key in the lock, she told her friend she had arrived at her building and her friend said, "I'll stay on with you until you get into your apartment."

Upon opening the door, Katie B. became aware of a man she had never seen before, with what looked like a pizza delivery box on his shoulder, who managed to slip into the building behind her before the door shut. Her intuition told her not to take the elevator as usual but to take the stairs up to her fifth-floor apartment.

As she began to climb the stairs, the man attacked her from behind and her phone flew out of her hand. Somehow, the speaker feature on the phone engaged as it hit the floor. While Katie B. screamed for help, her friend also kept screaming into the phone that she had called 911 (on her roommate's phone), the police were on their way, and she and her roommate were en route in a cab. Meanwhile, Katie B. had fallen on the stairs and had her two feet on her attacker's chest, trying desperately to keep him away, even as he tried to rip off her clothes. As Katie B. continued to scream and hold him off and her friend continued to scream from the phone, he finally ran from the building. The next day as Katie B. left her apartment, she overheard her neighbors in conversation. One of them said, "Did you hear that screaming last night? I was so scared I had a bat behind my door." Katie B. was heartbroken to know that she had been heard but no one had come to help her.

There is not much question that Katie B.'s friend knew what her job was. Once on the phone, she stayed on the line to make sure Katie B. got all the way into her apartment, not just her building. Obviously, she had a mother like us, always telling our kids to wait until someone is in their car—and it starts—or gets inside their house when dropping someone off. But then Katie B.'s friend was thrown into the terrifying situation of knowing that Katie B. was being attacked and having to make potential life-or-death decisions.

But what about the neighbors in Katie B.'s building who chose to hide behind their doors and their fears? It recalls a story we heard at the Tattered Cover Book Store in Denver. A woman told us about coming home from a first date with a man who had begun to make her feel uncomfortable. They were at the glass front door of her apartment building when the man suddenly put his hands around her neck. As she struggled, a neighbor inside the building opened his door and peered out, prompting the man to quickly leave and allowing her to get in the door safely. She never knew whether the neighbor heard a commotion or somehow sensed something was amiss.

In Katie B.'s situation, it was obvious to anyone who could hear that she was in trouble, and yet they chose to do nothing. This is the opposite of being the miracle for someone else, and yet we humans are capable of either choice: doing nothing or choosing to say yes instead.

These stories of ordinary people rising above the circumstances they face, putting their own needs—maybe even their own lives—second to another's, are remarkable. We share these stories because we hope to inspire ourselves and others to rise to the occasion should the situation come knocking at our door. We always have a choice to do the right thing or to turn away. Fortunately, most of us heed the call at least some of the time. Of course, to be the miracle, to say yes to the job with your name on it, does not always involve inconvenience, trauma, or even conscious effort. Sometimes a simple smile will do, igniting the spark of connection.

There is not a story in this book that does not share ingredients like coincidence or generosity of spirit, understanding the whole is greater than the sum of its parts, or simply taking the time to notice. In the case of Katie B., it was certainly synchronicity that her phone popped into speaker mode and that she was on the phone in the first place because she had run into the friend of an old friend at a bar. It is like the story of Zygmunt in the last chapter. His story is as much about being the miracle for a family that will never know of his generosity as it is about forgiveness. Or remember the woman on the Pacific Crest Trail who called 911 for a young woman who was not even missing yet? Being the miracle is all about stirring the ingredients of awareness and connection and understanding that meaning lies somewhere in the aftermath.

As Richard Rohr wrote, "Whatever your personal calling or your delivery system for the world, it must proceed from a foundational 'yes' to life."[8] If you like to pretend you are in control like we do, you can always choose to be someone else's miracle. Go ahead—give the Divine an assist and say yes first. It may be the only miracle that is coming, and it beats waiting around for a thunderbolt from the sky.

TAKE A MIRACLE MOMENT

Employment Opportunities: Do you know what your job is? How can you be the miracle for someone else?

....

....

....

....

....

....

....

....

CHAPTER FOURTEEN

Daring to Dream

Whatever you can do, or dream you can, begin it.
Boldness has genius, power and magic in it.
—Johann Wolfgang von Goethe

What fun we had as children sending our wishes into the universe and thinking we only had to wait for the stars to align in answer to our dreams. Life was simple and we thought anything was possible—think it, and it can happen, no questions asked. Our dreams, too, were simple—I wish I were... a princess, a scholar, an astronaut, or an Olympian. The list was endless and changed with regularity. At the time, we didn't understand that it took more than wishing to make things happen. On the way to adulthood, we lose that childhood innocence and realize achieving our dreams goes far beyond waving a magic wand. It is up to us to "proceed from a foundational 'yes' to life" by saying yes to ourselves first. Blaming others for our own shortcomings or for derailing our dreams can be a result of our own insecurity or the misfortune we think the world has dealt us. It is up to us to manage the uncertainty in our lives that causes us to silence the wistful voice within. Sometimes, the bigger we get, the smaller we dream.

To dream is to give our lives purpose and passion. As children of God, it is our responsibility to become our best selves, to set goals, and to secure steps toward meeting them. Daring to dream is about freedom of choice, giving yourself permission to make a change and pursue your life's purpose. Joan was reminded of this at a recent event she was invited to attend. Instead of Tupperware or clothing, it was a goddess party, welcoming attendees to find their "inner goddess." Not a concept usually found in Joan's comfort zone, but how often does one get asked to a goddess party? As an avid 90 percent rule follower, she had to go.

There she met Kathryn Ford, the lovely woman whose words of wisdom have graced previous chapters. Kathryn had traveled a path not always of her own choosing but the one she was destined to create. She suffers from a life-threatening chronic illness, and after years of researching how she could thrive and live a life of excellence in the face of her disease, she decided to write a book to share what she had learned that allowed her to become a medical miracle in the eyes of those who treated her.

As a first-time author, Kathryn had all the usual trepidation as she approached the book's completion, but she was clear on one very specific thing. She knew who she wanted to write the book's foreword. She had fallen in love with his writing, his view of the connection between health and spirit, his grounding in Western medicine, and his understanding that we are so much more than mere cells working in unison—we are spiritual beings in need of nourishment. She was sure he was part of her story.

While Kathryn had devoured everything he had written, she neither knew this prominent physician nor knew anyone who might know him. However, she was not deterred, and with all her heart she put her message out into the universe—he is the one. He must write the book's foreword. Keeping this dream in mind, she worked on completing her manuscript, and as she approached the book's final draft, Kathryn was asked to speak at an online international event. Why not? she thought, and said yes. Several weeks later, when she submitted her informative presentation to the meeting coordinator, Kathryn decided to look up the bios of the other speakers. There he was, the physician she was longing to meet, also presenting at the conference.

Kathryn called the meeting coordinator and asked if she would be willing to pass along her information with a request to speak with him. The coordinator was happy to oblige, and the call was arranged. Kathryn was somewhat deflated when he would only commit to taking a look at the manuscript. He cautioned her not to get her hopes up, because it was highly unlikely that he would agree to write the foreword, as he does not put his name on very many things and is extremely selective. A gracious woman, Kathryn said she understood, but honoring her commitment to herself, she agreed to send the manuscript regardless. Imagine her joy when this world-renowned physician emailed a few days later with the miraculous news: "I scanned the book and love it because we think alike." She knew he had agreed to her erstwhile request.

Daring to dream is an important life lesson most of us have to relearn. While it facilitates empowerment and passion, it also requires honesty and the willingness to ask for help. First, we have to start by acknowledging the reality of where we are. Once we recognize and accept that reality, the ensuing questions become much more obvious. Where would you want to be in the next one, five, or ten years? And how would you begin this journey? While it may be a rewarding exercise to answer these questions, it is not easy to turn our dreams into reality. To begin, you have to ask yourself more specific questions. Are you feeling empowered in your current life and how important is that to you? Can you identify your passions? Is your intellectual curiosity fulfilled? Are you happy with your degree of social engagement? Are you where you are supposed to be, doing what you are supposed to be doing? And the hardest question of all for many: Do you truly believe you are worthy enough to deserve your dreams? Without believing in your own worthiness, dreaming can become a minefield of false starts, disappointments, and self-fulfilling prophecies of failure, instead of the achievement of success by meeting milestones en route to your goal.

Daring to dream is about giving ourselves a personal blessing to appreciate our uniqueness, to find the courage to allow ourselves to try something new, and to act with honesty and open-mindedness. The stories of our lives provide the clues to taking the next steps, by revisiting activities where we have found joy and fulfillment. We must believe we are worth having a dream in the first place, as well as having what it takes to go after it. A dreamer himself, and someone who left an indelible mark on the entertainment industry, Walt Disney lived his belief that "all our dreams can come true if we have the courage to pursue them."[1]

Holding on to the idea that the "person I think I am" acts in a particular way or is not willing to do what needs to be done serves no one. In order to dream, first, we must recognize the barriers that we put in front of ourselves. Some of these are internal roadblocks, like fear of failure, while others are external, like where we live, what we do, what our resources are, and, perhaps most importantly, how we interact with those around us. Are we empathetic or judgmental; generous or unkind; understanding or dismissive? If we are honest with ourselves, most of us have had moments of all of the aforementioned.

Saint Ignatius challenged us "to seek out and find God's will for our lives and our ultimate good."[2] It takes intention and time to recognize our ultimate good. Where do we have potential for greater connection, collaboration, passion, and usefulness in the universe? Researching our options and seeking feedback from others are not always straightforward, but the clues uncovered are an essential part of the process.

Kathryn found this out as she left her safe career in human resources in order to do something new and go after a dream with the confidence to achieve it. Joseph Campbell, the anthropologist who researched, wrote about, and spoke extensively on the world's cultures, from ancient times through the twentieth century, observed, "We must let go of the life we have planned so as to accept the one that is waiting for us. The old skin has to be shed before the new one can come."[3] Life coach Martha Beck likens this phase to the cocoon of the caterpillar before it emerges as a beautiful butterfly. The caterpillar does not just grow wings while hidden inside; it must decompose and the nebulous goo it forms becomes a necessary part of the process of reincarnating itself into what it was meant to be. Since none of us will live forever, we must make the most of our one true life.

So, where do we start? Once we dream it, we must begin it. And we are the only ones who can. Beginning always starts the same way. As the Chinese proverb says, "The journey of a thousand miles begins with a single step." And once begun, we must continue to take one solid step after another. It is the only way that ever works.

Meb's journey with Liz started out just that way, a step at a time. After Liz was shaken so violently by the babysitter, not only did she have to relearn how to move again after being paralyzed, but she also had to learn how to maneuver as a blinded person in a sighted world. While Meb's job was to support Liz, Meb also took on the daunting task of changing policy toward child safety in the state of California. As Meb said, "I learned that if I could just take one step and then another, trusting that I was the instrument of a change that needed to happen, I could achieve what some thought impossible." In an environment wrought with funding shortfalls, she dared to dream that California would institute background checks on childcare workers to prevent people like Liz's abuser from working with other children. Now, thirty years after the TrustLine Registry became California law, thousands of people have been screened and numerous children have been spared injury at the hands of their caregivers.

The tipping point in Meb's journey came early on with a call she initially hesitated to make. Summoning her courage, believing in her mission, and trusting her instincts, she convinced the state representative on the other end of the line to champion her bill. Many of us sabotage our effort to take the first step, and it would have been simple for Meb to fall into this trap. After all, she was learning to help a child with a disability and had another small child at the time. It would have been easy to think, *I can't do this. It is one more thing in an already overcrowded life. How could I ever be successful in changing a law in the huge state of California? I am just one person!* Fear of failure is one reason to hold back from what is possible. Meb had to believe she could not fail as she watched her daughter work hard to achieve small miracles each day, never underestimating what one committed person could do.

"What would you do if you knew you could not fail?" asked Steve Jobs in his famous Stanford commencement address. It is a question we all must ask ourselves, time and time again. Asking this question is a way to check in with our inner self and to ensure that we continue to shine our light into the world without getting sidetracked or waylaid. Are we truly doing what we are called to do and what we want to do in our heart and in our soul?

Katie had the experience of seeking her true purpose in the midst of writing our first book. She was plagued by a fear of failure. Her thinking, unconscious though it may have been, went something like this: "Publishing has changed, we don't have an agent, no one will publish us newcomers, and our experience is in other areas..." As long as she kept thinking and not doing, she could never fail. Katie was enacting what many of us do and became a saboteur of her own life. As August Wilson wrote, "Confront the dark parts of yourself, and work to banish them with illumination and forgiveness. Your willingness to wrestle with your demons will cause your angels to sing."[4]

Sometimes, in order to hear the angels sing we must take the next step, whatever that step seems to be. A former banker and soon-to-be empty nester, Katie decided for her fiftieth birthday to enlist the help of a life coach who saw the passion in Katie's eyes whenever she spoke of our miracle exploration. The life coach explained it was up to Katie alone to commit to making writing a profession. It became the push she needed to commit fully and wholeheartedly to our book.

Even if we had tried (which we did not), we could not have scripted a more perfect scenario than the moment Joan called with the news of the acceptance of our *Miracle Chase* manuscript for publication. Katie was literally on her way out the door of the home she had lived in for twenty years for the last time to move three thousand miles across the country.

"Hi, Katie; it's Joan."

"Got to call you back, just waiting to hand over the keys to the Realtor."

"No!" came Joan's uncharacteristic response. "Actually, you might want to sit down."

"Very funny, Joan—I've got no furniture. Okay, sitting on the stairs. What's up?"

It was clear to anyone who spoke to us that we found our passion in our miracle quest and the spiritual journeys that followed. Our motivation to continue was in the constant gifts of stories we received and in the apparent liberation of those who told them. Coco Chanel once said, "Success is often achieved by those who don't know that failure is inevitable."[5] We were those people! We found that once your life has been touched by the Divine, anything becomes possible. Wrong turns or detours transform into opportunities. Our vulnerability and our uncertainty became secondary as we forged a new path forward. As the stories kept coming, we miracle collectors kept getting affirmation that we were on the right path.

Following our heart can take us down many roads at different times of our lives. One of the most common is the dream of starting a family, something we both understand from our own experience with mother-hood. While many are spared the difficulty of conceiving a child, others are tortured by testing, injections, high cost, and disappointment. The birth of a child is one of life's greatest miracles and yet to many it is out of reach.

Joan met Tanisha at a local nail salon while Joan was primping in advance of a wedding she was attending. Though she had frequented the establishment at random times over the past twenty years and Tanisha had worked there for over ten years, it seemed strange their paths had never crossed. In the process of Joan's manicure, they shared the usual small talk. When Joan returned from rinsing her hands and paying the bill, Tanisha was admiring a polished silver charm that looked like a military dog tag. Joan was intrigued and asked what it was. She could tell by the look on Tanisha's face it was something with substantive meaning and was impor-tant to her. Tanisha showed Joan the picture of the strapping baby boy in the photo framed on her workstation. "He's my miracle," she said, not car-ing who knew how she felt.

Tanisha explained she had numerous miscarriages and the doctors blamed the uterine growths that had precluded her successfully carrying a baby to term. Beaten down, she kept her strong faith but felt as though the real life goal she had to be a mother would never occur. Then while she was sleeping one night, she had a dream where she heard confirmation that she would have a child and what his name should be. After misdiagnoses and numerous procedures, her physician and her pastor told her just to try one more time. Sure enough, she became pregnant and as the baby grew, so did the tumor surrounding it. She prayed daily to her guardian angel to protect her baby. And each day she did not deliver was one more gift. Her pastor explained that he knew God had sent his angels to protect her and that all would be well. Her son was born full-term and healthy. Tanisha had commissioned a charm to wear around her neck, where above the baby's name the words GOD GAVE US A PRECIOUS MIRACLE were engraved.

Tanisha was not alone in her miracle delivery. We got a call from Cece, an ardent miracle believer who had printed MIRACLE CHASE T-shirts after reading our book and had them for sale in a local gift shop. She called to say she was ordering more shirts, because the grandmother of a miracle baby named Chase, whose parents had tried for years to conceive, had come in and bought out the store's entire supply.

So many couples try for years to achieve this dream and many do, whether through foster parenting, adoption, the wonders of science, or nature taking its course. Why is this dream one we strive for and stay constant to, while so many other dreams fade away? Do we think our other dreams and aspirations are not as important or as meaningful to us? Committing wholeheartedly is the recognition that we are worth the effort to be or to do what we are meant to be or to do.

Gina, a friend of Joan's, disclosed a miracle story that helped her know that she and her family were where they were supposed to be. Joan has known them for years, going back to their children's grade school days. With parents committed to teaching their children the value of volunteering and of helping others who are less fortunate, theirs is a family dedicated to contributing to the world through service.

Shortly after the Indian Ocean tsunami in 2004, the family traveled to India to help with the cleanup of the devastating destruction that occurred there as a result. They had a trip already planned to the area, but it took on a whole new dimension after this disaster. While several others who were scheduled to join them chose not to go on the trip, they went anyway. As

Joan and Gina rode bikes side by side on a New England bike path years after their return, Gina expressed how the near incomprehensibility of a disaster this massive stirred her soul to the edge of despair. What saved her from absorbing so much suffering herself was a family she encountered that she felt she was destined to meet.

It was the day after Christmas when the tsunami hit without warning. In a city along the coast of India, a young mother caught in the fury was grasping her infant child in her arms when she was abruptly swept away by the rising water. Though she had tried with all her strength to keep the baby safe, the force of the water pried her child away from her. She awoke much later in a makeshift hospital bed, alive but bereft at the loss of her child. She knew she was blessed because she was eventually reunited with her husband, even though initially they ended up in different refugee camps. Like so many other families, they posted pictures and filled out forms with their baby's description, but as the days went by and amid such powerful destruction, their situation felt hopeless. There was no way an infant could be expected to survive.

The power of the tsunami swept inland before it ultimately receded and left debris and chattel of all types in its wake. Miles away, upriver, in a usually dry part of the country, as the townspeople came out of their huts to clear the rubble from their waterlogged town, a baby's cry was heard. There, on a piece of flotsam, lay a healthy baby, safe, but far from home. The story of survival Gina witnessed, when she saw the reunited parents with their child, was an affirmation of the importance of connecting to the greater good and making the choice to make a difference.

As Gina recounted the experience, it was as though Joan was there with her in that moment of wonder. Joan held her breath in anticipation of what she hoped would be the story's happy ending, but it seemed so unlikely she prepared herself for the worst. It was yet another example of how sharing defining moments reinforces the power of the experience for the teller and changes the listener as well.

While the unification of one family buoyed our spirits, it does not erase the tragedy of the massive loss of life in the disaster. Recognizing the blessings that do arise in the aftermath of destruction allows us to keep going instead of falling prey to feelings of powerlessness. We have no choice; we must be willing to find forward motion in the nuggets of grace and goodness that surface, even in the midst of great suffering.

At the heart of daring to dream is the answer to that one overarching question: What would you do if you could not fail? We must be willing to take stock and see who we really are before we can truly know what is important to us and what we wish to accomplish in the world. As an exercise in self-discovery, it may just lead the way to overcoming our defenses to reveal our soul. For some, it may be to become a princess, a scholar, an astronaut, or an Olympian, but for the rest of us, the words of psychiatrist David Viscott ring true: "The purpose of life is to discover your gift. The work of life is to develop it. The meaning of life is to give your gift away."[6]

TAKE A MIRACLE MOMENT

Dream Catcher: Consider your purpose and passion. What would your ideal personal mission statement look like?

CHAPTER FIFTEEN

The Gift of the Present

Life is a miracle. We, all of us are creator beings.
We are the joyful choice makers.
—Sakshi Chetana, *Laughing Buddha:*
The Alchemy of Euphoric Living

Daring to dream is about being the miracle for yourself and stirring up universal energy in the process to light the signposts along your way. With commitment, we are better able to navigate our path in the right direction, without guarantees, but with hope for the future and gratitude for the good that finds us.

Like a kaleidoscope, ever changing and working in tandem with every turn, gratitude emerges as the touch point where awareness, connection, and meaning meet. Cicero wrote, "Gratitude is not only the greatest of virtues but the parent of all others."[1] Awareness of the moment is really about being grateful *for* the moment, making the connection, whether to each other or to the Divine, with a sense of appreciation of where God, the eternal Presence, can be found. It is not in yesterday's worries or tomorrow's plans but only in that eternal now. By finding a way to keep gratitude as a constant companion, the blessings of joy and contentment become our reward. With intention and practice, gratitude becomes a way of life.

Sometimes gratitude fills the void left by loss. Remember the coincidence Katie and her brother experienced when choosing the burial plot for her father? A year later, Katie and her husband were moving from an apartment to a town house across town to make room for their first baby, who was soon to arrive. As they drove down the freeway with a car full of belongings, Katie began to cry, "I know you'll think I'm crazy, but Dad won't know where I am now." Jim did his best to soothe her feelings but there is only so much we humans can offer when feelings of loss engulf us. The next day, there was a knock at the door of their new home. The man at the door gave them their code for the neighborhood gate. It was forty-one, the same number as her parents' home address and her father's burial plot. For Katie, it was the sign she needed, confirming that he knew exactly where to find her.

When Laura was born months later, it coincided with a mix of emotions—mostly euphoria and joy, but also the resurfacing of a deep sadness that her dad would never know his granddaughter. One night a few weeks after her birth, Katie explained she had what seemed like a dream. "Dad was at the bottom of the stairs, not in a form I recognized; I simply understood his presence there. He was looking up in anticipation before he ascended the stairs and wandered into the nursery where he lingered next to Laura's crib. He then crossed the hall to our bedroom where I sensed him inside the doorway, his visit there more fleeting." Katie said she woke up, one moment to the next seamless, as if the dream were taking place in what seemed like real time and space. "What a gift this was to me."

Henri Nouwen, a renowned twentieth-century priest and author, wrote, "Gladness and sadness are never separate, joy and sorrow really belong together, mourning and dancing are part of the same movement."[2] Even the recognition of all that we have never inoculates any of us from suffering. Some of the time, it may seem to make our suffering worse, because we have fully appreciated and taken advantage of joyful circumstances or allowed ourselves the full measure of friendship and love. When we embrace the gifts of the moment, we have left ourselves vulnerable to their loss, making their absence seem even more profound. Yet to be grateful is to embrace life fully, to live it all. Gratitude is a spiritual exercise that puts us in touch with divine possibility.

Like loss, fear is also an emotion that can become transformed by gratitude. Sorour and her family lived in California when her husband was diagnosed with an incurable late-stage cancer. With one son in college on the East Coast and another son still in high school, she did not know how she would cope without him. Less than a month before he died, Sorour had a dream. She was walking on a deserted beach on the Caspian Sea where the four of them had vacationed before leaving Iran to immigrate to the US. In her dream, she had her young boys by the hand, and it was just the three of them walking along. Sorour felt overwhelmed, alone, and frightened. Turning toward the water, she was confronted by an enormous wave, neck high, coming straight for them. She knew they could not overcome it. Right then, she and the boys turned around, their backs toward the oncoming wave. The previously deserted beach was now filled with people, lined up several deep, and in her heart, she knew that they were there for her.

The dream had a profound effect on Sorour and completely changed her outlook. A few nights after her husband's burial, she accidentally set the table for four, prompting an emotional response from all three of them. Sorour told her boys that their dad trusted them to live their lives and knew they would all be okay. She even insisted that her younger son, who was willing to stay close to home for college, go east, since she knew deep down that was what her son wanted to do. For the next year, her house was full of family and friends who came to stay and visit for periods of time. She was grateful for the courage and the love they shared that helped her go on in spite of her grief.

Just like we have the choice to be the miracle for someone else, we also have a choice to be grateful or not. It seems to come naturally to some and requires a big shift in focus for others, like the glass half-full/half-empty analogy. The thing is, grateful people's lives are not filled with more gifts or more things to be thankful for; they simply acknowledge, remember, and see the good. And, as happened with Sorour, it can change the way you see your life and positively impact the lives of those around you.

Katie has always found it helpful to keep a gratitude journal. Looking back at her entries, she is stunned by the things she would otherwise have forgotten. Like the April morning an early spring snow blanketed New York City. She was on her way to greet the day with her grandsons as she did most weekday mornings. When she opened the window shade in her two-year-old grandson's room, the swirling, dancing snow mesmerized him. Then he began to laugh, shaking down to his toes, a pint-size bundle of mirth. There is nothing like a toddler to remind you that you can experience heaven on earth. Committing memories to a journal ensures that precious moments are not lost in the muck of everyday life. Being grateful is more than remembering, though. It is an ongoing shift in perception on how to view whatever circumstances arise. A practice of gratitude gives us needed perspective to soften the adversity that is part of all of our lives.

Perhaps gratitude is also a key ingredient for remembering miracle stories. Maryann, the woman we met who is a survivor of the Miracle on the Hudson, shared a story from the early years of her marriage. Her husband Ron's best friend, and the best man in their wedding, had just committed suicide. They decided to drive their new car from Nashville, where they lived, to Chicago to support the grieving widow and attend his funeral. They had not been in Chicago long when Maryann received an emergency call that her father had suffered a massive heart attack in New York. He was in the intensive care unit (ICU) and they were not sure whether he would live.

They made a reservation to fly out of Nashville the next morning so they could bring their car back home. That meant that in order to make the flight, they would have to drive all night from Chicago. As they traveled along a remote road in a blinding rainstorm at about 1 a.m., their car broke down. As they were stopped by the side of the road, rain pelting the roof, Maryann began to sob, her worry over her dad and her frustration at their predicament overwhelming her. All of a sudden there was a knock on the driver's side window. It was a minister, his priestly collar on, who wondered what was wrong and offered to help. He had a house that was not far away and brought Maryann and her husband there. While his wife gave them milk and cookies, he called a couple of parishioners, one of whom was a mechanic with the skill to repair the new kind of engine that was in their car. Within a short time, they were on their way again and made their flight by ten minutes. As an added blessing, her dad survived the heart attack.

Sometimes, without tipping our hand or a preemptive story to lead the way, miracle stories find us. It is as if we have some magnetic pull to attract stories from random encounters. We cherish these sudden miracle connections like the one that Katie experienced on a flight to Denver. Halfway through the flight, her seatmate, Susan, asked Katie if the book she was reading had a dog in it. It did, Katie responded, and Katie gave her a quick synopsis about *The Friend* by Sigrid Nunez. Susan then began to tell Katie about her beloved dog Daisy, who had died two years before. She said the dog had been a miracle in her life and a gift from God. Susan felt this was quite a revelation, since she is not religious or much of a believer. She explained that at the time, her husband had recently left her, and while it had occurred to her that maybe a dog would be a good idea, she had decided against it. After all, she was a busy physician who worked long hours and did not need, or want, the responsibility.

A few days after making that decision, she came across three adorable puppies up for adoption, snuggled in a playpen on busy East Eighty-Sixth Street in Manhattan. They were surrounded by passersby who could not resist a look. Susan wandered over and asked if she could hold the only tan one. It looked exactly like a dog she had seen at the park whose looks most appealed to her. As she stood there, the puppy trembled in her arms. All of the things she had to do, all of the reasons she should not get a dog flashed before her, but she also heard a voice—her own—say, "I'll take her." Coincidentally, Susan had the next week off so she could get settled with her new responsibility.

Daisy became the "love of her life" for the next fourteen years. Susan welcomed her walks in the park and around the city where she met new friends, proud to show Daisy off to the young and old, who constantly approached her to "ooh" and "aah" at her cuteness. Daisy was also an overwhelming focus and responsibility that, while challenging, supplied more joy than Susan had thought possible. Susan believes there is a "Being up there" who understood it was what she needed, knew she was resistant, and intentionally put a puppy in her path so adorable that she was powerless to refuse. "*That* was God's gift to me."

In a subsequent conversation, Susan admitted she thinks "God is an absolute frame of reference." As a scientist and doctor, she had always been disturbed by Einstein's theory of relativity where the concept of absolute goes away, and everything becomes relative to something else. But she believes the more you know as a scientist, it seems more likely it is all guided by a higher power and that there must be an absolute frame of reference, and that absolute must be God. She did not ever think she would believe

God could intervene on a personal basis, but Daisy may have changed her mind on that.

We tend to appreciate in retrospect things like a warm spring breeze in the dead of winter, a loved one's smile after leaving for the airport, our own good health when illness comes calling. Usually, gratitude requires commitment and effort. Life can be mundane and predictable like the nature we are surrounded by: leaves eventually lose their color and fall, and the sun comes up every day. Ho hum. Gratitude adds sparkle to the ordinary and energy to the complacent. The constant pull of gratitude that Susan felt (literally and figuratively, because sometimes Daisy walked Susan and not the other way around) after meeting Daisy makes it more difficult to take people, pets, and circumstances for granted. When we look at our lives through the lens of gratitude, our blessings gain in stature and depth; they rise to the top and prompt us to consider new meaning in our lives.

G. K. Chesterton said, "Gratitude is happiness doubled by wonder."[3] This was certainly true in the synchronistic events that began to unfold one August day in 2019. The Riggs family wanted to give their toddler, Cameron, a sense of normalcy after the birth of her younger sister, Hadley, just thirteen days earlier. The new family of four decided on an outing to Cameron's favorite place, the Denver Zoo. At around 10:30 a.m., just outside the sea lion exhibition, the girls' mom, Sarah, noticed Hadley turning blue. And then, Hadley stopped breathing. Sarah began screaming for help.

Meanwhile, paramedic James Boyer was watching his boys play in a nearby sandbox when his wife alerted him that she heard someone scream, *She's not breathing*. Boyer instinctively swung into action, quickly locating tiny Hadley. He scooped her up and began CPR. Family practice physician Carolynn Francavilla Brown also heard the screams and came to assist in the rescue effort, handing her own eleven-month-old over to a complete stranger. The two professionals alternated efforts for the next twelve minutes, one doing chest compressions while the other blew fresh oxygen into Hadley's lungs until the ambulance arrived. Erik, Hadley's dad, stood away from the scene with Cameron, terrified by the desperate measures being taken to save his baby daughter.

Thanks to the lifesaving efforts of Boyer and Brown, Hadley survived to be diagnosed with a congenital heart defect that could be repaired. A few more coincidences and a heaping dose of gratitude would bring the three families together again, once Hadley had recovered. Eventually, Dr. Brown got in touch with the Riggs family and heard the good news. Sarah Riggs also reached out on a Facebook page for the City Park neighborhood where she lives, hoping to connect with the people who saved her daughter's life. And who administers that page? James Boyer's wife, Tanya, who happened to be back at the Denver Zoo when she saw the post.

It should surprise no one who believes in synchronicity that the Children's Heart Foundation's Congenital Heart Walk, an event that rotates around the country and one that Joan's family has frequently supported after their own experience with a congenital heart defect, had been scheduled for that fall in Denver, at the Denver Zoo. It was a logical opportunity for the Riggs family to honor Boyer and Brown. "The new mother said, her voice breaking, 'I've never been more grateful to anyone in my life than these two people.'"[4] The perfect series of events that saved a life and a family spread gratitude throughout the community. Gratitude makes the world a little kinder and gentler; it reminds us that this is a place we want to inhabit.

Joan has lived her life feeling grateful for many things. As a six-year-old, she remembers waving goodbye to her mother at the front door, asking her to please bring back a sister from the magical hospital where siblings seemed to come from—no more brothers! When her wish was granted, she remembered to say thank you and has been saying thank you ever since. Part of it is attributable to her upbringing, but also it is in recognition of the gifts that surround her, of family, of friends, and of things that have not been as bad as they could have been. As a breast cancer survivor, she is grateful every day, knowing that she was fortunate that hers was a cancer that could be treated.

As part of her positive outlook and as an avid cook, Joan loves to host large dinner parties. In addition to serving what she hopes will be a delicious meal, Joan loves to serve up inspiration as well, as each guest is asked to share their favorite part of the day. Many times, these are moments that might not have been remembered, much less shared with anyone, but once spoken aloud, it makes the experience more real and even more appreciated. The universal message that comes through these vignettes is a sense of joy and gratitude. Everyone present experiences how these insights reveal a part of who we are. It creates an air of sensitivity and respect for each other and often turns out to be the most important course of the meal.

Gratitude can be a two-way street. It cultivates increased awareness by shining the spotlight on something or someone else, leading to connection, and providing benefit to both the giver and the receiver. It can become a virtuous circle spreading good in the world. Numerous research studies have shown that gratitude is good for your health and may help cultivate other virtues like patience, humility, and wisdom.[5] It can even improve academic performance! One study indicated that gratitude among middle school students "can foster an increased sense of hope and trust in others and fuel a desire to give back to their community."[6] While the myriad benefits of a gratitude attitude are all encompassing, we have to be careful not to take gratitude itself for granted.

Like miracles, expressions of gratitude can be big or small or anywhere in between and are not in the sole purview of holidays or special occasions.

The important thing is to stop and take the time to recognize the people, places, and things in your life that make gratitude tangible.

Gratitude is a gift that keeps on giving. Just ask Karen, who found a way to wrap it up in a box and tie it with a ribbon. Some thirty years ago she gave a gold Tiffany bracelet to a friend, Anne, who was leaving New York City to start a new life in Washington, D.C., after a challenging divorce. A few years later, when Karen left New York herself to move across the country, Anne gave it back, a talisman for good luck. When Anne, and then Karen, got breast cancer, the bracelet went back and forth again. By this point Karen understood the symbol of love and caring the bracelet represented and decided she would make it available to anyone who needed it. Her only stipulation was that when the bracelet was returned, a note accompany it saying what wearing the bracelet meant to each person as she went through her individual trial.

Since then, the bracelet has been worn by two women battling lung cancer, five women battling breast cancer, one with Guillain-Barré syndrome, and others who were facing difficult life changes. Karen herself has had more than one miraculous escape while wearing the bracelet, including an additional cancer and a temporal artery bleed. All of the women are alive and well. The notes Karen received expressed similar sentiments: "It helped me realize that other women had struggled with things and made it through"; "That there were people who I didn't even really know that cared about me and could understand"; "That I wasn't alone"; "It gave me the strength and courage to push through." The women felt connected to each other, grateful to Karen for the "good energy, positive thoughts and the strength of every woman" who had worn it before them.

The Magic Bracelet, as they all call it, would be powerless without the love, courage, and gratitude associated with it. The good news is we all possess that power, even if we don't wear it on our sleeve.

TAKE A MIRACLE MOMENT

Make My Day: Is there someone in your life, past or present, who deserves your gratitude? Have you told them? What would be a good way to thank them?

CHAPTER SIXTEEN

Miracle Courage

Courage is what it takes to stand up and speak;
courage is also what it takes to sit down and listen.
—attributed to Winston Churchill

Gratefulness and courage are closely intertwined, like the yin and yang of speaking and listening. Twentieth-century clergyman James Faust recognized a grateful heart as the foundation for courage. Each is magnified when they are aligned together. It takes courage to find gratitude for the difficult things in our lives that have taught us humility and wisdom. But what else is courage? Is it soldiers marching into battle? Climbers reaching the highest peak? Parents dealing with a terminally ill child? Saying goodbye to an elderly parent? Courage allows us to face fear and do it anyway. Nelson Mandela learned that "courage is not the absence of fear, but the triumph over it."[1] Without fear, courage does not exist, and without gratefulness, courage is diminished.

Courage assists us each day in the choices we make: whether to show up or not, whether to speak out or not, whether to face reality or not. Courage is our not-so-secret weapon to take on more than we think we can handle and do our best in the face of overwhelming odds. It is courage that allows us to find the path forward when our road becomes unclear.

It can take courage to get up in the morning, to recover from a tragedy, to stand up for ourselves, to turn the boat toward danger, to comfort and assist the homeless, or even to admit a foray into another dimension. It takes courage to forgive, to dream, and to be yourself. Showing up, living by the 90 percent rule, doing the right thing, and putting someone else's needs above our own all take courage too.

We saw courage in those who shared their stories with us. It is as simple, and as complicated, as accepting that, "Yes, this really happened." While miracle stories encompass a universal language, it takes courage to stand up and say, "My life has been touched by a miracle." Miracles can be messy and uncomfortable and force us out into the open. Sharing a story out loud becomes a powerful equalizer of the collective human spirit by inviting others to be by our side. Enabling each other to validate our struggles helps each of us in our lifelong search for meaning.

We have wondered why it takes some people a lifetime to share a story, while others find it easier to be more forthcoming. As someone who held a miracle story close for a long time, Katie knows how hard it is to share a story that defines part of who we are. "We are forced to reconcile the experience with who we thought we were, or how we thought the world worked, or even perhaps whether we are still here for some purpose." As Katie says, it is "big soul-searching stuff we need to make peace with and learn to trust ourselves again."

Other times, even in cases where we would be happy to share, we do not recognize life's events as miraculous. That was certainly the case for Joan, who, left to her own devices, would never have considered her son David's medical journey to be miraculous. Even after her friends' prodding, it took the words of Willa Cather in *Death Comes for the Archbishop* for her to finally acknowledge the miracle out loud. "Miracles seem to me to rest not so much upon faces or voices or healing power coming suddenly near us from afar off, but upon our perceptions being made finer, so that for a moment our eyes see and our ears can hear what there is about us always."[2]

This intensified sense of hearing and seeing is a common experience with miracles. It is why we began this book with a section dedicated to the importance of becoming aware. But that is only a part of the equation. Finding the vocabulary to express not just the facts of what happened but the emotions and sensations that occur takes the courage to accept the consequences of what others might think. Some people who hear the stories we share tell us, "Well, that's not a miracle," as if they have been deputized as special miracle police. But that is not our point. Some have even asked what is the best, aka biggest, miracle we have heard. But that is not the point either. As Teddy Roosevelt said, "Comparison is the thief of joy."[3] This opinion is as true for miracles as it is for other aspects of life.

The point of a miracle is a process of self-recognition and the acceptance of an encounter with the Divine that leaves us changed, regardless of whether or not it is classified by some as a miracle. George Bernard Shaw wrote, "A miracle, my friend, is an event that creates faith…if they confirm or create faith, they are miracles."[4] It is what is behind the idea of miracles as signs. While signs can be personal, they can also be universal.

No religion has the market cornered as far as miracles are concerned. All faith traditions and cultures have a concept of the supernatural where "signs and wonders" are included in business as usual. In the Catholic Church there are strict criteria for what classifies as a miracle. Many events are reported, though over the centuries few have been deemed miraculous. The story behind Our Lady of Guadalupe is one such verified example. In 1531, the indigenous peasant Juan Diego, now a saint, encountered Our Lady, the Blessed Mother, on Tepeyac Hill near Mexico City. Our Lady instructed Juan Diego to go to the bishop and ask that a chapel be built on the spot where they stood, so that she might share her love and compassion with all the people. But the bishop wanted a sign that what Juan Diego said was true. In a subsequent vision of Our Lady, he was instructed to go to the top of the hill and pick flowers to bring to the bishop. Though it was winter, he found beautiful Castilian roses, not native to the area, in full bloom. When he returned to the bishop and opened his cloak to reveal the roses, there was also an impression of a pregnant Blessed Mother imprinted on the cloak. Twenty million people make a pilgrimage to the shrine of the Basilica of Our Lady of Guadalupe each year where the cloak, which has not deteriorated in the ensuing centuries, is on display.

Katie's mother-in-law, Monica, was devoted to Our Lady of Guadalupe, having spent much of her childhood in Mexico. She kept the iconic image from the cloak framed in her bedroom. When she died, the priest was told of her special devotion and brought his own framed image to her funeral Mass where he told the story of Juan Diego. Before flying to the East Coast for her funeral, Jim had gone to his local parish, Saint Monica, to ask that the next available 9 a.m. Mass upon his return be said for his mother. Several weeks later at the appointed Mass in California, the priest announced they would continue their month of devotions to the Blessed Mother. This was news to Katie and Jim, as they had never heard of such a devotion at the church before. When the special speaker walked up to the altar to give the homily, he brought with him the same iconic print of Our Lady of Guadalupe and began by telling the story of Juan Diego.

Miracle stories are one way to bridge the gap between religion and spirituality. While the designation of a miracle can be left to the person who receives it, saying it out loud can contribute to our comprehension that a significant event in our life may just be a miracle. In spite of the cynicism of our current culture, where religion has often been hijacked by human failings, miracle courage exists as that willingness to say yes to the original core messages of love and wisdom.

Sometimes, telling one miracle story opens the miracle memory box and we are able to recall other stories. After Patricia shared the story of her nephew baby TJ, she relayed another miraculous tale. This one occurred with her adult daughter on a trip to Mexico, a favorite vacation spot of theirs. On a road trip between Cancún and the pyramid in Chichén Itzá on the Yucatán Peninsula, they decided to stop at McDonald's. Her daughter had gone in and returned with a blond-haired, blue-eyed, English-speaking woman who insisted they take a different road than the one they were on. When asked for a photo with her, the woman refused. She gave them directions and they followed her advice. The next day they read about a murder that had taken place on the road they would have traveled. While it rarely involves risk to life, sometimes courage is listening to advice from others and being willing to make a change midcourse.

Katie heard a talk to a group of newly minted medical school students that compared being the best student and doctor to the famous trio from *The Wizard of Oz*. Of course, it takes brains like the Scarecrow and heart like the Tin Man, but most especially, it takes courage like the Cowardly Lion. Courage, the speaker said, requires you to be willing to do two things: first, to ask for help when needed, and second, to be able to say, "I don't know." Not as simple as it sounds but vital for all of us. There is a humility required in acts of courage because we risk being minimized in someone else's eyes. There is also courage inherent in the admission "I was wrong" and in honestly saying, "I'm sorry."

Courage comes in many forms. Sometimes, it is as simple as having faith in yourself when life takes you in a different direction than you had planned. You know the feeling—something happens, and you sit behind the wheel of your car before turning it on and start to shake or shed a tear or pound the dashboard, asking, "Why me? How did this happen?" Fear grips you and is compounded by the other emotions it lets in: uncertainty, grief, disappointment. Sue told the story of sitting behind her steering wheel one morning, after having just signed her divorce papers; just like that, she felt that decades of her life had diminished. Suddenly, her phone pinged with a message. Instinctively looking down, she saw it was from a Jesuit friend who, not knowing where she was or what she had just done, sent a message of inspiration: "Remember a new life, like a new birth, starts with pain." In that moment, she learned two things: one, she knew she had the courage to face the new road ahead of her, and two, God knows how to text.

Fear is an emotion we have all felt and can comprehend. Imagine how muted and confined life would be if we only stayed within our comfort zone. For some, this is a smaller space than for others. As Anaïs Nin said, "Life shrinks or expands in proportion to one's courage."[5] Courage is what allows us to face our fear head-on and move beyond it, or at least be willing to coexist with it.

We have each experienced great fear, even terror, in the stories that ignited our miracle journey. But having courage is an ongoing and necessary part of life. Courage is a requirement if we are to point ourselves in the direction of wisdom, fulfillment, and joy. In thinking about what courage means to us, we asked each other this question: Where have we had to exercise courage?

Katie: "Joan, you know the answer. Public speaking! But I practiced and prepared and practiced and prepared, and eventually I got more comfortable with it. I even came to enjoy it on occasion. If you make me go deeper, I would say being open about having faith and what it means to exercise it. That's really hard for me."

Joan: "That could be true for a lot of people. I feel like my courage is tested every day. It seems there are so many people counting on me to provide support, a shoulder to cry on, advice, or just a fresh perspective. While I love it, the ongoing responsibility takes courage. Just you wait—it's probably because I am older than you are that I have these conversations so routinely."

Miracle courage does not come easily. "Nobody is born with courage. You have to develop courage the same way you develop a muscle,"[6] according to Maya Angelou. The stronger miracle courage becomes with practice, the more we feel empowered and assured of our own self-worth. It is a recognition of our existence as a whole person with physical and spiritual components side by side, complementing each other. It may take a while, but eventually, if we let it, miracle courage facilitates meeting the challenges life will throw at us.

Sometimes the journey is a literal one like the opportunity that arose for a group of soldiers on a routine trip to carry equipment between military bases. On January 12, 2012, an eighteen-wheeler truck overtook a car on a bridge in Santa Barbara County, California.[7] While the truck flipped and careened off the bridge, the mangled and flattened car it sideswiped dangled precipitously from the guardrail. It was nearly impossible to believe anyone could be alive inside, but they were. In the car was a mother, her ten-year-old daughter, and her six-month-old baby girl. The police and fire responders were called by the surrounding drivers, traffic was stopped, and the rescue operation began. Unfortunately, with the car teetering on the guardrail and overhanging a deep ravine, getting the passengers out safely was not a task that would be easy to accomplish. One false move and the car would fall off the bridge and explode into flames as the truck had already done, taking the life of its driver with it.

Stuck in the resultant traffic, though they were going in the opposite direction, was a convoy with four servicemen who were members of the Naval Construction Battalion (Seabees). They had been ordered to transport a number of pieces of equipment and machinery back to their home base. On the trailer of one of the vehicles was a last-minute addition to the convoy, and one they had waited to load, which caused them to get on the road later than they were originally scheduled. Realizing the seriousness of the accident, the Seabees identified themselves to the on-site commander and offered to help. They were initially rebuffed by the local experts, who felt that they had the necessary training and were unwilling to take any additional chances on unknown personnel, so the soldiers were sent off to help with traffic control.

The rescue stretched out for more than an hour, with each moment adding to the medical risk of the helpless family trapped inside the car. The Seabees were aware that the situation was dire and getting worse, but they also were military men who were well trained in the importance of adhering to the chain of command and following orders. Countermanding a direct order is not to be taken lightly. They also knew that the very unusual and specialized piece of equipment they were carrying was designed to pick up heavy machinery, including cars and trucks, and manipulate them in any direction without causing damage—a kind of superhero's forklift. They recognized what they needed to do.

It was an opportunity where miracle courage meant saying yes to a job that had their name on it. Together, they approached the officer in charge and insisted that they get involved in helping in the rescue operation. Perhaps he saw the determination on their faces, or perhaps he knew he needed a miracle. Whatever the reason, he gave them the go-ahead. They drove their vehicle to the bridge, and ever so cautiously, so as not to injure the inhabitants any further, they stabilized the car. Finally, the passengers could be safely extricated and taken to the hospital for treatment.

Who knows why the Seabees were on the road at the exact right time that day, why their orders had suddenly changed that morning to include adding the specialized forklift to their convoy, and why they were bringing this piece of equipment to a place it had never been before. It was a case of synchronicity meeting miracle courage, and instead of complete tragedy, three lives and their family unit were saved.

The crisis that ensues from a serious traffic accident sometimes leads to a miracle moment. One story came from a woman who was not expected to live, according to the words she overheard from her rescuers. "An angel," who looked human, was at her shoulder as she waited to be extricated from the car and told her she would recover. Joan's aunt had a similar experience. She recounted how after her own traffic accident, a man—a nurse, unusual in those days—appeared at her side to reassure her that all would be well; once the police arrived, he was no longer there. Another story came from a woman who swore to us that she met her guardian angel, who helped her narrowly avoid the fatal crash ahead by guiding her car with his flowing robes as she drove down the highway. It takes courage to recover from the potential of what might have been and greater courage to relive the experience and share the story.

After a talk one evening, Joan was approached by a mother and daughter clearly intent on making a connection with us in order to share their story. The raw emotion Joan sensed between them was palpable. The mother had attempted suicide and was just back home after having received inpatient medical care. They had come to our miracle talk together to see if there was any morsel of wisdom they could find that would help them in their journey to reestablish trust and their faith in one another. They told Joan they enjoyed the conversation and they believed that her survival had been a miracle, but as they continued in their search for answers, they wondered whether there was anything else Joan could tell them that would be helpful.

As it turned out, a couple of months earlier, Joan had been at an author's event where her dinner-table partner was a woman who had written a book about her own mother's suicide, how she coped, and what she wished she would have known. Pulling out her handbag, Joan handed the pair the business card of the author, a psychiatrist whose practice was within traveling distance. They knew they had been given what they had come to find.

The courage this mother and daughter displayed by showing up and being all in, honestly asking for help at a time of uncertainty, was a reminder that sometimes we need to be miracle conduits to listen and hear what is needed. Not everyone or every moment requires a thunderbolt miracle. Sometimes what is needed is a referral, a shoulder to lean on, or a simple act of kindness or understanding. As our fellow *Miracle Chase* author Meb says, "Sometimes miracles happen when we show up as ourselves and do what we can, when we can, and the world is made a better place by our simply being who we are meant to be."

Whether it is in something as simple as the courage to participate in the Ice Bucket Challenge[8] that raised over $220 million for charity, or a more complicated long-term commitment, stories of selfless giving are equally inspiring, as we have seen over and over again.

In Oakland, California, the story of sixty-seven-year-old Mick Myers is a saga of survival and courage that no one could have predicted. Mick was not always homeless—it only seemed that way, especially to the policeman who was half his age and finally took the time to talk with the panhandler he had asked numerous times to move along. The officer found out that Mick had no identification, and without it, he could not prove his eligibility for assistance, including Medicare. Helping him get his ID seemed like a way to offer practical assistance and was a task the officer took on willingly, not having any idea how difficult it would become. On a subsequent local TV news spot about Mick and his Good Samaritan, the words Mick spoke about being alone resonated with a viewer. The viewer, in turn, was associated with a nonprofit group called Miracle Messages that attempts to reconnect individuals experiencing homelessness with their long-lost loved ones. In Mick's case, it worked. Not only did he find his eighty-five-year-old birth mother who, wanting to give him a better life than she could provide at the time, had put him up for adoption at age two, but he also reconnected with his brother and a host of extended family members. For a man who had lived on the streets for thirty years in fear and isolation, it was a miracle that altered the lives of all involved.[9]

What would make a law enforcement officer take the time to worry about Mick? Perhaps the better question is what makes any first responder do whatever it takes to rush into a burning building, face down a potential killer, or put themselves in mortal danger? It is the courage that military personnel call on daily in their service to our nation. At times of extreme stress or fear, everyone wants to believe in, or hope in, a higher power; it is a place where miracle courage is born.

Like gratefulness, kindness and a willingness to be of service to others are also at the foundation of miracle courage. The act of offering someone—anyone: the grocery clerk, the post office employee, the bus driver—an expression of gratitude reaps rewards far beyond a simple thank-you. There was a kindness challenge Joan read about online that asked, "Is there any-thing I can do that would brighten your day?"[10] The results were impressive; simple acts of kindness flourished and appreciation flowed. The courage to be kind is a challenge we can all embrace.

In being the miracle for someone else, it often takes courage to speak up or to go out of our way. It can be risky. As the Oakland officer learned, it is daunting to ask a question when you do not already have the answer, but the reward is usually worth the effort. We are relieved that the wife of the man Jim rescued from his hazardous driving didn't accuse Jim of kidnapping or stealing his car, but a cynical response is always a potential result.

Knowing that not all problems can be solved makes it even more dif-ficult for us to ask how we can help. It takes courage to think that we can be an effective part of the solution, or even make a difference. The essence of miracle courage is to let our light shine and help in a way that only we can.

Joan's fitness instructor, Charley, had the opportunity to exercise her own miracle courage one morning while driving to work. When Joan got to class, she wondered why a dog was leashed to the ballet barre. Even for a community that allowed dogs in all sorts of places, this was unusual.

Charley explained, "As I saw the stopped traffic, I wondered, *Would I be like the drivers ahead of me who passed by the car that was turned precariously into the bushes, or would I stop and see if something was amiss in the out-of-place vehicle?* There was just something wrong about it."

While she knew if she stopped, she would surely be late, her soul sent a different message. After parking her car, Charley anxiously peered into the window and was greeted by a frantic dog that wanted out. "Once I shifted a bit, I could see his owner slumped against the steering wheel and I called nine-one-one. Since I couldn't get inside the locked car, I spoke to the dog, hoping to soothe him." Relieved that she had listened to her spirit, she explained, "The ambulance couldn't take the dog, so I took him with me and put a note with my name and phone number in the man's pocket as well as with the paramedics." As the dog joined our class that morning, we each thought of our own fathers, brothers, and husbands who could have been in this very situation. What a miracle it was to the driver's family that someone stopped to assist him in his moment of need, and he was not alone.

Courage is required in all facets of life. Sometimes we have to wait out the easy decision for a better one that we hope will be around the corner. Yet, what if it is not? What do we do then? It takes courage to help others, but it also takes courage to dare to dream and to await the right move or person or next step in our own lives. At a talk we gave at Kepler's Books in

Menlo Park, California, Diane relayed her own story of miracle courage. She had finished her PhD at a time when positions in higher education were scarce. Pressured to get a job with the burden of paying back her student loans weighing on her, her friends and family were stunned when she turned down not one but two promising opportunities. It took courage to believe in herself and to feel certain that the right job was out there, soon to be hers. She told us she felt that it was a miracle not only that she got the job of her dreams a week later, but that she had the strength to wait for it amid the growing external pressure to settle for less.

Miracle courage is required to make the most of the gifts and good fortune we have been given. It is essential that we turn on the light within and shine it outward into our corner of the world. Miracles change us forever, whether in the simple events of day-to-day life, or in extraordinary events of tragedy and near misses. The miracle of the human spirit, the force within us that calls us to celebrate ourselves, takes us forward into the unknown, step-by-step. As Thomas Merton said, "At the center of our being is a point of nothingness…It is like a pure diamond, blazing with the invisible light of heaven."[11] Courage propels us out from that center to become more aware, to consider different perspectives, to go deeper with each other, and to finally recognize that meaning is personal and sometimes illusive, a moving target. But *finding* meaning, the search itself, gets us closer to God and our ultimate spiritual connection.

TAKE A MIRACLE MOMENT

Nerves of Steel: Today, do one thing you are afraid of doing—speak up, speak out, or share a story.

CHAPTER SEVENTEEN
The Ripple Effect

*Like throwing a rock into the middle of a quiet lake, energy ripples
outward in ever-widening waves until lake meets land and the force
of the wave washes onto the beach, dissipating its energy onto
the shore. With a miracle, the wave ripples outward, adding
amplitude and force until it returns to the shore of the eternal.*
—The Miracle Chase: Three Women, Three Miracles,
and a Ten Year Journey of Discovery and Friendship

Inspiration hits us in many ways, perhaps as something we have read, seen, or heard: a story that speaks to us like the ones in this book, a person's deeds that challenge us to get involved, or simply the beauty of a new dawn that reminds us that we are alive and life is a gift. Awareness, connection, and an ongoing search for meaning are the spiritual tools that prompt us to embrace our life with zeal. We often return to the words of Mother Teresa, who knew that "I alone cannot change the world, but I can cast a stone across the water to create many ripples."[1] When we acknowledge our unique place in the world and recognize the miracle experiences that come our way, we have the opportunity to set off a ripple effect that emerges and sets sail in directions we cannot anticipate. Initially, we thought we were chasing after miracles; it turns out miracles have chased us instead.

Miracle experiences prompt us to reconsider our way of looking at the world and to discover connections never before considered. The idea that God could act in such a personal and directed way is manifested in stories like Sue's text, Sorour's dream, and the two of us, who found our lives enriched by a spiritual journey and the myriad ripples set in motion as a result. The unfolding of a miracle takes place as our original experience and intentions expand, and our journey becomes altered in unexpected ways.

Some ripples are small, like doing our part to create a kinder world, even something as simple as a nod of understanding in the comforting of a friend that makes her feel less alone. Other ripples cover more ground, like the synchronicity that began at the Denver Zoo when Hadley's life was saved and continued to reverberate throughout the community. The consequences of these ripples remind us of the commonalities in the human spirit: our desire to be of assistance, our relief in the rescue of another, our joy at making a new connection.

Joan had one such experience after her son David's wedding. Given the distances between the families of the bride and groom, the wedding festivities on Nantucket (an island off the coast of Massachusetts) provided the first opportunity for many of the extended family members to meet each other. Over the course of a few days, Joan had a number of conversations with one of her new daughter-in-law's aunts, Carole, who was from the Midwest. Carole was intrigued when someone told her about the miracle book Joan had written with two friends. Numerous times during the course of the weekend, she asked Joan for a signed copy, but it was not until the last possible moment that Joan was able to get her a book, though in the bedlam of everyone leaving, it was left unsigned.

The letter Joan received in thanks emphasized not only the wedding weekend but the "treat she had in reading the book." Carole went on to explain that she told her good friend about Joan, the wedding, and her book, and the topic of miracles had sparked immediate excitement. Earlier that year Carole's friend had been invited by one of *her* friends to a lecture in Chicago where she'd heard Joan speak. She bought one of Joan's books for Carole and asked for it to be signed. She could not believe Joan was the mother of the groom and that Lirra married her miracle son, David. The friend ran and found the book she bought and gave it to Carole. When she opened it, she could not believe what she read: "To Carole: Miracles Abound!! Joan Luise Hill." Suddenly, there was no need for Carole to ship hers back for Joan to sign. Seems like Somebody knew their paths would cross before they did. In light of this story, Joan joked that not only do ripples extend beyond the shores of islands, but she now had her own modern version of a biblical wedding miracle, water into wine not included.

While the ripple of that miracle connection is a gentle wave where shared interest meets coincidence and spreads the miracle message to a new group of friends, the ripple of another woman's experience carries a broader impact. She contacted us to share her story because she, too, understood the importance of the ripple effect. She was a mother whose son had suffocated by being placed in an unsafe crib. She was determined to make the death of her child mean something, to ensure that no other family would suffer what happened to her own. But she was not sure how to begin.

She googled other women who had turned tragedy into advocacy. She found Meb and the work she had done to establish the TrustLine Registry. But it was *The Miracle Chase*, which also came up on Google, that she said actually launched her advocacy. She bought the book and saw how we uncovered what the miracles in our life meant to us. She explained that the wonder and nature of miracles soothed her soul and inspired her at a time she really needed it. It was the impetus she needed and why she decided to go to an upcoming childcare conference. She wanted to learn how to use her own voice and her family's experience to try and make a difference.

At the conference, she heard that the bill to renew the Child Care and Development Block Grant, which had been in effect for over a decade with the goal of making childcare safer, was being held up by a lone congressman. The bill would die in session if the vote were delayed as the lawmakers in Washington, D.C., approached the Christmas holiday break, and the important funding provided would cease.

It was her own hometown congressman who held the lone vote required for passage of the bill. In that moment, not only did she know that her job was to pay him a visit, but she knew she had to say yes and do it, even though it was out of her comfort zone. As mothers ourselves, we know just how strong our instincts for protecting our children are, and a mother who is inspired by miracles is unstoppable. Miracle courage fortified her as she turned her heartbreak into a personal crusade to continue the funding of this important federal legislation.

She walked into her legislator's office and told him about her son, explaining why what happened to her family must "never again" be any other family's experience. In sharing her story and making a passionate plea for the congressman's support, she was able to accomplish what many others who had tried before her were not. He relented and the legislation passed. As the adage says, the river cuts through rock, not because of its power, but because of its persistence.

Like many of us in a time of crisis, this woman became clearer in her mission, knowing what job had her name on it. She was able to rise to the challenge of changing the status quo. Perhaps when we are most vulnerable, whether it is facing a topic that is deeply personal like improving child safety, or confronting sickness or death, space opens up to allow for the possibilities that surround us. In this case, the ripple continues, as Meb ensures that the services made available through the Child Care and Development

Block Grant are optimally utilized by providing technical assistance to states and territories throughout the US.

Activism is often sparked by tragedy. MADD, the Susan G. Komen Breast Cancer Foundation, and California's TrustLine Registry are all examples of turning personal trauma into ripples that benefit us all. The death of someone close to us can propel us headfirst into initiating our own ripple. After the senseless murder of her son's college roommate, Mark, by gang members when he went to an ATM in Brooklyn, New York, Susan knew she needed to leave her teaching job at a comfortable suburban school outside Philadelphia to offer her talents to inner-city children. She wanted to help avoid the hopelessness that so often results in the despair that drives people to do the unthinkable.

Susan met her own incarnation of Mother Teresa in a nun who was willing to think outside the box about how to help her students, and an idea was born. The popularity of the TV show *Dancing with the Stars* and the buzz around contestant and NFL star Emmitt Smith's show-stopping dance performance, together with the fact that New York City had launched a successful dance program in their schools, combined to ignite the initiation of Philadelphia's own Dancing with the Students (DWTS) program. Initially begun with a trial at one school, DWTS now covers twenty-five inner-city schools in Philadelphia and has taught manners, respect, body mechanics, and ballroom dancing to over five thousand students.

Compliments of Susan and her fellow dancing angels, the program's graduates have found a way to emerge from their personal tragedies and learn to communicate with each other and find a reason to smile. When Susan shared the experiences of her students, some of whom were living on the streets and another who had witnessed the murder of a parent, she explained it is the resilience of the students that motivates her to continue.

As Susan said, "After Mark's senseless murder, I had to do something. I couldn't be complacent about kids growing up in circumstances that offered no hope. The biggest thing I had to learn was to listen to God. I realized I had been telling God what to do in my own life, but listening was a lesson I needed to learn. It was also one I could pass on. We teach the students how to speak with one another. When they speak over each other, I remind them that, 'What you say, I value. I want to hear you.'" Her students continue to amaze her as they move on through their lives, graduating from college, establishing careers, and becoming parents themselves. She watches the ripple continue and rides the virtual wave of their success.

While DWTS rippled throughout the community, becoming a force for good in those students' lives and changing the way they viewed the world, it went beyond the impact on the students. Parents who had never shown up before began coming to the school to see the recitals and got involved in new ways, both with the schools and with their children. Students felt rewarded for their positive contributions, and barriers were broken down as self-esteem and a sense of community were built up.

Often a ripple effect results in an amplification of our original intentions. Jen, a two-time cancer survivor, rides her bicycle 192 miles each summer in the Pan-Mass Challenge. She never intended to be a role model for cancer survivorship. Yet through her volunteerism, she has touched numerous lives and continues to inspire and be inspired by those she encounters. As she said in her thank-you note to her supporters, "I thought of all of you and your dedication…I thought of my oncology team in 2005 and again in 2019, who made me well again. I thought of my buddies, Zachary (doing great! Biking, running, hiking, being a kid!!!), Ady (she really is brave and awesome!) and Cam Bam (what a golf swing!). I thought of those of you who have heard that news, been in that johnny, had those side effects, living your lives every day. I thought of friends and family and people I know. I thought of what it takes to get through the tougher moments and the inherent joy in so many others." Jen says she rides not only to pay back her caregivers, but to help advance the knowledge leading to a cure for these deadly diseases.

In the Jewish culture there is a principle called *tikkun olam*, which is described as any activity that improves the world. According to Rabbi Tzvi Freeman, "Each act of tikkun olam is a fine-tuning of our world's voices. With each tikkun, we are creating meaning out of confusion, harmony from noise, revealing the unique part each creation plays in a universal symphony that sings of its Creator."[2] It is a way to think about the practical ripple each of us can initiate by contributing to helping the condition of others. The beauty of this concept lies in its simplicity as we go about our lives, dancing, riding, advocating, or simply caring about another. There is no need for heroics, grandiose plans, or huge infusions of cash. It is a system based upon small moments, individual contributions to the whole that reflect our humanity—our better angels, so to speak. According to Rabbi Freeman, Rabbi Isaac Luria taught that "our job is to find those divine sparks, select them and reconnect them to their original, higher purpose."[3] He goes on to explain that according to Jewish oral traditions, any *tikkun* performed "reverberates through all the rest of the world. Each tikkun has the potential to change everything."[4] Like *tikkun olam*, the ripple effect brings you to the next, and the next, as the universe encourages you to bring about extraordinary change by ordinary means whenever you can.

Paying it forward has become today's version of going out of your way to do a kind deed. The stories we hear, like funding the elderly man with his paleta cart in Chicago, offering to buy a cup of coffee for an exasperated taxi driver, or literally giving someone the shirt off your back in an emergency, all spread their own ripples of goodness into the world. Sometimes, the impact of a courageous act becomes magnified when it is so unexpected that it changes the lives of a multitude. The sea evacuation of Manhattan on September 11th was one such event. Even Mr. Rogers came out of his TV retirement following 9/11 to offer his message of hope and love for one another. "Thank you for whatever you do…to bring joy and light and hope and faith and pardon and love to your neighbor and yourself."[5] He created a ripple able to cross dimensions from the Neighborhood of Make-Believe to the land of twenty-first-century reality. In Seattle, this message translated into the formation of the Interfaith Amigos by a priest, a rabbi, and a Sufi minister who preach that what is important is to "appreciate the oneness that absolutely interconnects all of us."[6]

The announcement of commencement speaker Robert F. Smith at Morehouse College[7] is another example where a ripple effect magnifies generosity several times over in the people whose lives are changed. The students in the graduating class of 2019 experienced a miracle both personal and profound when he disclosed that the Smith family had agreed to provide grants to eliminate the student debt of the entire class of nearly four hundred students. In addition to the obvious immediate advantage to the students and their families, a ripple effect of that degree of magnanimity and kindness will multiply and flow to future generations. According to Morehouse president David Thomas, "This will allow them [the students] to pursue their dreams…as opposed to serving the debt."[8] Extraordinary change indeed.

Some miracles, like the one at Morehouse where student debt was repaid, are created in one fell swoop. Joan likens it to what happens whenever she tries to skip a stone into the water and the stone sinks—*kerplunk*—creating a big splash. While it is entertaining to watch, she is still practicing at achieving the small gentle ripples that occur when the stone is skipped perfectly. These ripples are more subtle, like the thousand little ways that a life well lived affects us all.

Katie's college friend Martha, whom we met in the first chapter, described facing her own mortality as your life being "turned upside down in a flash." After meeting with her spiritual adviser, Martha wrote on the chalkboard in their kitchen, "Nothing has changed." That way she could be constantly reminded that she was already living her life's purpose and contributing her gifts to the world. As her widowed husband later wrote, "Often the shock of knowing the days are numbered causes major outlook changes…what's important, how to conduct yourself, focus on charity, people to forgive; a packing up routine so you can discard your baggage. But not so much in Martha's case." To realize in those circumstances that nothing needs to change is to know your life has held meaning. What a miracle gift to leave behind.

The ripple effect offers each of us an invitation to enhance our lives by fostering and creating our own ripples that will continue long after we are gone.

TAKE A MIRACLE MOMENT

Endless Summer: Think about a ripple you have sent out into the world. What happened next, and after that, and then what?

Epilogue

When we are truly awake and present in ourselves and to each other and the world around us, miracles abound. While we have shared numerous stories of wonder, joy, and mystery, we leave you with one final story, manifesting itself in a meaningful miracle mix-up. It is the story of a woman with three special cats that she showered with love and tender care. She was bereft when her dear twenty-year-old cat, Mercy, died. To soothe her heartache, she decided to spend the upcoming weekend watching videos and staying close to home. Thinking it was an important movie to see, and not wanting to be completely self-absorbed, she ordered the movie *Dunkirk* from her mail-order vendor. When the movie arrived in her mailbox, instead of finding the one she had requested, in her hand was a copy of a very different movie: *Love & Mercy*. She knew it was a message from Mercy, sending her regards.

In the end, all miracles come down to love and mercy. Love is at the foundation of miracles because love, and the forgiveness it encompasses, is the language of the Divine. When we see or experience miraculous events, we open ourselves to the part of the Divine mystery that we can absorb and understand. The power of love is unstoppable—it is the energy behind the ripples of a miracle as they move beyond the horizon of our sight to gently roll onto unknown shores. By becoming aware of all the world has to offer us, deepening connection with each other, and finding compassion in our relationships, we are able to reap the meaning of our lives to the fullest extent possible.

Acknowledgments

Our deepest gratitude to our very own miracle worker, Maureen Egen, who has encouraged and guided us over the years and ultimately acted as agent extraordinaire. And to the people at Hachette/Worthy Books who have championed our miracle chasing and collecting, including Rolf Zettersten, senior vice president and publisher (ret.) of Hachette Nashville; our dedicated editors, Jeana Ledbetter and Karen Longino, and editorial assistant Morgan Rickey; social media expert Katie Norris; our creative publicist Laini Brown; and Hachette's committed sales team.

To Mary Beth (Meb) Phillips, our original co-author, friend, and soul sister, for her thoughtful reading and valuable commentary on the manuscript, her heartfelt foreword, and her continued inspirational guest writing on our blog. You will always be the miracle chaser by our side.

To those who gave us feedback on our proposal and manuscript, especially Patty Gebhardt, Margaret Sharkey, Tonia Hsieh, Paula Morgan, and the devoted members of our Moraga book group: thank you all for helping us focus our efforts.

To all of those who were brave enough to share their miracles with us and generously agreed to add their stories to this book, with special thanks to Martha's husband Joe McRoskey and to Andrea Bierce, friend and miracle magnet who became an honorary miracle collector herself.

To the miracle messengers who have proactively promoted our message and helped us reach our audience: the Council for Women for Boston

College, Santa Clara University, Elita Balfour, Gayle Snider, Johanna Ohlsson, Tanya Schmidt, Kim Kimball, and Susie Stangland.

To Jim Fox for his sage legal counsel, Professor David Weddle for his thoughtful questioning and steadfast support, Father Mike Russo for his ongoing friendship, and Sydney Sharek for her technological wizardry.

To our siblings, who have had faith in us and who have applauded and contributed to our miracle journey over the years.

And to our husbands for providing us the time, support, encouragement, and inspiration to follow our miracle dreams. And for cheering us on for the past four decades!

Lastly, to our children and grandchildren for reminding us every day that miracles really do happen.

Notes

PROLOGUE

1. "Religion among the Millennials," Pew Research Center, February 17, 2010, https://www.pewforum.org/2010/02/17/religion-among-the-millennials/.
2. Joan Luise Hill, Katie Mahon, and Mary Beth Phillips, PhD, *The Miracle Chase: Three Women, Three Miracles, and a Ten Year Journey of Discovery and Friendship* (New York: Sterling), 2010, 172.

PART ONE
CHAPTER ONE: TERMINAL COURSE

1. John Lennon, interview by David Wigg, *Scene and Heard*, BBC Radio 1 program, May 8, 1969.
2. James Connor, *Pascal's Wager: The Man Who Played Dice with God* (San Francisco: HarperCollins, 2006), 183.
3. Sangye Khadro, *The Nine-Point Meditation on Death*, PDF file, 2002, https://www.kadampa-center.org/sites/default/files/DeathHO5.pdf.
4. Charles Dickens, *A Christmas Carol*, in *The Christmas Books of Charles Dickens* (Ann Arbor, MI: Tally Hall Press, 1996), 71.
5. Fred Rogers, *You Are Special: Neighborly Words of Wisdom from Mister Rogers*, reprint ed. (London: Penguin Books, 1995), 160.
6. Bronnie Ware, "Regrets of the Dying," *Bronnie Ware* (blog), accessed June 21, 2020, https://bronnieware.com/blog/regrets-of-the-dying/.
7. John Whittier, *The Poems of John Greenleaf Whittier* (Norwalk, CT: The Easton Press, 1973), 6.

CHAPTER TWO: IT REMAINS TO BE SEEN

1. Doug Aamoth, "Study Says We Unlock Our Phones a LOT Each Day," *Time Magazine*, October 8, 2013, https://techland.time.com/2013/10/08/study-says-we-unlock-our-phones-a-lot-each-day/.
2. Leo Tolstoy, *What Is Art? & Wherein Is Truth in Art, Essays on Aesthetics and Literature, (1899)* (Musaicum Books, OK Publishing, 2017).
3. Ralph Waldo Emerson, *Nature* (Boston and Cambridge: James Munroe & Company, 1849), 7.
4. Ralph Waldo Emerson, *The Poems of Ralph Waldo Emerson, Each and All* (Norwalk, CT: The Easton Press, 1945), 9.

5. Deborah Franklin, "How Hospital Gardens Help Patients Heal," *Scientific American*, March 1, 2012, https://www.scientificamerican.com/article/nature-that-nurtures/.

6. Steve Hartman, "Mother's Hunch Helped Save a Hiker's Life on the Pacific Crest Trail," CBS News, November 9, 2018, https://www.cbsnews.com/news/mothers -hunch-helped-save-a-hikers-life-on-the-pacific-crest-trail-washington-2018-11-09/.

CHAPTER THREE: MORE THAN MEETS THE EYE

1. Christopher Chabris and Daniel Simons, "The Invisible Gorilla," accessed December 11, 2019, www.theinvisiblegorilla.com/videos.html.

2. Stephen Covey, *The 7 Habits of Highly Effective People* (New York: Free Press, 2004), 24.

3. Noah benShea, *Jacob the Baker: Gentle Wisdom for a Complicated World* (New York: Ballantine Books, 1990), 19.

4. Soren Kierkegaard, *Training in Christianity* (New York: Vintage Books, 2004), 109.

5. Alexandra Larkin and Sophie Lewis, "Boy, 8, Says 'Angels' Helped Him Free Dad from Collapsed Car," CNN, March 9, 2017, https://www.cnn.com/2017/03/09/us/idaho -boy-saves-dad-angels-trnd/index.html.

6. Deepak Chopra, "A Science of Miracles—No Longer Optional?," The Chopra Foundation, October 6, 2014, https://www.choprafoundation.org/consciousness /a-science-of-miracles-no-longer-optional/.

7. Fritjof Capra, *The Tao of Physics* (Boston: Shambhala, 2000), 11.

8. K. P. Shashidharan, "Cosmic Dance of Shiva," *Times of India*, January 11, 2012, https:// timesofindia.indiatimes.com/Cosmic-dance-of-Shiva/articleshow/10485316.cms.

9. Capra, *The Tao of Physics*, 68.

10. Ibid., 24.

11. C. S. Lewis, *Miracles* (New York: Simon & Schuster, 1996), 229.

12. Joel Landau, "'Mysterious Voice' Led Utah Cops to Discover Child Who Survived for 14 Hours in Submerged Car after Mom Drowned," *NY Daily News*, March 10, 2015, https://www.nydailynews.com/news/national/mysterious-voice-leads-police-baby-car -crash-article-1.2142732.

13. Richard Rohr, *The Naked Now: Learning to See as the Mystics See* (New York: The Crossroad Publishing Company, 2019), 27.

CHAPTER FOUR: CO-INCIDENTAL

1. Kathleen Hattrup, "If God Is a God of Surprises, What Is My Response, Pope Asks in Easter Homily," Aleteia, April 1, 2018, https://aleteia.org/2018/04/01/if-god-is-a-god -of-surprises-what-is-my-response-pope-asks-in-easter-homily/.

2. "Eucharistic Crusade: The Story of St. Dorothy," Society of Saint Pius X in Canada, accessed August 6, 2019, http://www.Fsspx.com/EucharisticCrusade/2006_November /St_Dorothy.htm.

3. Carl Jung, *Synchronicity—An Acausal Connecting Principle* (London: Routledge and Kegan, Paul, 1972); Herbert Read, Michael Fordham, Gerhard Adler, eds., W. McGuire, executive ed., R. F. C. Hull, trans., *The Collected Works of C. G. Jung*

(London: Routledge and Kegan Paul, 1953–1980), vol. 8: *Structure and Dynamics of the Psyche (1916–1952)*.

4. Deepak Chopra, "Nothing Is Coincidental—Everything Is Meaningful," The Chopra Center, October 19, 2018, https://chopra.com/articles/nothing-is-coincidental -everything-is-meaningful%20&?utm_source=Newsletter&utm_content=181106, accessed November 10, 2018.

5. Vincent DiStefano, "Forgetting Jung's Tree," August 31, 2011, http:// thehealingbprojectweblog.blogspot.com/2011/08/forgetting-jungs-tree.html, accessed March 31, 2016.

6. "Synchronicity," Wikipedia, accessed June 21, 2020, https://en.wikipedia.org/wiki /Synchronicity.

7. Hamed Aleaziz and Kevin Fagan, "Window Washer Survives 11-Story Fall from S.F. Building," November 21, 2014, https://www.sfgate.com/bayarea/article/Worker -plunges-from-downtown-San-Francisco-5909289.php.

8. Ibid.

9. Julian of Norwich, *Revelations of Divine Love*, trans. Clifton Wolters (New York: Penguin Books, 1966), 110.

10. The Trinity 3.9.16; quoted from Augustine, *The Trinity*, trans. S. McKenna, *The Fathers of the Church*, vol. 55 (Washington, D.C.: The Catholic University of America Press, 1963), 112.

11. John Henry Newman, *Lectures on Present Position of Catholics in England, Summer, 1851* (London and Bombay: Longmans, Green, and Co., 1896), 306.

CHAPTER FIVE: LET THE LIGHT SHINE

1. Kenneth Woodward, *Making Saints: How the Catholic Church Determines Who Becomes a Saint, Who Doesn't, and Why* (New York: Touchstone Books, Simon & Schuster, 1990), 201.

2. Paul Tritschler, "Why Stories Matter," Daily Good, June 10, 2017, http://www .dailygood.org/story/1607/why-stories-matter-paul-tritschler/ (article originally appeared in the Transformation section of Open Democracy), accessed September 17, 2017.

3. Robert Waldinger, director of the Harvard Study of Adult Development (1939–2014) based on the Grant Study and the Glueck Study, summarized in the *Harvard Health Letter*, "Can Relationships Boost Longevity and Well-Being?," June 2017, 5.

4. Marianne Williamson, *A Return to Love: Reflections on the Principles of "A Course in Miracles"* (New York: HarperCollins, 1992), 165.

5. William James, *The Will to Believe and Other Essays in Popular Philosophy* (New York: Dover Publications, 1956), 62.

6. Bangambiki Habyarimana, *The Great Pearl of Wisdom* (self-pub., by CreateSpace Independent Publishing Platform, 2015).

CHAPTER SIX: IT'S A WONDER-FULL LIFE

1. Dacher Keltner, "Why Do We Feel Awe?," *Greater Good Magazine*, May 10, 2016, https://greatergood.berkeley.edu/article/item/why_do_we_feel_awe.

2. Sarah Butler, "The Chilean Miners' Miracles: How Faith Helped Them Survive," CNN, August 4, 2015, https://www.cnn.com/2015/08/02/world/chilean-miners -miracles/index.html; Héctor Tobar, "Sixty-Nine Days," *The New Yorker*, June 30, 2014, https://www.newyorker.com/magazine/2014/07/07/sixty-nine-days.

3. David Weddle, *Miracles: Wonder and Meaning in World Religions* (New York: New York University Press, 2010), 2.

4. Sean Flynn, "Miracle at Tham Luang," *GQ*, December 3, 2018, https://www.gq.com /story/thai-cave-rescue-miracle-at-tham-luang.

5. David Weddle, *Miracles: Wonder and Meaning in World Religions*, 22.

6. Dennis Overbye, "Darkness Visible, Finally: Astronomers Capture First Ever Image of a Black Hole," *New York Times*, April 10, 2019, https://www.nytimes.com/2019/04/10 /science/black-hole-picture.html.

7. "Joseph Campbell: The Goal and the Meaning of Life," *Excellence Reporter*, July 21, 2015, https://excellencereporter.com/2015/07/21/joseph-campbell-the-meaning-and -the-goal-of-life/.

8. Matthew Fox and Lama Tsomo, "How Silence Leads Us to Awe," syndicated from *Yes Magazine*, October 20, 2018, http://www.dailygood.org/story/2122/how-silence-leads -us-to-awe-matthew-fox-lama-tsomo/.

PART TWO
CHAPTER SEVEN: THE SECRET SAUCE

1. "Why Give? Religious Roots of Charity," Harvard Divinity School, November 26, 2018, https://hds.harvard.edu/news/2013/12/13/why-give-religious-roots-charity#.

2. Chuck DeGroat, *Toughest People to Love: How to Understand, Lead, and Love the Difficult People in Your Life—Including Yourself* (Grand Rapids, MI, Cambridge, UK: Wm. B. Eerdmans Publishing Company, 2014), 113.

3. Brené Brown, *Daring Greatly* (New York: Gotham Books, 2012), 8.

4. Thomas Moore, *Dark Nights of the Soul: A Guide to Finding Your Way through Life's Ordeals* (New York: Gotham, 2004), 131.

5. Katie Steedly Curling, "Feeding the Good Wolf: A Gratitude Conversation with Ferial Pearson," syndicated from http://www.gratefulness.org, May 6, 2018, http://www .dailygood.org/story/1919/feeding-the-good-wolf-a-gratitude-conversation-with-ferial -pearson-katie-steedly-curling/.

6. Julian Treasure, "Julian Treasure on 5 Ways to Listen Better," TEDGlobal, December 15, 2017. http://www.dailygood.org/story/1844/julian-treasure-on-5-ways-to-listen -better-julian-treasure/.

7. Ibid. Also, Erik Palmer, *Teaching the Core Skills of Listening and Speaking* (Association for Supervision & Curriculum Development, 2013), 67.

8. Stephen Covey, *The 7 Habits of Highly Effective People: Powerful Lessons in Personal Change* (New York: Simon & Schuster, 1989), 239.

9. Antoine de Saint-Exupéry, *The Little Prince* (New York: Reynal & Hitchcock; France: Éditions Gallimard, 1943), 87.

CHAPTER EIGHT: TELLING STORIES

1. Myron Eshowsky, "Myron Eshowky [*sic*]: A Deeper Listening," interview with Gayathri Ramachandran, ed. Bonnie Rose, syndicated from Awakin Calls, October 8, 2018, www.dailygood.org/story/2032/myron-eshowky-a-deeper-listening/.
2. Kate Swoboda, "How to Live a More Courageous Life," syndicated from Greater Good, December 14, 2018, http://www.dailygood.org/story/2158/how-to-live-a-more-courageous-life-kate-swoboda/, accessed March 24, 2019.
3. Theresa Wiseman, "A Concept Analysis of Empathy," *Journal of Advanced Nursing* 23, no. 6 (1996): 1165.

CHAPTER NINE: BEYOND THE BEYOND

1. Kathryn Ford, *Be Well! A 7-Step System for Radical Healing* (Los Angeles: Excellence Institute, 2016), 19.
2. Kelly Bauer, "'Paleta Man' Accepts Check for $385,000, but He Won't Give Up Work," DNAinfo, September 21, 2016, https://www.dnainfo.com/chicago/20160921/little-village/paleta-man-accepts-385000-check-but-he-wont-give-up-work/.
3. Kent Nerburn, *Make Me an Instrument of Your Peace: Living in the Spirit of the Prayer of Saint Francis* (San Francisco: HarperOne, 1999), 54.
4. Viktor Frankl, *Man's Search for Meaning* (New York: Simon & Schuster, 1984), 12.
5. Pablo Esparza Altuna, "The House That Saved Refugee Mothers from the Spanish Civil War," OZY, February 7, 2018, https://www.ozy.com/true-and-stories/the-house-that-saved-refugee-mothers-from-the-spanish-civil-war/83378/.
6. Rich Tenorio, "How One Swiss Nurse Hid Hundreds of Pregnant Women and Their Kids from the Nazis," *The Times of Israel*, March 12, 2019, https://www.timesofisrael.com/how-one-nurse-hid-hundreds-of-pregnant-women-and-their-children-from-the-nazis/.
7. Mark Nepo, *The Book of Awakening* (Boston: Conari Press, 2000), 210.
8. Donald Spoto, "What Would St. Francis Do?," *San Francisco Chronicle*, October 3, 2002.
9. Larry Chang, *Wisdom for the Soul: Five Millennia of Prescriptions for Spiritual Healing* (Washington, D.C.: Gnosophia Publishers, 2006), 355.

CHAPTER TEN: LET THE SPIRIT MOVE YOU

1. Bianca Alexander, "Understanding the True Purpose of Yoga," Conscious Living TV, December 14, 2019, https://consciouslivingtv.com/yoga/true-purpose-yoga.html.
2. Margaret Mikkelborg, "The Spirit of the Times: Introduction to the Red Book," September 18, 2012, https://www.psychotherapyinsights.ca/carl-jung/the-spirit-of-the-times-introduction-to-the-red-book/.
3. Ibid.
4. Paulo Coelho, *The Alchemist* (New York: HarperCollins, 1993), 150.
5. Brené Brown, *The Gifts of Imperfection: Let Go of Who You Think You're Supposed to Be and Embrace Who You Are* (Center City, MN: Hazelden Publishing, 2010), 64.

6. Anita Moorjani, *Dying to Be Me* (New York: Hay House, 2012), 146.

7. Fox5 News, "4-Year-Old Child Falls from 2nd-Story Window in Lakeside," September 19, 2016, https://fox5sandiego.com/news/4-year-old-child-falls-from-2nd-story-window-in-lakeside/.

8. William Wordsworth, *William Wordsworth: Selected Poems* (New York: Penguin Books, 1992), 209.

9. Ibid., 211.

10. Sally Kempton, "Spiritual IQ: Is There Such a Thing?," Patheos, August 31, 2011, http://www.patheos.com/resources/additional-resources/spiritual-IQ-Sally-Kempton-09-01-2011.

11. C. S. Lewis, *Miracles* (New York: Simon & Schuster, 1996), 217.

CHAPTER ELEVEN: THE 90 PERCENT RULE

1. "Melissa Freeman," Wikipedia, accessed November 8, 2019, https://en.wikipedia.org/wiki/Melissa_Freeman.

2. *Blessed Mother Teresa*, pamphlet preceding her beatification (London: St Pauls Publishing, 2003), 4.

3. Willa Cather, *Death Comes for the Archbishop* (New York: Random House, 1927; renewed 1955, paperback, Vintage Books / Random House), 50.

4. Julianne Holt-Lunstad, Timothy Smith, M. Baker, T. Harris, and D. Stephenson, "Loneliness and Social Isolation as Risk Factors for Mortality: A Meta-Analytic Review," *BYU Scholars Archive*, 2015, 2.

5. Vivek Murthy, "Work and the Loneliness Epidemic," *Harvard Business Review*, September 2017, 1.

6. Ibid., 3.

7. Ibid., 6.

8. Daniel Hoffman, "Why Don't Miracles Happen to ME?," *Mysterious Ways*, August/September 2017, 19.

9. Ibid.

10. Ibid., 21.

11. Ibid., 21.

12. Thomas Merton, *The Seven Storey Mountain* (New York: Harcourt Brace, 1948), quoted in Elena Malits, *The Solitary Explorer: Thomas Merton's Transforming Journey* (Eugene, OR: Wipf and Stock, 1980), 94.

13. Oprah Winfrey, "Here We Go," *Oprah Magazine*, August 2019, 23.

14. Joan Luise Hill, Katie Mahon, and Mary Beth Phillips, *The Miracle Chase: Three Women, Three Miracles, and a Ten Year Journey of Discovery and Friendship* (New York: Sterling, 2010), 188.

CHAPTER TWELVE: FORGIVENESS' SAKE

1. Mitchell Landsberg, Richard Winton, and Ari Bloomekatz, "Concern Grows for Young Survivors of Covina Shooting Victims," *LA Times*, December 29, 2008.

2. Robert Enright, "Eight Keys to Forgiveness," October 15, 2015, https://greatergoodberkeley.edu/article/item/eight_keys-to-forgiveness.

3. Ibid.

4. The Associated Press, "Survivor of Covina Christmas Massacre to Join Protesting Students in Pasadena Walkout," March 14, 2018, https://www.pasadenastarnews.com/2018/03/14/survivor-of-covina-christmas-massacre-to-join-protesting-students-in-pasadena/.

5. Kathryn Ford, *Be Well! A 7-Step System for Radical Healing* (Los Angeles: Excellence Institute, 2016), 109.

6. Arthur Boyle, *Six Months to Live: Three Guys on the Ultimate Quest for a Miracle* (New York: Crossroad Publishers, 2014).

7. Desmond Tutu, *No Future without Forgiveness* (New York: Doubleday, 1999).

8. Wayne Dyer, "How to Forgive Someone Who Has Hurt You: In 15 Steps," *Dr. Wayne W. Dyer* (blog), accessed December 11, 2019, https://www.drwaynedyer.com/blog/category/forgiveness/.

9. Robert Enright, *8 Keys to Forgiveness* (New York: W. W. Norton & Company, 2015).

10. Philip McGraw (Dr. Phil), "There Is Power in Forgiveness," *Oprah Magazine*, January 2015, 41.

PART THREE
THIRTEEN: BE THE MIRACLE

1. Lois A. Cuddy, *T. S. Eliot and the Poetics of Evolution* (Lewisburg, PA: Bucknell University Press, 2000), 98.

2. "The Butterfly Effect: Everything You Need to Know About This Powerful Mental Model," FS Blog, accessed July 7, 2020, https://fs.blog/2017/08/the-butterfly-effect/.

3. Nicole J. Phillips, "Kindness Works As a Trifecta," accessed July 7, 2020, https://nicolephillips.com/kindness-works-as-a-trifecta/.

4. Regina Brett, *Be the Miracle: 50 Lessons for Making the Impossible Possible* (New York: Grand Central Publishing, 2013), 10.

5. *Boatlift*, a video narrated by Tom Hanks (Eyepop Productions, September 7, 2011).

6. Jessica DuLong, *Dust to Deliverance: Untold Stories from the Maritime Evacuation on September 11*, reported in "The 9/11 Rescue That We Need to Hear More About," CNN, August 20, 2017, https://www.cnn.com/2017/08/20/opinions/911-boatlift-rescue-opinion-dulong/index.html.

7. Simran Khurana, "Helen Keller Quotes," accessed July 7, 2020, ThoughtCo, https://www.thoughtco.com/helen-keller-quotes-2832699.

8. Richard Rohr, "From Being Driven to Being Drawn," accessed December 31, 2017, https://www.awakin.org/read/view.php?tid=2245.

CHAPTER FOURTEEN: DARING TO DREAM

1. Jim Bickford, *American Comeback* (Las Vegas: American Comeback—Publishing, 2013), 56.

2. Tim Muldoon, *The Ignatian Workout: Daily Spiritual Exercises For a Healthy Faith*, (Chicago: Loyola Press, 2004), 8.

3. Roma Downey, *Box of Butterflies* (New York: Howard Books/Simon & Schuster, 2018), 121; Joseph Campbell, "The Hero's Journey (On Living in the World)," quoted in Diane Osbon, *Reflections on the Art of Living: A Joseph Campbell Companion* (New York: HarperCollins, 1991), 21–24.

4. Elsie Jones-Smith, *Strengths-Based Therapy: Connecting Theory, Practice, and Skills* (Los Angeles: Sage Publications, 2014), 105.

5. Linda Faulkner, *Taking the Mystery out of Business: 9 Fundamentals for Professional Success* (Bedford, IN: Norlightspress.com, 2010), 18.

6. David Viscott, *Finding Your Strength in Difficult Times: A Book of Meditations* (Chicago: Contemporary Books of Chicago, 1993), 87.

CHAPTER FIFTEEN: THE GIFT OF THE PRESENT

1. Marcus Tullius Cicero, *Oratio ProCnaeo Plancio*, XXXIII, per WikiQuote.

2. Robert Jonas, *The Essential Henri Nouwen* (Boston and London: Shambhala, 2009), 64.

3. G. K. Chesterton, *Collected Works* (San Francisco: Ignatius Press, 2001), 463.

4. Andrew Kenney, "They Saved an Infant at the Denver Zoo. Then They Got to Meet Her," *The Denver Post*, September 23, 2019, https://www.denverpost.com/2019/09/23/denver-zoo-infant-rescue/.

5. Summer Allen, *The Science of Gratitude*, Greater Good Science Center, May 2018, https://ggsc.berkeley.edu/images/uploads/GGSC-JTF_White_Paper-Gratitude-FINAL.pdf.

6. Sarah McKibben, "Tapping into the Power of Gratitude," *ASCD Education Update* 55, no. 11 (November 2013): 1.

CHAPTER SIXTEEN: MIRACLE COURAGE

1. Nelson Mandela, *Long Walk to Freedom* (New York: Back Bay Books, 2013), 622.

2. Willa Cather, *Death Comes for the Archbishop* (New York: Random House, 1927; renewed 1955, paperback, Vintage Books / Random House), 50.

3. Theodore Roosevelt, *La Follette's Weekly*, May 1910, see https://www.britannica.com/topic/The-Progressive.

4. George Bernard Shaw, *Saint Joan* (scene II), in *Bernard Shaw's Plays*, ed. Warren Smith (New York: W. W. Norton and Co., 1970), 166.

5. Anaïs Nin, *The Diary of Anais Nin, 1939–1944* (New York, London, San Diego: Harcourt Brace Jovanovich, 1969), 125.

6. Maya Angelou, quoted in Nina Lesowitz and Mary Beth Sammons, *The Courage Companion: How to Live Life with True Power* (New Delhi: Viva Editions, 2010), 65.

7. Jesse Sherwin III, "Seabees Rescue Family from Car Crash," Navy News Service, story number NNS120114-11, January 14, 2012, https://www.navy.mil/submit/display.asp?story_id=64768; "Trapped," *Dateline*, June 28, 2013, updated January 21, 2014.

8. "Ice Bucket Challenge," Wikipedia, accessed December 6, 2017, https://en.wikipedia.org/wiki/Ice_Bucket_Challenge.

9. "Kindness Reunites 67-Year-Old Homeless Man with Birth Mother," KPIX 5, CBS SF Bay Area, March 15, 2018, accessed November 9, 2018, https://sanfrancisco.cbslocal.com/2018/03/15/kindness-reunites-67-year-old-homeless-man-with-birth-mother/.

10. Bonnie Rose, "Stranger Kindness," syndicated from dailybeloved.org, October 6, 2018, http://www.dailygood.org/story/2109/stranger-kindness-bonnie-rose/.

11. Thomas Merton, *Thomas Merton: Spiritual Master—The Essential Writings*, ed. Lawrence S. Cunningham (Mahwah, NJ: Paulist Press, 1992), 146.

CHAPTER SEVENTEEN: THE RIPPLE EFFECT

1. Hooseo Park, *The Eight Answers for Happiness* (Xlibris, 2014), 104.

2. Tzvi Freeman, "What Is Tikkun Olam?," Freeman Files, https://www.chabad.org/library/article_cdo/aid/3700275/jewish/What-Is-Tikkun-Olam.htm.

3. Ibid.

4. Ibid.

5. Fred Rogers, "Helping Children Deal with Tragic Events in the News," Fred Rogers Productions' Vimeo page, 2011.

6. Sarah Van Gelder, "9/11 Brought Them Together. They've Been Preaching Love Ever Since," syndicated from *Yes!* magazine, October 13, 2018, http://www.dailygood.org/story/2123/9-11-broughtthem-together-they-vebeen-preaching-love-ever-since-sarah-van-gelder/, accessed November 9, 2018.

7. "Billionaire Robert F. Smith Tells Morehouse College Grads He'll Pay Their Student Loans," CBS News, May 19, 2019, https://www.cbsnews.com/news/billionaire-robert-smith-morehouse-college-students-loans-paid-class-of-2019-commencement-speaker-sunday/, accessed May 21, 2019.

8. Ibid.

Take the Miracle Moment Challenge!

Take some time on your own, with a friend, or with your favorite group to do some soul searching about these provocative questions. You may be surprised by what you discover.

BECOMING AWARE

1. **Life Saver:** If you found out you had a week to live, what are the first three things you would do? When the reprieve comes, is there anything you would now change?

2. **Full Stop:** Take one minute to stop and look, sit on a nearby bench, find a favorite window view, or enjoy a sidewalk café. Are you surprised by what you see when you make the effort to notice?

3. **Hidden Pictures:** Think about someone or something you encounter every day but take for granted. Find something new or different you had not noticed before. Are you surprised by what you see?

4. **Fate or Fortune:** Think of a recent or memorable coincidence or circumstance that seemed fated and consider the possibility of deeper meaning. Has your interpretation of this experience changed over time?

5. **Let There Be Light:** What would it look like to let your light shine brighter today? How might you ask the universe to assist you?

6. **Awe-Some:** Reflect back to your most recent experience of wonder. What could you do to capture that feeling more frequently? How do wisdom and wonder intersect?

DEEPENING CONNECTION

7. **All Heart:** Find an opportunity to incorporate generosity of spirit today by being kind or giving someone the benefit of the doubt. Smile.

8. **Inside Scoop:** Everyone loves a good story. Practice empathic listening. See what it takes to uncover a story you have never heard before.

9. **The Sky's the Limit:** Consider what the greater good or the purpose of life means to you. What steps could you take to share your own gifts and talents with a cause or purpose that is bigger than you are?

10. **Soul Mate:** What does it mean to you to be spiritual? Do you have spiritual traits or spiritual states? How would you nurture that part of yourself?

11. **Be There or Be Square:** Consider the last time you showed up for someone or something you were tempted to skip. Were you all in? Did anything unexpected happen?

12. **Woe Is Me:** Begin the process of forgiving someone today; it can even be yourself.

FINDING MEANING

13. **Employment Opportunities:** Do you know what your job is? How can you be the miracle for someone else?

14. **Dream Catcher:** Consider your purpose and passion. What would your ideal personal mission statement look like?

15. **Make My Day:** Is there someone in your life, past or present, who deserves your gratitude? Have you told them? What would be a good way to thank them?

16. **Nerves of Steel:** Today, do one thing you are afraid of doing—speak up, speak out, or share a story.

17. **Endless Summer:** Think about a ripple you have sent out into the world. What happened next, and after that, and then what?

Reading Group Guide

DISCUSSION QUESTIONS

1. Do you believe a miracle could happen to you? Did *The Miracle Collectors* encourage you to look at any of your own life experiences differently?

....

....

....

....

....

2. Were you surprised that people shared their miracle stories, sometimes for the first time? Are there stories you have kept to yourself that you would now be willing to share?

....

....

....

....

....

3. What do you think of generosity of spirit as a secret sauce? Did this idea bring to mind any special ingredients you might add?

4. Has our techno-savvy social media culture caused us to lose our ability to truly connect with each other? Are there any ways you could deepen your connections?

5. What is your favorite miracle story from *The Miracle Collectors*? Are there stories in *The Miracle Collectors* you struggled to believe or understand?

6. Do you now recognize that you have been the miracle in someone else's life? Has anyone ever been the miracle for you?

7. What does miracle courage mean to you? Have you ever practiced your own version of miracle courage? What does it look like?

8. They say there are no atheists in foxholes. Have you ever been in a situation where you were desperate and needed help and it caused you to instantly change your outlook toward God or a higher power?

9. Albert Einstein wrote, "There are only two ways to live your life. One is as though nothing is a miracle. The other is as though everything is a miracle." Do you agree? Are miracles an all-or-nothing proposition?

10. Through becoming aware and deepening connection, were you helped by *The Miracle Collectors* to uncover a path to finding greater meaning in your life?

About the Authors

Joan Luise Hill's introduction to miracles evolved as a series of coincidences that ultimately could not be ignored. With a lengthy career in medical administration advancing innovative medical solutions, her expertise was put to the test to save the life of her son. She has a master's degree from the University of Connecticut and a bachelor of science degree from Boston College. Having lived in a number of states and with three adult children and family spread across the country, Hill and her husband are avid (and constant) travelers who split their time between Palm Beach, Florida; Pebble Beach, California; Aspen, Colorado; and Nantucket, Massachusetts.

Katie Mahon became a miracle expert the hard way. At nineteen, she walked away from serial killer Ted Bundy with the help of a stranger who appeared seemingly out of nowhere. Mahon has a bachelor of science degree in psychology from Santa Clara University and spent nearly twenty years in banking before staying home with her two daughters. A transplant from the San Francisco Bay Area, Mahon now lives in New York City with her husband and enjoys chasing more than miracles with her four grandchildren.